FROZEN TO THE CABIN FLOOR

THE BIOGRAPHY OF BABY DOE TABOR
1854-1935

Tracy Beach

outskirts
press

Frozen to the Cabin Floor
The Biography of Baby Doe Tabor 1854-1935
All Rights Reserved.
Copyright © 2019 Tracy Beach
v4.0

The opinions expressed in this manuscript are solely the opinions of the author and do not represent the opinions or thoughts of the publisher. The author has represented and warranted full ownership and/or legal right to publish all the materials in this book.

This book may not be reproduced, transmitted, or stored in whole or in part by any means, including graphic, electronic, or mechanical without the express written consent of the publisher except in the case of brief quotations embodied in critical articles and reviews.

Outskirts Press, Inc.
http://www.outskirtspress.com

ISBN: 978-1-9772-0046-4

Cover Photo © 2019 History Colorado Designed by Master Printers. All rights reserved - used with permission.

Outskirts Press and the "OP" logo are trademarks belonging to Outskirts Press, Inc.

PRINTED IN THE UNITED STATES OF AMERICA

Table of Contents

1. A Painted sky and the blind folded Mystic 1
2. A vial of ink and the broken promise 12
3. A bucket of soapy water and the bloody politician 25
4. A dead bartender and the hidden box of diamonds. 40
5. Massive marble fireplaces and ornate chandeliers 50
6. The child bride and the canvas backed duck. 60
7. The murdered Priest and a handful of gold coins 71
8. A stable full of peacock feathers and the two brothers. 80
9. And when the bough breaks, silver will fall. 94
10. A stack of firewood and the shovel full of gold 111
11. A cup full of leeches and the ring of flowers 126
12. A Queen's Diamond and a tin of chewing tobacco 141
13. Stolen mining stock and the dead millionaire. 152
14. Missing Silver ore and the man who owns the Earth. 163
15. A deadly snowball fight and the loving hand of God 174
16. The Presidents hunt and the Scientific Method 188
17. Stolen Virtue and the Taxidermied Lion. 203
18. A river full of quicksand and the lost ring. 219
19. The frozen Boa constrictor, the blue bird and another bout of appendicitis. 232
20. The angry Circus midget and a dead German fighter pilot. . . 245
21. A freshly baked pie and the diamond necklace 257

22. The buried steamer trunk and a box full of pomegranates ... 268
23. A tiny mesh cage and the friendly Pharmacist............278
24. The stench of embalming fluid and the heart wrenching lie..291
25. A tub of lard and the dancing squirrels..................304
26. A false name and the undiagnosed brain tumor 320
27. Piles of beautiful gifts and the burning Newspaper........333
28. A shotgun named Trusty and the cloaked visitor..........345
29. A town full of scavengers and the joyful reunion 359
30. A stack of chairs and the twisted flashlight..............376
31. Elizabeth Tabor's personal recipes and home remedies 389
32. Endnotes 398

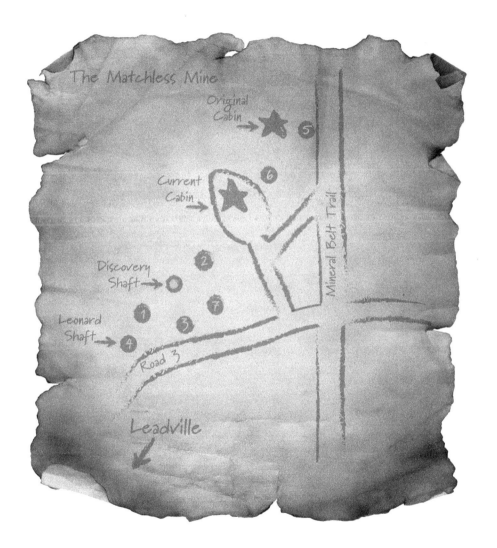

A Painted sky and the blind folded Mystic

"**Ladies and gentleman,** if you could please find your seats, the performance will begin in 15 minutes."

With a friendly smile and a round of firm handshake's, Horace Tabor excused himself from his theater patron's and headed back towards his private box, where his lady love awaited. Tonight's performance had been advertised as a once in a life time experience and he didn't want to miss a minute of it.

Despite months of elaborate productions, Operas and grand Choirs filling his newly completed Denver Opera house, Horace still found himself surrounded by theater goers who wanted to thank him for bringing such glamour to their little western city.

Determined to cement his name into the history books, Horace had spared no expense when he designed this Opera house, only a few years earlier. He had traveled around Europe, to gaze upon its amazing architecture and to order the finest fabrics and rugs that Denver had ever seen. And as he walked through the lobby of his finished master piece, he still marveled at what he had created.

Inside of the Tabor Opera house-The Denver Public Library, Western History Collection X-24748

Above his head, he could see his beautiful 70 ft. by 20 ft. stained glass ceiling reflecting its colors onto the immense crystal chandelier, which hung in the center of the lobby, while under his feet, he could feel the thick, velvety texture of the carpet he personally ordered from Brussels. Only the best would do, as this Opera house and the building it was located in, would be his legacy.

As he walked upon the crimson carpet, with its forest green boarders, he finally entered his private box and sat down next to Elizabeth. Of all his possessions, he prized her most of all. Her strawberry blonde hair, youthful face and piercing blue eyes made him feel like a young man again. She was his Elizabeth…his Babe.

As he took his seat, he ran his hand across the silky, mohair fabric he had personally chosen for the chairs upholstery and the Japanese cherry wood he had hand selected for the frame and smiled. When he had commissioned the Opera house's construction, which was built inside his Tabor Grand office building, he knew it had to be perfect.

When the local Denver contractors had originally heard about Horace Tabor's vision, they smugly expected to be given the contract, but were instead shocked to hear that he had hired a contractor from Chicago instead. With a bid of $850,000, Charles Cook had won the contract and began construction in 1880.

To construct Tabor's vision, he had used stone cut by inmates from the Illinois State Penitentiary, sandstone from Ohio and boilers from Saint Louis. Making sure to include Colorado in some of the buildings construction, Horace Tabor decided to order the heating pipes from Pueblo and employed local craftsmen to help complete his addition to Denver's downtown skyline.

But before the finishing touches on the fourteen little roof top towers were even complete, the offices and store fronts had been quickly snatched up by local merchants. With the building fully rented, it guaranteed Tabor a steady income and collateral in case he ever needed to borrow against it. Curtis St. and 16th had never looked so good.

"Ladies and Gentlemen, the doors to the Opera house will be locked following the commencement of tonight's weird and marvelous entertainment. No one will be admitted or allowed to leave after the doors are closed."

As the announcer exited the stage, Horace casually leaned back in his chair and soon found himself glancing up at the wonderful woodwork that framed his theater's murals. When his Opera house was still under construction, he had hired painters to add beautiful murals, including one of the daytime sky, which contained just a hint of white clouds to catch the eye. With the ceiling 65 feet above the floor, the mural bathed the entire seating area below in European elegance.

Soon the lights inside the Opera house dimmed and a hush washed over the crowd, as the announcer returned to the front of the stage and stood at attention until the crowd had silenced.

"Good evening. Dr. Alexander J. McIvor-Tyndall welcomes you to tonight's performance and wishes for me to enlighten you, on what you are about to experience tonight." The announcer began, as she glanced around at the 1,500 attendees, who were hanging on her every word.

"The reason that we are locking the doors to the theater, is on account of the peculiar nature of tonight's weird and remarkable entertainment." She continued, as the rear doors of the room were closed, which quickly caused whispers to fill the auditorium.

"To thank you for attending tonight's performance, gifts have arrived from the east and each person attending tonight's wonderful occultation of mystery and marvel will be a recipient of a gift. These gifts are from the International Swastika Society and Dr. McIvor-Tyndall will personally hand out the presents, which include an occult message and a blessing."

With the use of the word Occult, Horace found himself getting slightly uncomfortable. Despite the fact that he was fully aware of the subject of tonight performance, he was also reminded of the controversy that followed James Belford five years earlier, as he ran for Colorado's

House of Representatives in 1876.

Known as the "Red headed Rooster", James Belford was attacked in the Newspapers during his campaign and accused of attending spiritual séances and infidelity. Horace was already in the spot light for infidelity, having left his wife Augusta a year earlier and he didn't need his bid for a second run as Lieutenant Governor of Colorado, to also be marred with talk of a spiritual nature.

"Ladies and Gentleman…Dr. McIvor-Tyndall!"

The applause snapped Horace out of his self-induced trance and caused him to turn his attention towards the young man, who was now walking across the stage.

Dressed in the height of Victorian fashion, the man walked to the front of the stage, placed his hands behind his back and took a number of slight bows. With a serious expression, he then stood at attention and awaited his chance to speak, once the applause quieted down. He was quite a striking looking man, with deep set eyes and a thick tousle of dark hair.

"Ladies and Gentleman, my name is Dr. J Alexander McIvor-Tyndall. I am a hypnotist, a clairvoyant, a mind reader and a seer. I am also the Pastor of the First Spiritualist Church in Syracuse, New York." He began, introducing the audience to his Queen's English accent.

"Tonight, I will talk about man's secret powers and how to use them. I will talk about Psychic phenomena, clairvoyance, thought transference, telepathy, psychology and various other mystifications of psychic and occult power. I will illustrate the value of man's higher faculties, which are ours for the taking." He explained, as he removed his lamb skin gloves and tucked them inside his jacket pocket.

"I will need a gentleman volunteer from the audience." He announced, as he walked back toward the center of the stage and with the wave of his hand, guided a large prop to its pre-determined location.

As his assistant led a volunteer up onto the stage, Dr. McIvor-Tyndall walked back to the front of the stage and shook hands with the man, before continuing with his explanation.

"My teachings are very broad and naturally cause many quakes of fear in those who are inclined to be tied and fettered by so called authority, down in his heart." the Mystic explained, as he motioned for his assistant to lead his volunteer over to the center of the stage.

"Here you see a prop wall, like you would normally see used in a play or stage production. My stage hands have covered it in wallpaper simply for aesthetics." He pointed out, as he quickly ran his hand over the floral print, before giving it a quick tap with his knuckles.

"I will now ask my volunteer to inspect the wallpaper for any holes he might find." He added, as the man was led over to the prop. After running his hands over the paper numerous times, it was found to of passed the man's inspection

Dr. McIvor-Tyndall then walked towards the left side of the stage, turned his back to the prop wall and dramatically removed a black, silk blindfold from his jacket pocket.

"My assistant will now hand our gentleman volunteer my lapel pin, which he will stick into the wallpapered wall, any place he chooses." He explained, as his assistant walked over and removed the pin from the lapel of the Mystics jacket. Dr. McIvor-Tyndall then showed the audience both sides of his blindfold, before tying it around his eyes.

As the audience quietly watched, the volunteer took the pin from the assistant, walked over to the prop wall and carefully studied the floral pattern, in an attempt to find the perfect spot to stick the pin. Satisfied, the man then stepped away and waited further instruction.

As though in a trance, the Mystic turned around and skillfully walked toward the prop and stopped within arm's length. With a gasp from the audience, Dr. McIvor-Tyndall quickly plucked the lapel pin from the floral print and held it out for the audience, who loudly cheered his success.

As the show continued and his skills put to the test, Dr. McIvor-Tyndall amazed the audience with bouts of hypnotism and mind reading, before the final curtain.

With the show complete, the mystic's assistant once again took the stage and reminded the audience to pick up their free gift in the lobby and sign up for private readings, which would be held the following day.

As the Opera house doors were unlocked and the elite of Denver began to trickle out into the lobby, Horace Tabor motioned for Elizabeth to stay seated just a while longer. The fear of a newspaper reporter catching him leaving a production, which involved an Occult theme inside his own Opera house, was not something he wished to experience right now.

Adding to Horace Tabor's disgust with reporters, newspapers as far as New York City had been printing stories of his personal life, since

Dr. J. Alexander McIvor-Tyndall-Legends of America

his first run for Lieutenant Governor of Colorado and they had gotten much more critical, since he had left his wife Augusta the year before.

He had read numerous stories that labeled his lady love Elizabeth as a Strumpet, while Tabor's own wife Augusta was informing everyone that she was holding Horace to their wedding vows…for better or for worse. The newspapers were having quite a field day with his personal life.

Months before, when Horace Tabor's Opera house had held its opening night, he was hoping to celebrate it with the introduction of his Babe to Denver's high society, but unfortunately that was not to be the case. On September 3rd, just two days before opening night, his estranged wife Augusta had sent him a letter begging his forgiveness and a second chance:

Dear Husband,

I am in town and would very much like to go to the Tabor Grand and witness the glory that you are to receive. Believe me that none will be more proud of it than your broken —hearted wife.

Will you not take me there and by so doing, stop the gossip this is busy with our affairs?

God knows that I am truly sorry for our estrangement and will humble myself in the dust at your feet, if you will only return. Whatever I said to you was done in the heat of passion and you know the awful condition that I was in when it was said.

Pity, I beseech you and forgive me. And let us bury the past and commence the anew. And my life shall be devoted to you forever.

You're loving,
Wife

Despite refusing Augusta's request to attend the opening night of his Opera house, Tabor feared she would still show up and insist on sitting in his private box. As a sinister ploy, Horace ordered a large floral arrangement, which spelled out TABOR, to be placed in the box instead and instructed his workmen to place the arrangement in front of the seats, to block the view of the stage.

September 5th 1881 saw the opening night of Horace Tabor's Opera house, which was filled to capacity with the finest people Colorado had to offer. He found he couldn't stop smiling, as he shook hands with everyone who approached him and eagerly listened as they gushed about the elegance his Opera house had brought to their city.

As the grand opening ceremony began and the audience finished settling into their seats, Horace chose a seat in the front row, closest to the stage's staircase. Glancing over at his beloved Elizabeth, who was just a few seats away, he gave her a wink, which made her quickly blush. As the lights dimmed, Horace could hear the whispers of the audience as they commented about the Opera houses beautiful ceiling, which was trimmed in gold, maroon, blue, orange and black and framed a painted daytime sky.

As the curtain finally began to rise, the audience saw a handsome, ebony table set in the center of the stage, on which sat a bound book and a small casket. Before anyone could begin to question the table's purpose, the Honorable I.E. Barnum strutted out onto the stage towards the foot lights.

Mr. Barnum had been a delegate during the 1879 State Convention and in so doing, had become friends with Horace Tabor, who he had helped to elect. Seeing Tabor in the front row, Mr. Barnum gave him a friendly smirk and a quick nod, as he waited for the applause to settle.

"If Governor Tabor is in the house, will he kindly step upon the stage." Mr. Barnum inquired, as he pointed his hand toward Horace. To a vociferous applause, which echoed through the opera house, Horace Tabor quickly stood up and walked up onto the stage.

With an eager handshake, I.E. Barnum welcomed Horace Tabor onto the stage and motioned for him to stand next to the small table. With his arms behind his back, Horace made eye contact with Elizabeth and gave her a slight smile.

"As an appreciation of the love which you have bestowed upon Denver and her people, I present to you this autograph album and this golden watch fob. This gift was made possible by one hundred citizens who had subscribed $5 each." Mr. Barnum announced, as he picked up the small casket that had been lying on the table.

The beautiful watch fob was constructed of solid gold and consisted of three links, connected with close fitting hinges. On the top was a small hand grasping a large ring, which would allow it to be attached to a pocket watch and on bottom was an ore bucket filled with tiny pieces of gold and silver. The center consisted of three links, which represented the steps Tabor had climbed to fortune and success and were decorated with tiny silver ladders, which graced each side of the fob.

After a hardy round of applause, Horace stepped forward and raised his hands to quiet the crowd.

"It has been sixteen months since I commenced the building of this opera house. At that time I looked Denver carefully over with its people and here I found a town at the base of the Rocky Mountains- a city of 30,000 or 40,000 inhabitants: the finest city I think, of its population on the American continent. I said if Denver is to have an Opera house, it should be worthy of the city. Here is the Opera house; I shall leave it to your judgment if I have done my duty in this respect. Here is this beautiful album and fob chain- as beautiful as can be. I shall prize them every hour I live. I shall prize them not for their price value, by for the spirit in which they are given."

As a round of applause once again filled his theater, Horace took another bow and glanced upon the approving faces of Denver's high society. But as he continued to stare into the crowd, he began to notice that the faces of his theater guests were slowly beginning to lose their clarity and the Opera house's lights were starting to dim…

"Mr. Tabor? Mr. Tabor Sir? Sorry to bother you, but the show has ended." The usher announced as he lightly tapped Horace on the shoulder.

Feeling the sensation though his evening jacket, Horace quickly turn around and saw the nervous face of one of his uniformed ushers. As the memory of the Opera house's opening night quickly faded away, Horace turned back around and found himself staring at an empty stage, which now only held a man yielding a broom. Pulling out his watch, to check the time, Horace smiled at the sight of his beloved watch fob, that he had been gifted that glorious night.

Peering down into the theater, which was now only occupied by ushers who were busy brushing the upholstered seats, Horace Tabor turned and smiled at his beloved Elizabeth, before taking her gloved hand and escorting her out to their waiting carriage.

But unknown to Elizabeth, the night spent watching the Mystic had just begun. As a surprise, Horace had arranged a private Psychic reading for the next day and he knew it could be nothing but good news.

A VIAL OF INK AND THE BROKEN PROMISE

As Horace Tabor and his lady love ate breakfast the next morning, inside their suite at Denver's Windsor Hotel, Horace informed Elizabeth that he had made an afternoon appointment with the Mystic for a psychic reading. Out of respect for her religious faith, he explained that the appointment was only for himself, but Elizabeth quickly enlightened him to what this upcoming reading could mean for his soul…and hers.

Elizabeth had been raised a devout Catholic and she quickly explained to her lover that by simply accompanying him to this visit with the Mystic, that it would still add to her now numerous sin's against God. She was already doing daily Penance for her sexual relationship with a married man and she knew that the sin of visiting a fortune teller, would go far beyond the realm of a simple prayer and confession.

Father John B. Guida, who was Elizabeth's spiritual counselor at Denver's Sacred Heart Catholic Church, would have described her attendance to Dr. McIvor-Tyndall's performance the night before at the Opera house, as a "Venial sin". This type of sin is considered a forgivable sin, in the eyes of the church, if it is done out of stupidity or for fun…but now Horace wanted to take it one step further.

Fortune telling, Palm reading and Tarot cards, Catholics believe, violates God's first commandment and it appeared Elizabeth would be adding this visit, to her already long list of sins.

Arriving for the appointment with the Mystic, Elizabeth walked into the rented office suite with Horace, where they were greeted by Dr. McIvor-Tyndall's secretary. With a friendly smile, the young woman explained that a full reading, which was normally $5, was now only $2.50 and a short reading was simply $1, to ensure that everyone would be able to benefit from a reading.

Within just a few minutes, the office door opened and a well-dressed gentleman walked out looking rather pleased. With a smile, he turned and shook the Mystic's hand and thanked him for his reading, as Elizabeth took a deep breath, knowing that it was now their turn.

After watching the man leave the suite, Dr. McIvor-Tyndall looked over at his secretary to inquire who was to be his next client. With a subtle motion of her hand, the secretary gestured towards Horace and Elizabeth. With a satisfied smile, the Mystic walked over and politely introduced himself. After formal introductions, the Mystic was thrilled to learn that his next client was none other than the Lieutenant Governor of Colorado, Horace Austin Warner Tabor.

After signaling for Horace and Elizabeth to enter the adjoining office, inside his rented suite, Dr. McIvor-Tyndall began to discuss his personal credentials with them. He began by talking about how he was the son of an eminent surgeon and that he even belonged to one of the most Aristocratic families in Leicestershire, England.

"I was originally educated in the medical profession." The Mystic explained, in an overly rehearsed tone. "But my power in thought reading was so remarkable, that I just had to abandon the beaten track of human science."

After offering Elizabeth a seat, the Mystic began his instructions concerning the anticipated palm reading. His elegant way of speaking, in his native Queens English, made the entire experience feel very sophisticated.

"Governor, if you could please wash your hands before we begin. I will need them to be free of any dirt or oils for the reading", Dr. McIvor-Tyndall informed Horace, as he pointed over at a nearby wash basin. Standing off to the side with a small towel, the Mystic waited until his client had finished rinsing his hands free of soap and drying them, before approving Horace for the next step in the reading.

With his newly cleaned hands, Horace was then led over to a table which contained paper, a glass vial of ink, a small porcelain saucer and an ink roller. Pouring a small amount of the black ink into the saucer, Dr. McIvor-Tyndall placed the small roller into the dish and proceeded to coat the entire roller pad, front to back, with the ink. Satisfied, the Mystic motioned for Horace to hold out his dominate hand, which he carefully inspected using the light from a nearby table lamp.

Choosing two pieces of white paper from the pile, the Mystic laid them on the table side by side. Taking Tabor's hand, the Mystic placed it palm side up and using the ink coated roller, covered Horace's palm with a layer of the black ink.

Pleased with the coverage, the Mystic flipped over Horace's hand and carefully placed the inked palm onto the center of the white paper. With an added gesture, the Mystic then asked Tabor to place his free hand on top of the inked one and press it hard against the paper. When Horace lifted his hands up, he saw a dark ink print of his palm. The Mystic then had him repeat the same motion on the second piece of paper, which produced a lighter palm print, but one with clearer lines.

Satisfied with the prints, the Mystic led Horace back over to the nearby basin and asked him to again wash his hands. As Dr. McIvor-Tyndall held out a towel for Mr. Tabor, he explained that soon the Palmograghs would be dry enough for him to read.

As they walked back over to the table, Dr. McIvor-Tyndall began to explain the art of palm reading. "The lines of your palm accurately reveal the important events of your life… past, present and future." the Mystic explained, while the palm prints continued to dry. "Successes and failures are plainly marked, as are general characteristics and tendencies."

Picking up a nearby magnifying glass, Dr. McIvor-Tyndall began to study the still damp prints, as they lay on the table.

"As the world's greatest authority on the science of palmistry, thousands have benefited from my private readings" he explained, with a prideful tone, as Horace leaned over the table to check out his palm prints.

"I have read the palms of many prominent people, which is why I've done two prints of your hand." He explained, as he put down the magnifying glass and handed a pen over to Horace. "If you could be so kind as to autograph your print for my personal collection, I would be honored."

As Horace began to add his signature to the darker of the two palm prints, the Mystic continued to boast. "I have prints from the Lieutenant Governor of British Columbia, the Earl of Norbury, The Sultan of Turkey, the Countess Wachtmeister and even Mark Twain himself!" the Mystic explained, as Horace finished signing his name.

Satisfied that the prints were dry enough, the Mystic picked up his magnifying glass and began to study the lines and curves of the print. He quickly began talking about relationships, marriages and children before discussing past events and future events…but with that, he got quiet and studied the prints closer.

With a serious look, the Mystic turned to Horace and alerted him to an upsetting discovery. It appeared that Tabor's life line contained a gap, which meant that something dangerous was coming. The more the Mystic studied the palm print, the more certain he was that Horace's life would not be a long one.

Disappointed that he had to give Horace bad news, the Mystic informed him that choices that he makes every day can alter his life path and can cause the lines to change shape. With a firm hand shake,

Horace and Elizabeth left the Mystic's office and headed back to the Windsor Hotel.

It seemed the die had been cast…

Finding herself quite shaken up, and fearful of the possibility the Mystic was right about Horace, Elizabeth found her thoughts wondering back to her childhood and about the road she had traveled to become the mistress of a multi-millionaire. A relationship, if the Mystic was right, might be short lived.

Elizabeth was the 5th daughter and 6th child, out of the fourteen children born to Peter and Elizabeth McCourt. Her childhood had started out at the height of privilege in Oshkosh, Wisconsin, only for her to end up the mistress to one of the wealthiest men in Colorado. This, unfortunately, came with a glowing badge of shame wherever she went, which she hoped to discard once she had a wedding ring on her finger.

Elizabeth's father Peter had owned a wonderful clothing store and Tailor company back in Wisconsin, which had allowed her to grow up in a beautiful house and have every wonder imaginable at her fingertips.

But the fire of 1875 changed everything.

The flames had sparked to life on April 28, 1875, at the local saw mill and spread quickly throughout the wood framed neighborhoods and nearby lumber yards. The St. Paul Depot and freight yards were soon engulfed, as was the Harding Opera House, which only took 20 minutes to become a pile of burning debris.

The fire then raced down Main Street where Elizabeth's parents found themselves powerless to stop the fire from reaching their store and instead were forced to watch it burn. They saved what they could, but without a building to work out of, they couldn't support their large family or their opulent lifestyle. Luckily, through the grace of God, the fire had skipped their home.

Eager to rebuild, Peter McCourt and his business partner Mr. Cameron managed to borrow $4,000 from the bank and build a two story , brick building at 62 Main street, but found few customers once they opened their doors. Cameron and McCourt clothing store sat unprofitable, as it appeared that after the fire, the residents of Oshkosh had more important things on their mind than new clothes.

The McCourt family home-The Oshkosh Public Museum —P1939.19

As the years passed, Elizabeth and her siblings made due and continued to enjoy their life in Oshkosh. As her older siblings married and started their new lives, Elizabeth decided that she wanted to marry into an opulent family and be assured that she would never have to worry about money. She had no desire to marry a shop keeper or a common laborer like some of her sister's had, so she set her sights on the richest family in town.

The man she had her eye on was Harvey Doe, the son of Oshkosh, Wisconsin's certified tycoon William Harvey Doe Sr. He had made his fortune by accumulating mining claims in Colorado and investing his money in the lumber trade, which had paid off handsomely.

But his family was Protestant.

As a devout Irish Catholic, Elizabeth's upbringing in the church had taught her that this was quite unacceptable. A marriage between a person of the Catholic faith and a person of the Protestant faith, was seen as extremely tragic and about as far down the social scale as you could possibly go.

But thankfully, Elizabeth's father chose to look past the Doe family's only real flaw and looked at how this union could possibly benefit his own social standing. Mr. McCourt's only demand was that a Catholic Priest would conduct the wedding ceremony, as he refused to allow his daughter to be married by a Protestant Pastor.

So, despite the Reverend F.B. Doe being not only a Pastor, but Harvey Doe Jr's Uncle, the wedding was conducted by Reverend James O'Malley, from the McCourt's church of St. Peter's.

But not inside the church itself.

To keep the gossip at a minimum, the wedding was held at the McCourt family home, on June 27, 1877 and attended by two families split by their religious up bringing's.

And as 22 year Old Elizabeth Bonduel McCourt walked down the aisle, her father beamed with the thought of how this union could help his business and social standing, while both mothers remained silent and cold, filled with the knowledge that they were allowing this shame upon their families.

But luckily the shame was kept hidden, with the decision to send the new couple off to live in Colorado. Placed quickly on a train, soon after the ceremony, Elizabeth found herself watching her childhood home disappear behind her, as the towering Rocky Mountains appeared over the horizon. Accompanied by Harvey's father William, Elizabeth and her new husband Harvey would soon be introduced to Central City, Colorado and their own mining claim christened" The Fourth of July".

A wedding gift from Mr. Doe Sr.

With the train making its first stop in Denver, the newlyweds chose to honeymoon at The American house Hotel, while Elizabeth's new father-in-law continued up to Central City, to check out his mining claims. William Doe Sr. intended on having his son follow in his footsteps, with his pretty, little daughter-in-law Elizabeth producing him Grand-children. He had it all planned out and he beamed with pride with the thought of it.

A young Elizabeth McCourt-The Oshkosh Public Museum-P2001.47.3

But unfortunately for the newly crowned Mrs. Elizabeth Doe Jr., her husband didn't take to mining the claim his father had gifted to him or even to the town of Central City for that matter. As soon as

Harvey Doe Jr. - Legends of America

his father left town, Harvey Jr. began spending his days gambling and drinking himself into a stupor.

Working the claim herself and managing her own crew, Elizabeth quickly received ridicule, but her ability to make a profit soon began to fill her bank account. With money to spend, it was while out shopping that she ran into the man with whom she would have her first affair, but soon one affair turned into two. But it was with her second affair that she was offered a life style more luxurious than she could ever imagine.

But it did come with a hefty price tag and the extreme risk of failure.

In order to prove to her newest lover, the married Horace Tabor, that her love for him was true, she needed help in getting rid of her current husband Harvey Doe Jr. Not just a divorce in the eyes of the State of Colorado, but an annulment in the eyes of God.

And this could only happen, if Harvey has an affair.

Unfortunately, for Elizabeth, Harvey wasn't the one who had strayed from the marriage, but she still had to find a way to make it look like he had.

And now with the unwanted union with Harvey hanging over her head and a Mystic's prediction that her married lover might not live to a ripe old age, she desperately needed that divorce. If her lover was to die before she got that diamond ring on her finger, she could be facing the rest of her life either in a Brothel or a sweatshop sewing on buttons.

These thoughts flooded her mind, as Elizabeth and Horace walked the short distance back to their suite at the Windsor Hotel, after their very eventful visit with the Mystic. Seeing that his beautiful Babe was in deep thought, Horace stopped walking and was pleased to find that she desired a divorce from her husband Harvey Doe, but understood that it would take some planning, as well as a few favor's.

Getting a divorce in the Victorian era was not easy, as the only acceptable reason was adultery, but Harvey had been a saint in his duties as a husband. With many witnesses to attest that Harvey had been staying pure to his wife Elizabeth, despite her affair 's and even more witnesses aware of Elizabeth's cheating ways, proving herself as the victim in this marriage was going to be difficult.

In regards to her Catholic faith, she desperately needed to get an annulment from Harvey, if she ever expected to marry Horace and have it excepted by God. The Catholic Church refers to an annulment as a "Declaration of nullity" and the bible has reasons for its followers that explain why it is so important.

An annulment would help Elizabeth wipe the sin of adultery from her soul and allow her to start going to confession and serve out any penance she might be handed. But going to confession right now would do her no good, as she was planning to continue living in sin, with Horace, until her annulment was granted.

> *Proverbs 6:32-33*
> *But those whoso committeth adultery lacketh understanding : he that doeth it destryeth his own soul*
> *A wound and dishonor shall he get: and his reproach shall not be wiped away*

Sparked with the realization that his young mistress wished to marry him, Horace began talking with some influential friends and a dastardly plan was hatched, in order to obtain this gift of deceit for his Elizabeth.

And the woman behind his scheme, was none other than Mrs. Lizzie Preston.

Lizzie was a Madam down on Holiday Street, which was the premiere location of the best Parlor houses in Denver. Combined with at least 17 known Opium Dens and numerous Saloon's, the entire area was the perfect place to be caught doing something wrong. Now they just needed a way to get Harvey into Lizzie's Parlor house.

And Elizabeth knew just the thing.

When Elizabeth and Harvey had first gotten married, his father had gifted them with a mining claim in Central city called "The Fourth of July" and she had a strong hunch that he might want to sell it.

And with this, the plan was set into motion.

On March 2, 1880 Harvey received a telegram from a man who said someone was very interested in buying his mine. Desperate for money, Harvey quickly met up with the unknown man, who told him that they had to act quickly if he wanted it sold. It seemed that the interested party was leaving town the following morning and he had been seen entering Lizzie Preston's Parlor house on Holiday Street.

At this, Harvey stopped short. Despite his wife's affairs and his broken heart, he still loved Elizabeth and didn't want the temptation that would accompany going into a house of ill repute. If Elizabeth ever found out he had gone inside, he might never win her back.

As he stood on the street corner, faced with the prospect of finally selling his mine, the unknown man convinced him to join him inside to find the buyer.

> Just a quick look around and we will be right out...
> It will just take a minute...
> I thought you wanted to sell your mine...

With a heavy sigh, Harvey headed up the steps of the Parlor house and as the girls swarmed him and begged for a date, Elizabeth made her move.

Quickly coming out of the shadows, Elizabeth stood outside the Parlor house with Officer Edward Newman and waited. Desperate for

Denver Brothel- History Colorado-10049683

her evidence of adultery, that she needed to show the judge in order to secure her divorce, she gave a silent prayer that he would come out of the door with a lady of the evening on his arm.

But Harvey had no intentions of accepting a date from any of the painted ladies and instead spent his time following around a stranger, who never turned up the promised buyer for his mine.

Discouraged, Harvey left within five minutes of walking inside, but it was too late. To his surprise and extreme confusion, his wife Elizabeth was standing outside with a police Officer.

"Harvey? Harvey Doe, is that you?"

"Elizabeth? Oh sweetheart, I can explain…"

And with a smile, she took hold of Officer Newman's arm and headed back to the Windsor Hotel.

A BUCKET OF SOAPY WATER AND THE BLOODY POLITICIAN

March 4, 1880 found Elizabeth Bonduel Doe inside a Denver Court house, happily filling out Divorce papers. Wearing a torn, outdated dress and worn out shoes, she made sure to complete her outfit with a tattered coat and a pitiful cry, as she filled out the paperwork placed in front of her.

Elizabeth B. Doe-against- William H. Doe Jr...

The first question on the document read, "The said action is brought-"…and with a sly smile and a peek over her shoulder, Elizabeth wrote in her answer.

"To obtain a divorce from you on the grounds of adultery..."

As she finished writing these words on the required line, she made sure to become slightly more upset, since she wasn't sure who might be around to mentally record her reactions. She then wiped the invisible tears from her eyes and began writing the account of what happened, according to her of course. She would very get granted a divorce if she told the truth.

> *"I saw my husband, the defendant, out on the second day of March in the evening go into the house of ill fame of Lizzie Preston's on Holliday Street in the City of Denver. I went to the door and the woman came to the door asked me what I wanted. I told her that I had just seen my husband going in and I wanted to follow him. The woman told me that if I came in I would be in a house of ill fame too. I then pushed past the woman at the door and saw my husband in one of the rooms. I then turned around and came right out and went home. Mr. Newman, the policeman accompanied me home. I had no knowledge or even consented to him going there and never thought he would go in such a place."*

Fifteen days later, on March 19th, Elizabeth came in for her appointed divorce hearing and sat alone in the court room. At only 5'2" tall, with beautiful, bright blue eyes, she cast a pitiful appearance to the other people seated near her. To add to her air of the victim, she made sure to keep her handkerchief and rosary beads in her hands where everyone could see them.

But when it was finally her turn to approach the court, she held her head high and slowly walked up to testify. As she began to softly cry and wipe her eyes, making sure to keep her rosary in plain sight, she enlightened the court on the hardships she had endured at the hands of her husband Harvey Doe.

She talked about how he refused to work their mining claim in Central city and how she had been forced to work the mine herself. She described the shame of wearing man's overalls and working the horse drawn whim. How she had to personally sink the shafts deeper into their claim, while Harvey drank himself into a stupor night after night.

To add more of a sympathetic tone, she got up and handed the judge a newspaper clipping, before tearfully stepping back. The article was written in October 1877 by a Central City, Colorado newspaper called "Town Talk", under the section marked "The Mining Reporter."

> "I next reached the Fourth of July Lode, a mine which has not been worked for several years but started up some months ago under the personal supervision of the owner, Mr. W.H. Doe and his wife. The young lady manages one half of the property while her liege Lord manages the other. I found both at their separate shafts managing a number of workmen, Mr. Doe at his which is 70 feet and his wife, who is full of ambition, in her new enterprise, at hers which is sunk 60 feet. This is the first instance where a lady, and such she is, has managed a mining property. The mine is doing very well and produces some rich ore."

As the court read her article, Elizabeth decided to add the additional heart breaking story of being forced to sell her furniture, clothing and jewelry to support them both. With an added pout and some extra tears, she easily secured the divorce she sought and knew she would also soon have the annulment she desired.

As she walked out of the court room, with her head held high, she gave a silent wish that her lover Horace Tabor would do the same for her. She felt that only a divorce from his wife and a wedding ring on Elizabeth's finger would put her right with God.

Unfortunately for Elizabeth, Horace Tabor had more on his mind at that moment than obtaining a divorce from his wife Augusta, as he was busy being the Lieutenant Governor of Colorado. But Horace's life had not always been full of success, a net worth of almost $10 Million or a wardrobe full of tailor made suits, decked out with diamond buttons.

He instead started off like most of Colorado's fortune seekers, with a covered wagon full of supplies and a dream of finding gold.

Horace had begun his life in Holland, Vermont on November 26, 1830 and caught Gold fever in June 1859. Taking his young wife Augusta and new born son Nathanial Maxcy along, Horace joined the wagon trains that were heading to Pikes Peak, which was located in an area that was not yet named Colorado, but instead was part of the Territory of Kansas. This Territory was originally part of the 1803 Louisiana Purchase, which was later renamed The Louisiana Territory in 1805 and finally received the name of The Missouri Territory on June 4, 1812.

Young Horace Tabor
89.451.4076 History Colorado

When the large, vast Missouri Territory was broken up into smaller territories, starting on March 2, 1819, Horace Tabor's desired destination of Pikes Peak found itself located inside the Territory of Kansas on May 30, 1854.

Stopping in Denver City to stock up on supplies, the Tabors eagerly headed up to the promised riches of Pikes Peak and the piles of gold that were rumored to be laying on the ground, just eager to be picked up and make somebody rich. But unfortunately, the promised gold was sparse and was mainly found as dust along the inside edges of a gold pan, which was filled with ice water that had poured down from the mountains.

And with no gold making a profitable appearance and their food pantry running low, Horace Tabor's wife Augusta began to bake bread and wash clothes for the other miners, in order for their family to survive.

On October 24, 1859, still with no sizable amount of gold in his pockets, Horace discovered that his new home, located inside the Kansas Territory, had now been re-named The Territory of Jefferson. Unfazed by this turn of events, Tabor continued on his quest to strike it rich, while his wife Augusta continued being the sole support of their family.

Taking the reins once again, Augusta convinced Horace to open up a general store in the new mining town of Buckskin Joe in 1860. While Horace continued traveled the area looking for gold, his wife and son ran the store, which was their only source of income. But when the icy winter came and mining around the town was set to stop until spring,

Young Maxcy Tabor-
The Denver Public Library, Western
History Collection-X22009

the family packed up and headed to Denver City, where Augusta ran a boarding house to keep the family fed.

But before they arrived back to Buckskin Joe, in the spring of 1861, they discovered that President James Buchanan had signed legislation that organized the free Territory of Colorado, just a week before leaving office. The Territory of Jefferson was no more.

The Tabor family's pattern of staying up in Buckskin Joe in the warmer months and they spending the winter's in Denver City, continued for eight more years, until the 1868 discovery of more mining claims in the California gulch area. Packing up once again, Augusta easily convinced Horace to open up a dry goods store and a post office in the newly formed mining town of Oro City, which was Spanish for gold.

And just like in the past, Augusta found herself running the store alone with her son Maxcy, while Horace spent his time looking for new mining claims. Since he hadn't been able to strike it rich himself, Horace would often offer to give prospectors supplies and equipment from his store for free, if they agreed to sign an IOU, which would give Tabor a percentage of their mining claim if they struck it rich.

Horace's habit of doing this infuriated his wife Augusta, since she knew that many of the miners that came into their store didn't even have a claim, they just wanted free supplies, but her husband refused to listen.

In 1875 Horace heard that Lake County, which held his beloved town of Oro City, was having elections for their first county Treasurer and he quickly threw his hat into the ring. If

Young Augusta Tabor-The Denver Public Library, Western History Collection-X-21992

he was to win, this title would secure him the notoriety he desired and more money in his family's pockets, but he didn't realize how nasty his competition could be.

One of the main reasons for the invention of the coveted new office position, was the possibility of moving the Lake County boundary lines and making it part of nearby Park County. This caused more mudslinging then Tabor was expecting.

A newspaper called "The Canon City Avalanche" published a story in February 1876 that caused Horace to question if he really wanted the job of County Treasurer or not. With the tile of the article listed as "Domestic Tragedy in Lake County", it falsely reported that Horace was being charged with his wife Augusta's murder!

The story went on to mention that Horace had been jealous and cruel to his wife Augusta, which resulted in her elopement with a man named Ward Maxey from the town of Fairplay. The article ended with the story of how Horace Tabor discovered the betrayal and murdered his wife.

The humorous part of the story was that Horace and Augusta's 19 year old son Nathaniel Maxcy worked alongside his mother in their store and it appeared that the writer of the article, may have been implying that Augusta and her son were having an affair.

Luckily, the fire storm from this story quickly burned out, with the discovery of Horace and Augusta attending a nearby party alive and well, which allowed Horace to easily win the election.

And to add to the excitement, it was announced on August 1, 1876 that the Free Territory of Colorado, was now officially the state of Colorado. President Ulysses Grant signed the proclamation of statehood, despite President Andrew Jackson vetoing its first bid to become a state and join the Union.

In regards to Horace Tabor's victory, in becoming Lake County's first county Treasurer, Augusta and Horace decided to keep themselves in the spot light by opening up a second Dry goods store in the nearby mining camp of "Slab Town", leaving their son Maxcy to run the store back in Oro, City.

Horace's handling of the newly elected office of County Treasurer impressed so many residents of Slab Town, that he was soon appointed one of the commissioners and Election Judges of the "Perfect a town Organization" on January 10, 1878.

Joined by three other appointed members, their first task was to give their little mining camp a real name, instead of continuing to call it "Slab Town." As the town's people gathered around, names were thrown into a hat and voted on.

Agassiz?

Carbonateville?

Harrison?

Leadville?

With a winning vote, the town was officially re-named Leadville and to add to his ever increasing list of jobs, Horace Tabor was also named the town's Mayor on February 4, 1878, but he wasn't officially recognized until April 3, 1878.

While running his Leadville Dry Goods store on April 21, 1878, two hopeful miners came into Horace Tabor's store looking for supplies, but as usual, had no money. Their names were August Rische and Theodore Hook and all they owned was a pick, a shovel and a dog. As was his habit, Horace agreed to give them not only the supplies they desired, but groceries as well, for a 1/3 interest in their claim.

But this investment actually paid off.

After years of Horace investing into fraudulent claims and worthless mines, these two miners used their newly acquired supplies and stuck their pick axe into a thirty foot drift of high grade silver ore. The two men quickly christened their new mine "The Little Pittsburgh", named after the Pittsburgh steel mills that Theodore Hook had once worked at. With excitement and full of adrenaline, the two men quickly filled a wagon full of the ore and took it to the nearest smelter.

Elated to find that their new claim had produced such high grade ore and being paid $800 for the first wagon load, they decided to keep their acquired money a secret from Horace Tabor…but good news travels fast.

Arriving at the newly formed mine, with the signed document that listed Tabor as a 1/3 partner, the two men quickly admitted defeat and welcomed Horace onto the team. Luckily for them, Horace knew everything that was needed to make the new mine productive and within two months, the mine was producing $20,000 a month.

Horace Tabor was finally a rich man.

As Horace continued his many duties, which included being Leadville's Mayor, Post master and the County Treasurer, as well as helping his family run two General stores and working at "The Little Pittsburgh" mine, he discovered that his name had been put into the running for the Lieutenant Governor of Colorado, on July 22, 1878.

The current Lieutenant Governor of Colorado was Lafayette Head, who was elected to the newly formed post on October 3, 1876, only two months after Colorado became a State.

Mr. Head had been elected in 1875 at the Constitutional convention, as the United States prepared to grant Colorado Statehood and now his term was coming to an end. But Horace Tabor wasn't taking the idea of running for the position seriously, as he had no desire to have the job. Being Lieutenant Governor meant he would have to step in as Colorado's Governor, if the current one died or became too ill to do his duties and Horace just didn't have the time, so he declined to campaign or attend any of the conventions.

But he didn't say no to the nomination.

Unknown to Horace, a number of people were campaigning on his behalf and the slogan they chose for him was "A man of the people, a miner, and a man of nerve, force and excellent administrative ability." Horace Tabor smiled at the description, but still didn't have any desire to get involved, until he found himself face to face with a scoundrel named William Austin Hamilton Loveland.

Loveland owned a newspaper called "The News" and he seemed to enjoy attacking candidates in order to get more readers for his paper, but he had gone too far when he decided to mess with Horace Tabor.

William Loveland was the mayor of a Colorado town that had been named after him, so he felt he could attack anyone he wanted to, but on August 10, 1878 he started a fight he couldn't win.

He started off by accusing candidate Horace Tabor of "Cultivating friendly relations with our sister territory Utah" and then added in a second article, that Tabor was even in love with the territory and didn't have Colorado in his heart.

> "Was Tabor entirely off with the old love before he was on with the new? Two souls with but a single thought? Two wives that love as one?"
>
> "If both of Tabor's wives should take the stump, aided by his hundred Chinamen, what a red-hot canvas they would make! Did Tabor make his fortune by importing cheap labor, to the exclusion of the pioneer miner?"
>
> "Since Tabor is married to Utah, he must be a Mormon and it is known that infidelity and Mormonism go hand in hand!"

With this accusation, Horace Tabor felt he finally had to reply and make sure to steer the focus back towards his mining claim and away from the accusations of him having "Two wives and practicing infidelity". The infidelity claim, despite being directed towards his fictional love for the Territory of Utah, was beginning to stir up gossip concerning the real affairs that he was having with some of the actresses from the Opera house.

And in order to squash these accusations and keep his love affairs in the shadows and away from his wife Augusta, he was going to have to start campaigning to be the Lieutenant Governor of Colorado.

Horace started by contacting the local newspapers and informed the voting public that he had lived, in what was now the state of Colorado, for 19 years and had never brought in any Chinese labor to work his mine in Leadville. He also went on to explain that he was running as a Republican, where Mormon's in the Territory of Utah were all Democrat, so it was impossible that he favored Utah over Colorado.

But despite Tabor's best efforts to clear his name, William Loveland continued his vicious attacks on him. With a heavy heart, Horace began fiercely campaigning for the position of Lieutenant Governor, although he had no real desire to win the seat. Pulling out of the race now would just make Loveland think his vicious attacks had worked.

Finally, as a last resort, Horace Tabor filed a Libel suit against William Loveland for $30,000, which was the amount Loveland had paid for his newspaper and his printing plant. After a few more choice words against Tabor, Loveland soon turned his attention onto another candidate, who he accused of making insulting proposals to young ladies.

With the fire storm diverted, Horace immediately stopped campaigning and returned to his normal list of duties, but he had no idea the amount of attention his short burst of retaliation had attracted.

It appeared that Loveland's attack on Tabor, who was a fellow mine owner, had stirred up support for a candidate that people considered "One of their own."

On October 2, 1878, while Horace Tabor ate dinner and enjoyed a quiet evening at home, the ballots were counted and Tabor had secured 49.8% of the votes. He woke up the next morning as the second Lieutenant Governor of Colorado.

To celebrate his unexpected and unplanned victory, Horace Tabor began by contacting William Loveland and informed him that he would only drop his Libel suit, if Loveland printed a retraction in his newspaper and apologized.

```
"It is with profound regret that The
News was ever made the medium of Tabor's
attacks. Horace Tabor is a gentleman of
```

honor, integrity, ability, worth and an upright citizen."- William Loveland.

Winning the title of Lieutenant Governor, Horace soon discovered, also involved him moving to Denver and away from his beloved town of Leadville. With his mining ventures doing great and a bank account full of money, Tabor decided to treat his wife Augusta to a new home.

The three story tall mansion, he chose for her, contained over 20 rooms and had such lush grounds that it had to be tended by servants. Augusta was horrified, but Horace was ecstatic. He felt that this house mirrored his success and showed the City of Denver that he was a force to be reckoned with.

Augusta Tabor's Mansion-The Denver Public Library, Western History Collection-X22040

Having his wife packed away inside a huge home, also allowed Horace the chance to continue horsing around with other women. As he was still holding the position of Mayor in Leadville, he was able to find many excuses to spend time in Leadville and spend time he did.

One of his many conquests was an actress named Alice Morgan, who worked for the Globe Theatre Company, who entertained the crowds with her vaudeville style act of swinging Indian clubs.

Another actress that caught his eye was a woman named Erba Robeson, who worked with the Grand Central Theatre in Leadville, but Horace didn't just like actresses, he also had his eyes on ladies of the evening.

During his numerous visits to Chicago, on business involving the Governor's office, he found himself mixed up with a prostitute named Willie Deville who latched on a bit too tight. With some added effort to remove her from his life, he learned to keep his extra women at a distance, until he met Elizabeth Nellis Bonduel McCourt.

His Babe.

Despite enjoying his role as Lieutenant Governor, Horace knew he couldn't run for a second term in 1880. The firestorm that had surrounded his separation from his wife Augusta earlier that year and his ongoing affair with Elizabeth would be a field day in the newspaper's and he had no desire to put his mistress though that.

Luckily for Horace, a fellow miner named George Robinson was running for Lieutenant Governor in the 1880 election and had won Horace's position.

But unfortunately Mr. Robinson wouldn't live long enough to attend his own inauguration.

On November 26th, 1880 George Robinson was shot, at his own mine, by one of his guards. The employee who was on watch for claim jumpers, had mistaken his boss for a possible thief and had fired a warning shot in the direction of the suspected intruder. The bullet ricocheted off a nail and struck Robinson in the hip, which caused him to slowly bleed to death over a span of 36 hours.

His death on November 29th caused shock waves to flow through the Governor's office. Governor Pitkin solemnly contacted Horace Tabor and informed him that he would be remaining Lieutenant

Governor of Colorado.

For the second time, Horace Tabor had been handed the job of Lieutenant Governor of Colorado with no campaigning and no babies to kiss. He would be able to keep his social standing and his well respected job, all the while carousing with his mistress, as his wife sat in their mansion and pouted to the newspapers and local socialites.

And now that his Babe had proven her love for him, by securing a divorce from her husband- regardless of the fact it was fraudulent- Horace began to get a slight bit worried about the possibility of losing his beautiful Elizabeth to a single, younger suitor.

Horace Tabor understood, quite well, that an older man who was the current Lieutenant Governor of Colorado, was much more alluring to a young woman, than an older man who used to be the former Lieutenant Governor.

Sitting at his desk, inside the Governor's office and finishing up some last minute paper work, Horace was informed that Elizabeth was waiting for him down stairs. He hated that his lady love spent so many hours alone in their apartments at the Windsor Hotel and the fact she was shunned by the high society ladies, due to her role as his mistress.

His Mistress.

As he replaced his ivory pen back into its stand and pushed his chair away from his desk, he thought about that word.

Mistress.

Back at his Mansion on Broadway Street sat his wife Augusta, the woman who had struggled with him through the long, cold winters, the woman who had done so much to support their family and yet, she wasn't who he wanted anymore.

He had bought his wife diamonds and fur coats.

But she refused to wear them.

He had bought his wife a beautiful, three story tall Mansion full of servants, to take care of her every desire.

And she turned it into a boarding house.

He had bought his wife a beautiful carriage with matching horses. But she felt it was tacky.

Yet downstairs from his Government office, sat a young woman who loved to be spoiled and never complained. A young woman who had divorced her husband, so she could be with a man almost 24 years her senior.

His Babe didn't deserve to be shunned by the upper crust women of society.

As Horace grabbed his jacket off the back of the chair and slid his long, lanky arms into the sleeves, he thought about what he needed to do. He needed to give Elizabeth the respect she deserved and she deserved to be known as Elizabeth Bonduel Tabor.

A DEAD BARTENDER AND THE HIDDEN BOX OF DIAMONDS

"Sir, a letter has come for you", the concierge of the Windsor Hotel informed Horace Tabor, as he and Elizabeth walked through the front doors. "It arrived this morning."

Thanking the young man and returning his smile, Horace glanced at the return address and saw it was from his sister Emily. Anxious to read it, he offered Elizabeth a seat next to him in the lobby, while he opened it.

Horace's wife Augusta had been getting very vocal as of late, in regards to his abandonment of their marital home and his desire to get a divorce, which she was refusing to even discuss with him. To his relief, he saw that his sister hadn't taken Augusta's side in this matter.

Dear Brother,

I do not blame you for leaving her. You could not bear her fretting and complaining any longer. I saw enough when I was in Denver, never satisfied with one thing you did or one thing you got her, whether house, carriage, diamonds or anything you did ever pleased her.

I have gotten tired of her letters of complaints to me and have not written her for some time."

Emily

As Horace carefully folded the letter and returned it back into the envelope, he thought about how stubborn and cold his wife was being. He felt that if she really loved him, like she continued to profess that she did, then she would allow him to be with Elizabeth.

"Nobody in my entire family has ever resorted to divorce!" Augusta would always remind him, as her first line of defense, at any mention of the subject." And I come from a very large family."

"And look where that got your sister Rebecca." Horace would counter, as he would once again try to explain the benefits of divorce. "Her husband Folsom wanted a divorce and she refused. She has spent most of her married life separated from her husband because she wouldn't accept a divorce. She could have re-married!"

But Augusta still refused to budge. Her husband was a millionaire many times over and his income allowed her to live a very relaxed life style and travel at her leisure. And if she granted Horace a divorce, she was afraid she would be left penniless and destitute.

It would also be an admission of defeat.

And to Augusta, defeat was not a word she ever wanted to pass through her lips, especially in regards to that trollop Elizabeth Doe, who painted her face like a common whore. No God fearing woman would ever apply ungodly colors to her face!

Understanding of her worries and hoping to present her with a piece offering, Horace had a document drafted in March 1881, that gave Augusta the right to Will their Broadway Mansion and its property to whomever she pleased. And within two weeks, she had written up her new Will and even had it witnessed, but still refused to file for divorce.

Tired of waiting and not willing to give his ungrateful wife any of his fortune, Horace took his lady love Elizabeth on a trip to Durango, Colorado and caused quite a scandal while he was there. He decided that if Augusta wasn't going to file for divorce, then he would.

Stepping into the La Plata County Court house in January 1882, Horace declared himself a citizen of Durango, based on his numerous mining claims in the area and asked for a "Bill of Complaint" form.

Under the question "The said action is brought..." Horace went much further with his own lie, than Elizabeth had when she filed for a divorce from her husband Harvey. In Tabor's report he accused his wife Augusta of every crime he could think of, except drunkenness, due to her affiliation with the church. He knew that lie could be disproved.

One of his accusations against his wife was adultery, which was understandable for the time period, but raised eyebrows at the Court house, since Horace was filling out the form while standing next to his young mistress.

During the Victorian Era, when it came to a man seeking a divorce from his wife, the simple mention of a wife's adulterous behavior was usually excepted without question and would be a sufficient grounds for divorce. Unfortunately, the judge that signed the degree said "It could not be deemed legitimate because the circumstances were so suspect and irregular", which rendered the divorce request void and quite scandalous.

The newspapers and gossip channels were all the buzz over Tabors actions in Durango and to make matters worse, Horace's business partner William Bush had been visiting Augusta's home and had taken it upon himself to harass her.

With threats of her husband cutting her off without a cent, which was a husband's prerogative, Augusta found herself heading to the court house, but not for a divorce, but for alimony.

On April 26, 1882 Augusta applied to the Colorado courts for adequate financial support. She applied for alimony and proper maintenance.

1. *From the time of her marriage to the month of July 1880 lived and cohabited with defendant as his wife, and always conducted herself towards her said husband as a true, faithful and loving wife, forgiving her husband's faults and shortcomings, aiding and assisting him in their common business and sedulously striving to make their home and family pleasant, comfortable and happy.*
2. *That on or about the month of January 1881, said defendant disregarding the duty and solemnity of his marriage vow, willfully deserted and absented himself from the said plaintiff and ever since has and continues willfully and without cause to desert and abandon said plaintiff and to live separate and apart from her without sufficient cause or any lawful reason and against her will and consent.*
3. *That said defendant has often times offered to the plaintiff a portion of his large fortune if she would apply for and secure a divorce between herself and her husband from the bonds of matrimony, for which she has ample cause but each of said offers has been firmly rejected and is still declined by the plaintiff.*

She went on to list that "Their common, mutual exertions, patient industry and economy from more than 23 years, they had acquired real, personal and mixed to the estimated value of $9 million" and went on to claim that Horace had a present income of $100,000 a month.

For herself, Augusta asked the court to declare the Broadway Mansion her sole and separate property with the title in her name only and $50,000 annual support.

Her claim was denied.

The courts dictated that the Lieutenant Governor had already provided for his wife in a "Handsome and liberal manner" and yet she refuses his request for a divorce. The Court continued by saying

"This is generally considered as revenge and spite work on her part and has already resulted in expressions of sympathy for him, as it's being instigated by revenge."

With a divorce still unachieved, Horace turned his focus back onto his upcoming bid for Senator of Colorado. Unlike his two previous Lieutenant Governor runs, of which he never campaigned, he was eagerly trying to win this seat.

Tabor's Republican opponents for the 1883 Colorado Senate race were William Hamill, Thomas Bowen and Horace's own boss …the current Governor of Colorado, Frederick Pitkin.

Tabor's first opponent, Mr. William Hamill, was a silver miner, but unlike Horace, Hamill made his money in a very corrupt fashion.

When Hamill would discover a productive mine, he would buy up all the unproductive mines that surrounded it and then tangle the remaining mine owners in frivolous lawsuits. By forcing the mines into bankruptcy, he could then acquire the property at pennies on the dollar. Horace quickly realized that Hamill wasn't a threat. With Colorado full of miners and mine owners, nobody would cast their vote for a scoundrel like Hamill.

Tabor's second opponent was Mr. Thomas Bowen, a current member of the House of Representatives, which made him Tabors biggest threat.

Horace's only saving grace, in keeping votes out of Bowen's hands, involved a scandal the man was involved in a few years back. But even Tabor didn't know if that was enough to keep Thomas Bowen from winning the election.

Back in 1876, Thomas Bowen was elected the Judge of the Fourth Judicial Court, a position he held until the night of April 28th, 1880.

The night he found himself running for his life.

As a Judge who decided the fate and jail terms for numerous types of crimes, Bowen found himself face to face with a man who was facing murder charges. His name was John J. Hoover.

Hoover had walked into a bar in Fairplay, Colorado, shot the bartender and then declared himself the new owner of the hotel. But when the bartender died and John Hoover got arrested, he started to sing a different tune.

As he stood in front of Judge Thomas Bowen, Hoover declared himself temporarily insane, due to an old mining injury. The story he shared with the court involved him falling down a 65 foot mine shaft back in Oro City, which caused him to have "Temporary fits of insanity."

After hearing his plea and the reasons for his heinous actions, Judge Bowen reduced the crime to manslaughter and after subtracting time served, John Hoover was set to only spend 5 years in the Canon City Territorial Prison.

But that wasn't sitting well with the residents of Fairplay.

On the evening of April 28, 1880, Mr. Hoover was drug out of the courthouse and strung up by the friends of the deceased bartender. Judge Bowen watched the man's body swing from the second floor window of the Hotel for only a few moments, before he backed his bags and got out of town. He reigned the next day.

Horace Tabor's third opponent for Senator, was the current Governor of Colorado and Tabor's boss, Frederick Pitkin. As Lieutenant Governor of Colorado, Horace was quite aware of all of Governor Pitkin's short coming and didn't see him as a threat, in regards to Tabor's quest to be the next Senator of Colorado.

Frederick Pitkin had won his seat as Governor in 1878, but had already faced a few challenges that would still be fresh in the memories of the voters, as they showed him to be weak.

In 1879 Governor Pitkin was faced with the "Meeker Massacre", involving the attempted relocation of a tribe of Indians that did not want to move and then in 1880 he hid in Wyoming when he was desperately needed during another crisis, this one involving striking miners.

During Pitkin's term as Governor, the town of Leadville found themselves in the midst of a vicious mining strike, started by Union organizers who wanted to recruit new members. But when things got out of hand, the Governor Pitkin found urgent business that needed tending to in Cheyenne, Wyoming and left Lieutenant Governor Tabor to take the reins.

Horace felt his only real threat, in regards to winning the Senate seat, was Thomas Bowen and his own estranged wife Augusta. Her continued refusal, in regards to granting him a divorce and the lawsuit she filed demanding Alimony, was taking precedent over his Senate run.

It had to stop…

But while Horace wrangled with his options, in regards to his desired divorce, he would soon discover that he was going to be getting married to his lady love Elizabeth earlier than he expected.

Whether his wife Augusta liked it or not.

Tabor had discovered that when Elizabeth had originally started to fool around on her now ex-husband Harvey Doe, she had acquired numerous baubles from her many suitors. But since she was, at that time, still legally married to Harvey, she was afraid she might lose her shiny little trinkets to him if they were ever to divorce. After discussing her worries with her family, it was decided that she needed to ship them off to her brother James for safe keeping.

But now her brother was dead.

James McCourt had been killed in a racing accident in September 1882 and his creditors were already knocking on his widow's door demanding payment for his debts. But unfortunately for Elizabeth, they had also just discovered what was inside the safe deposit box.

Happy for a much needed distraction, Horace and Elizabeth boarded a train for her home town of Oshkosh, Wisconsin, to pay their final respects to her brother and retrieve her personal property.

If only it was that easy.

Upon arriving at the bank, Elizabeth and her brothers widow Amelia (who the family had nick-named "Dolly Bibbles") presented their safe deposit box keys to the bank employee, but they were refused access to the box.

It seemed that bank policy dictated that a divorcee, with no visible means of support, could not possibly be the rightful owner of the shiny, gem encrusted treasures located inside the safe deposit box. As a woman, the jewelry rightfully belongs to her now ex-husband.

After some discussion, the bank's manager went onto explain that the only way the former Mrs. Harvey Doe could retrieve her shiny valuables, was if her ex-husband retrieved them or is she was re-married. If not, the jewelry inside the safe deposit box, which had recently been appraised at over $15,000, would become the property of James McCourt's creditors.

With the bank agreeing to give the Lieutenant Governor a week to set things in order, Horace, Elizabeth and her brother Peter quickly boarded a train down to St. Louis, Missouri, where a Judge owed Horace a favor.

Arriving on September 30, 1882, Horace Tabor, Elizabeth and her brother took a carriage ride to the court house, located at 11 North 4th street and were greeted by a building that was truly a construction marvel.

The court house, completed in 1862, had been patterned after the St. Peters Basilica church in Rome, and the immense copper dome, which graced the top of the structure, was the epitome of elegance.

Walking inside, they were immediately hypnotized by the grand design of the building, which showcased solid stone pillars and white oak columns. The beautiful details of the majestic domes interior, which could be viewed from inside the center of the building, was the same design used in Washington, D.C. for their Capital building.

Locating the front desk, Horace Tabor was quickly allowed access to his friend Colonel D.P. Dyer, who welcomed his old friend with a firm handshake and a tip of his hat for the lady. Horace then introduced Colonel Dyer to Elizabeth's brother Peter, who quickly offered his hand as well. Mr. McCourt had come to be a witness to their marriage, as one of the stipulations for the bank.

Just as the Colonel was explaining to Horace that a Justice of the peace would have to do the ceremony, a gentleman named John M Young entered the Colonel's office and introduced himself. After exchanging handshakes all around, Mr. Young laid out the blank marriage license on the desk and proceeded to fill in a form that both Horace and Elizabeth knew was extremely fraudulent:

H.A.W Tabor of Colorado, over the age of 21, to Elizabeth B. McCourt of Wisconsin, over the age of 18 years.
Signed and stamped by Justice John M. Young of Saint Louis.

Despite the marriage not being legal, Elizabeth found herself over the moon with happiness. Horace really did love her! He loved her enough to risk public humiliation and even his bid to become the Senator of Colorado, just to retrieve her sparkly treasures for her!

With an extra bounce in her step, Elizabeth held the arm of her fictitious husband, knowing she was now only one step closer to becoming the real Mrs. Elizabeth Tabor.

Arriving back in Oshkosh, Wisconsin, Horace walked up to the bank Manager, who had caused so much trouble before and presented him with a marriage certificate. After putting up a bond, that matched the value of Elizabeth's jewelry, the couple was finally able to return to Colorado.

With Augusta unaware of her husband Horace's sudden fraudulent marriage, the court case involving the subject of alimony continued on her end.

On December 23, 1882, the case was addressed once again, in regards to the $50,000 a year in alimony Mrs. Augusta L. Tabor was demanding. As the attorneys argued, the judge made an unusual ruling and decided that perhaps he would try the case for alimony without a divorce, at the next hearing. Seeing this as a victory, Augusta continued to stand strong in regards to her husband's demands for divorce.

But people do change.

As the year was drawing to an end, Horace appealed to Augusta once more. He sat and talked to her about his desire to become a Colorado Senator and explained to her that his only true opponent was

Thomas Bowen, but he needed her help in defeating him. If she could just secure a divorce by January 9, 1883, before the votes were cast, he was sure to win.

On January 2, 1883 Augusta Tabor arrived at the Denver District court house, with her lawyer Amos Steck, and tearfully asked Judge Harrington for a divorce.

Massive marble fireplaces and ornate chandeliers

"**All rise, the** Honorable B.F. Harrington of the Denver District court presiding", the Bailiff announced, as Judge Harrington entered the court room.

Augusta Tabor stood in the court room alone. She was surrounded by curious onlookers, newspaper reporters and her Lawyer Amos Streck, but she was alone. Her beloved husband Horace, who had begged her for a divorce, wasn't even in the court room.

She was utterly and painfully alone.

As she looked around, she saw only the Judge, the county clerk, Sheriff Spangler, her attorney Mr. Streck and her soon to be ex-husbands attorney Mr. Rockwell.

"Mrs. Tabor, was there any collusion between yourself and your husband, in trying to procure this divorce?" Judge Harrington asked, as he looked through his paperwork." And with collusion, I'm referring to any type of conspiracy that you feel was put into place to deceive or cheat you."

"Yes, your honor." Augusta answered, as she found herself starting to tear up.

"Your Honor, collusion exists only as to Mrs. Tabor consenting to take a certain sum of money to procure the divorce." Augusta's Attorney Streck blurted out, in an effort to stop her from speaking. "That is it, your Honor."

With a nod of his head, Judge Harrington began signing the divorce papers, granting Horace Tabor his wish. As Augusta watched the coldness of the pen glide across the paper, which would end her almost 26 year marriage, she quickly spoke up.

"Judge, I wish you would enter upon the record, not willingly asked for. Oh God! Not willingly! Not willingly!" Augusta added, as she found herself bursting into tears." Not willingly!"

With a slight sigh of annoyance, at the show he felt his client was presenting to the Judge, Augusta's attorney walked over to the bailiff and retrieved the still wet divorce papers. As he approached the table, he slowed down his pace, to allow her time to wipe her eyes enough to sign her name.

"What is my name now?" Augusta asked her Attorney, in almost a scream. "What is it!" she asked again, as the tears started to flow.

"Your name is still Tabor, Ma'am", her Attorney replied, as he tried hard to show even the slightest air of compassion, "Keep the name, it is yours by right."

"I will. It was good enough for me to take, it is good enough for me to keep." She replied, as she slowly added her name below the name of her now Ex-husband.

But the instant Augusta finished adding the final letter of her name and before she even had time to lift the pen from the paper, she was approached by Horace's Attorney Mr. Rockwell. He had stood silently, until this point and now was ready to give Augusta her final blow.

"Ma'am, my name is Attorney Rockwell, I represent Horace Tabor." He announced, as he took Augusta's shaking hands into his own and gave them a quick squeeze. His Cheshire cat smile and his cold, damp hands, quickly brought back memories of how a Funeral director greets the family of the deceased.

"Mrs. Tabor," he began, as he quickly let go of her hands, so he could remove a piece of paper out of his briefcase and place it on the table in front of her. "I am here to inform you that my client, Horace Tabor, is willing to give you the sole rights of ownership to your home on Broadway Street in Denver, to do with as you see fit."

Shocked, Augusta quickly looked over at her Lawyer, before lifting up the document. Flipping it over, she found it was blank on the back.

"And support, yearly support! He promised!" Augusta added, in a demanding tone. But the look she received from Attorney Rockwell and the side to side shake of his head, said it all. Augusta's marriage was over and her now ex-husband, a man worth almost $9 million, had left her penniless.

No alimony.

No separate maintenance.

Not a dime.

As Augusta stood in shock, and watched the two Attorneys shake hands, she glanced back down at the deed. The deed to a three story home with over 20 rooms and gardens so lavish they needed to be attended to by a gardener. How will she feed herself? How will she afford to keep the oil lamps burning? How will he even afford to heat the house?

In a burst of clarity, Augusta wiped the tears from her eyes and confronted Horace's Attorney, as he clicked his briefcase shut. She suddenly knew how to keep herself from becoming a burden on her family.

How to keep herself from starving.

"I also want the La Veta Apartments!" Augusta demanded, finding her inner strength beginning to build. "Horace has enough properties. I want the apartments added and solely in my name."

Surprised by her sudden change of attitude, Attorney Rockwell turned to face his clients now Ex-wife and began to feel a slight tinge of respect for her, but just slight.

Clicking his briefcase back open, he pulled out a notepad and jotted down the information. "I'll be in touch." He added, as he now found Augusta Tabor standing tall and offering her own hand. Her now firm hand shake, added to his building sense of respect.

After Attorney Rockwell's meeting with Horace Tabor and hashing over the details of Augusta's demands, she was invited back to her Lawyers office to go over the details.

If she wanted the Apartments, she would have to pay for them.

In a shocking turn of events, Horace brought up the $100,000 gift he had given to Augusta, the night he became the Lieutenant Governor of Colorado in 1879 . The $100,000 was for her to spend any way she wished, but Horace was very aware that the gift was still sitting in the bank untouched.

And he wanted it back.

After getting over her initial shock, Augusta agreed to meet Attorney Rockwell and her own Attorney Mr. Steck at the bank, to make the transfer of the funds for the apartments and the transfer of both the deeds over to her.

"Now Mrs. Tabor, I need you to realize that by purchasing the apartment's from my client and excepting the home on Broadway Street, you are doing this in lieu of all claims for alimony, maintenance and support forever." Horace's Attorney informed her, as he slid the deeds to the properties across the table for her to sign. With a deep breath, and quick twist of the pen, Augusta added her signature and both properties became hers.

In 1883 Horace Tabor was worth over $9 Million dollars and he gave his wife of almost 26 years, the mother of his only child, the woman who dealt with freezing winter storms in desolate mining camps, the woman who rubbed her hands raw washing clothes for miners to keep her family from starving, the woman who ran the general store in

Leadville that helped produce his first productive mining endeavor... property valued at only $150,000.

And not a dime more.

The La Veta apartments, Augusta so wisely purchased from Horace for $100,000, were located in a very elegant section of Denver. Constructed with massive marble fireplaces, ornate chandeliers and formal parlors, they were the most fashionable in town. In total, the property contained 14 apartments, with each renting for around $150 a month.

With the income from this investment and the rooms she rented out inside her Broadway Mansion, Augusta would easily be able to support herself, but she wouldn't be able to ever look at Horace again without a twinge of disgust.

And with his desired divorce finalized, Horace Tabor could now focus solely on his race for Senator, but his current job as Lieutenant Governor just threw an unexpected wrench in his plans. Called into an emergency meeting, Horace was informed that Governor Frederick Pitkin, his boss and Senatorial race rival, was sick.

Again.

With only 6 days left in his term as Lieutenant Governor, Horace once again found himself in the Governors chair, but this time Tabor would finish his term of office as the official Governor of Colorado.

Frederick Pitkin had been dealing with a deadly illness for years, but unfortunately, this latest trip to the Sanitarium would prevent him from finishing his term as Colorado's Governor and could possibly ruin his chance to become Senator.

Frederick Pitkin was first diagnosed with Tuberculosis in 1873, which had prompted him to travel throughout Europe, in a desperate attempt to find a cure. Discovering that a sunny, dry climate helped to heal the lungs, he moved to Colorado in 1874, where he was able to finally find relief.

But the toll of being the Governor of Colorado, had spiraled his lung disease out of control and had left his Lieutenant Governor, Horace Tabor, saddled with the task of being the stand-in Governor more times than Pitkin would have liked. The fatigue, the weight loss and his severe coughing fits, which resulted in numerous bloody handkerchiefs, finally convinced him he had to throw in the towel.

Frederick Pitkin had no choice but to hand the full seat of Governor of Colorado, over to his Lieutenant Governor Horace Tabor.

And as Pitkin checked himself back into yet another Sanitarium, this one at an undisclosed location in the east, Horace found himself in full command of the Governorship, while still campaigning for Senator.

The first Caucus held for the office of Senator was on January 15, 1883 and found six people running, which consisted of four Republicans and two Democrats. Despite Frederick Pitkin being absent from the campaign, he was still listed as a candidate, as he was hoping for quick recovery.

As the campaign went into full swing, the newspapers had a field day with all the potential Senators, with one paper even coming up with a catchy little poem to commemorate the event.

> *"Sing a song of Caucus*
> *Senatorial pie*
> *Six or seven candidates and none of them are high*
> *While the Caucus wrangles O'er the precious prize*
> *Along comes a dark horse and nips it "Fore their eyes."*

The candidates had not been sure who this dark horse was, until they saw the name of the current Colorado Senator on the ballot, which made them laugh, since Senator Henry Teller had just recently quit, so he could change political parties.

Senator Teller and 24 other active Senators had stormed out, after the Republican National convention declared that gold, not silver would become the standard. The Senators had all left their seats vacant, with Senator Teller loudly declaring that he was so disgusted that he was changing his party to Democrat, as he stormed out of the Senate Chambers.

But when the caucus votes were tallied, on January 15, Horace Tabor found himself standing a bit taller. With a smile, he felt that his decision to force Augusta into a divorce had paid off after all.

Frederick Pitkin-21

Horace Tabor-16

William Hamill-10

Thomas Bowen- 4

Senator William Teller- 1

With 27 votes needed to secure the nomination, a second vote was cast on January 26th, with an upsetting turn around for Horace. Thinking that Governor Pitkin was his only real opponent and with Pitkin's medical diagnoses coming to light, Tabor was sure to be the winner. But it appeared that the man he feared could beat him all along, Thomas Bowen, jumped ahead for the win.

With the final votes cast, Thomas Bowen received the 27 votes needed to secure his nomination as the next Senator of Colorado, where Tabor received only 13. But as Horace felt his shoulders start to slouch and his tail begin to go between his legs, he and 23 other Governor's, from around the nation, found themselves being called into an unexpected meeting and were named temporary Senators.

With the 24 Senators, including Colorado's own Senator Teller, abandoning their seats, the current Governors of those vacated states found themselves in what was called "A hold."

And since Governor Pitkin had handed the reigns over to Horace Tabor, Horace discovered that he would be a Senator after all.

Even if it was just temporary.

With the next term of office not set to start until March 4, 1883, all active Governors were to be sworn in to fill the seats and with Governor

Pitkin still unable to perform his duties as the Governor of Colorado, Horace Tabor was to be sworn in as the Senator of Colorado.

For 36 days.

Elizabeth was ecstatic. As her and Horace packed their bags for their trip to Washington, Tabor had two telegrams sent. One was sent to Washington, with his instructions for the Senate and one to his Son Maxcy, who had kept his distance from his father, since leaving his mother Augusta in such dire financial straits.

Horace was hoping that this trip could help repair some of the hurt feelings and Maxcy had the blessings of his mother to join him. As Horace Tabors sole heir, Augusta didn't want to risk her child losing his rightful inheritance.

But as Horace, Maxcy and Elizabeth boarded the train bound for Washington D.C., the telegram he had sent ahead of him to the Senate, was causing quite an uproar. Newspaper editors quickly began printing stories that labeled Horace as a disgrace to Colorado and deeply criticized his request that the Senate stop all appointments and confirmations until he arrived.

Horace had no idea what type of hornets' nest he was walking into.

Arriving in Washington D.C., on Feburary 2, 1883, Horace Tabor and his son Maxcy greeted fellow Senators outside the Capital building, while Elizabeth was taken to their Hotel to rest. With Newspapers recording the historic event, Horace's visit was not painted fondly.

> "When Senator Tabor approached the Capital at Washington and began ascending the stairway in the rotunda, the marble goddess of Liberty bowed down to him and extended her hand to greet the fabled stick-in-the mud from the Silver State. As he walked arm and arm with Senator's Edmonds and Blaine, he did so with war horse steps and a gaudy mustache..."

As the temporary Senators filed into the Senate Chambers, they were greeted by President Chester Alan Arthur, who would conduct the ceremony, along with Chief Justice Waite. Normally, this honor is done by the Vice President of the United States, but right now there wasn't one.

On March 4, 1881, the man who had been sworn in as the 20th President of the United States was James Garfield, with Chester Arthur being sworn in as his Vice President. Unfortunately, the morning of July 2, 1881 changed the course of history and this change was blamed on direct orders from God himself.

A disturbed man by the name of Charles Guiteau felt that he had received a divine message from God to kill the President and he boarded the train that day to do just that. Shooting the President twice, once in the arm and once in the back, began the germ filled, downward spiral of a man who had only been President for less than four months.

Immediately after the shooting, nearby doctors carried the wounded President into a room at the train station and began digging dirty fingers and unsterilized instruments into the bullet wound in his back. Unable to locate the bullet, President Garfield was transported back to the White house, where he suffered through fevers, severe weight loss and finally blood poisoning. He succumbed to the infections that raged through his body, on September 19, 1881.

Which was quickly followed by Vice President Chester Alan Arthur being sworn in as President.

And with the temporary Senators standing inside the Senate Chambers, President Chester Arthur, asked them to all raise their right hands and repeat the Senate's oath of office.

"…I will well and faithfully discharge the duties of the office on which I am about to enter. So help me God."

As each new Senator approached the bench, to give a speech of thanks and commitment to their newly elected position, Horace Tabor patiently waited his turn to address the legislators.

> *"You have seen fit to factor me with an election to the short term, a baby term, which is only 30 days. It is not always that one who goes in for the big prize, is put off with one 72nd part of it as I have been, yet I am very thankful and am satisfied, especially as you have secured a very capable gentleman for the long term. As I will be in Washington but 30 days, I will be able to be of but little service, but I shall do what I can and I shall take especial pains to commend the State to the kind of consideration of the President."*

Quickly getting down to business, Horace Tabor found himself seated in his newly acquired senate seat, discussing a Tariff bill. Despite not quite understanding what the bill entailed or the correct way to address it, Horace stood up and made everyone in the room thankful that his term as Senator would be a short one.

> *"I have no personal acquaintance with this tariff bill, but what I have known of Buffalo Bill, Wild Bill and Billy the Kid has inspired me with the conviction that our glorious country has had quite enough to do with bills of every kind!"*

As Horace patted himself on the back and returned to his seat, he decided that his short run as Senator should be topped off with a once in a life time event. An event celebrated not only by family, but by the President of the United States himself.

He was going to marry his lady love Elizabeth, his sweet Babe, in Washington D.C.

The child bride and the canvas backed duck

With Horace spending his days as both the Governor and Senator of Colorado, he let his lady love Elizabeth plan her dream wedding. With all of Washington D.C at her finger tips and an endless supply of money to play with, she sat down with a wedding designer and decided on the perfect way to celebrate their love.
A floral filled fairy land.

Since Horace and Elizabeth were already staying in the Willard Hotel, she decided to secure their largest Parlor and fill it to the brim with roses, tulips, violets, gauze and streams of light fabric everywhere. She felt like a child in a candy shop, as she picked out every kind of flower available in all of Washington D.C.

Horace desperately wanted to give his lady love everything she desired, but unfortunately, there was only one thing he couldn't give his sweet Elizabeth, regardless of all the hands he shook and all the lunches he attended.

Willing wedding guests…

Despite sending invitations to all of Washington's elite, the entire

Senate and even the President himself, Horace found himself flooded with rejection letters full of excuses.

Hoping the invited would soon have a change of heart, Horace Tabor decided to focus his attention on trying to find a Priest willing to marry him and his Elizabeth. With all the stories floating around Washington D.C. concerning Horace and Elizabeth's personal life and the scandals surrounding their recent divorces, he needed to find a Catholic Priest who didn't follow the gossip pages.

In regards to the Catholic faith, anyone who has obtained a divorce in the eyes of the state but wishes to re-marry, must also obtain an annulment in the eyes of the church. Elizabeth hadn't' received her annulment yet, as her divorce had yet to be entered into the courts and Horace, who was a practicing Protestant, had only received his divorce papers 58 days earlier. But with Elizabeth's parents expecting a Catholic wedding, there was no other way around their problem, except to lie to a Priest.

With just a few weeks left before their wedding, Horace and Elizabeth walked up the steps of The Parish of St. Matthew of the Apostle for their Pre-Cana, or pre-wedding consultation. Accompanied by Elizabeth's parents, who would serve as witnesses, the collective sinners approached the steps of the Greek revival style church at 15th and H Street.

Holding her Rosary tight in her hands, Elizabeth followed Horace and her parents into the church, approached the font of Holy water and dipped her fingers inside. Making the sign of the cross, she approached the first available pew, knelt down and removed a bible from its cradle.

Proverbs 6:16-19
"Six things there are which the Lord hateth and the seventh his soul detesteth, naughty eyes, and lying tongues…"
God hates lies. God cannot be fooled. You cannot escape God.

"Father Chappelle will see you now." announced a young woman wearing a simple dress and a nun's habit, "Please follow me."

Entering the Chambers and accepting the offered seats, the group sat in shameful silence while they waited their turn to willingly deceive God.

As the Priest entered the room and began his routine questions, Elizabeth tried hard to smile, as she listened to the rules in regards to a "Mixed Marriage." This was a marriage between a person of the Catholic faith and a Protestant, which in itself was considered a sin.

As they sat, the Priest explained that all sacred rites are forbidden and that the wedding would have to take place outside the church, without the usual Nuptial blessings. Pleased to find that an alternative site for the wedding had already been arranged, Father Chappelle continued with questions regarding the raising of future children into Catholicism and the possibility of the husband converting to the faith.

But as the Priest continued to read through his list and ask his questions, the family waited for the question they dreaded, the question that would force Elizabeth and her parents to lie to a man of God.

"Now, on the subject of previous marriages, have either of you been married before?" Father Chappelle asked the couple, as he held his pen ready to enter their answer. With a confident look, both Horace and Elizabeth lied.

"And Mr. and Mrs. McCourt, the parents of the bride-to-be, can you testify, before God, that this is a true statement?" the priest asked, as Elizabeth looked over at her parents with pleading eyes.

Peter and Elizabeth Anderson Nellis McCourt had been members of the Roman Catholic church since they were born and had even held services in their home back in Oshkosh, Wisconsin and now their daughter was asking them to lie to a man of the cloth, before God.

And they did.

With a Priest chosen and victoriously deceived, Horace could now focus on the remainder of his term as both a Senator and Governor of

Colorado, while Elizabeth put the finishing touches on their wedding plans.

With the help of the chefs of the Willard Hotel, Elizabeth planned out a fabulous reception dinner of Canvas back duck, fillet of beef larded with mushrooms and French soufflés. From the center of the large banquet table she chose to hang a white wedding bell and a wreath of rosebuds. With the addition of linen napkins, fine china and polished silver, everything was perfect.

The evening of March 1, 1883 found Horace and Elizabeth's wedding guests arriving at the Willard Hotel in luxurious carriages and in the latest fashions. The parlor quickly filled with members of Washington's elite, who arrived dressed in expensive suits, adorned with gem encrusted lapel pins and joined by their wives and daughters who outshined them all, in beautiful gowns and stylish furs.

As the champagne was poured and the soft music began to play, the floral filled parlor took on an air of refinement and elegance. But as the guests mingled, they found themselves taken back by an unexpected and uncomfortable sight. As the elite of Washington D.C. had dressed for a night of merriment, they found themselves facing both men and women

Older photo of Horace Tabor-Legends of America

dressed in black funeral attire.

Unknown to most of the wedding guests, the bride-to-be had lost her older brother James the previous September and with her family being devout Catholic, they were still observing deep mourning. Standing quietly off to the side, the men were dressed in plain, black suits with black shirts and ties, while the women wore simple, floor length black dresses with long sleeves and gloves. To add to the morbid feel, the women were also heavily veiled, with black, lace fabric that draped down to the floor.

In regards to Catholicism, the death of a child entails the observance of heavy or deep mourning for a six month period, at which time the family begins the observance of half mourning for six more months and finally finished off with light mourning for an additional three months.

Deep morning, which the family was still observing, consists of black attire, no jewelry containing any colored stones and refusal of any and all invitations to public functions, including meals eaten outside the family home. The McCourt family had only observed the five month, nine day mark, before they found themselves attending, not only a public function, but a festive dinner party as well.

As 9pm approached, the guests quieted down and took their seats. Horace and his son Maxcy were the first to walk down the aisle, where they took their places near Father Chappelle, as Elizabeth was escorted into the parlor by her father Peter. Dressed in a beautiful $7,000 wedding gown, which was trimmed at the neckline and waist with feathers, she looked stunning. A newspaper reporter, who was invited to document the event, was found not to be as impressed with the night's spectacle, as he was the people in attendance.

The attending guest list was quite short, but also quite scandalous in itself, as anyone who was found to of attended the wedding would surely be questioned at length by their Capital Hill co-workers.

As the wedding ceremony continued, the reporter counted up

the guests, to the years most talked about wedding and discovered only 18 guests who were not somehow related to the bride or groom. With Senators, the U.S. Secretary and even the President himself in attendance, the reporter found it surprising that more people didn't want to watch Senator Horace Tabor marry a child bride.

Discovering this shameful twist, which was heavily based on the fabrication Elizabeth herself had invented to hide her true age, the reporter wrote his account of Governor Tabor's wedding. Elizabeth had touted herself at being only 22 years old, to help convince the Priest that she hadn't been previously married, where in fact, she was really 28.

With Horace Tabor being 52, Elizabeth's true age made for only a 24 year age difference, but with her fabricated age listed at only 22, this became a scandalous age difference of 30 years. When the reporter added Horace Tabors height at 5'11 to Elizabeth's tiny height of only 5'2", she seemed all the more innocent and childlike.

As the ceremony concluded and the newlyweds received their celebratory toast from President Arthur, the reporter just couldn't shake the image of a tiny, blue eyed girl marrying an older man with a big walrus style moustache. As he finished writing his story, he just kept thinking about the tiny, little divorcee Mrs. Harvey Doe, the child-like mistress who stole the Millionaire Silver King away from his wife and then married him in front of the President of the United States.

The baby bride, who only hours before had been known as Mrs. Harvey Doe.

> "On Thursday night, at Willards Hotel, Washington, Senator Tabor and "Baby" Doe were married"
>
> -The Republican

> "Mrs. Tabor is without a doubt the handsomest woman in Colorado. She is young, tall and well-proportioned with a complexion so clear it reminds one of the rose bush mingling with the pure white lily"
>
> -The Albany Journal

> There is nothing in Daudet so picturesquely vulgar as this gorgeous hotel wedding of a pair who had been married for months already, but were determined to have the eclat of being married over again in a senatorial capacity"
>
> -The New York Tribune

Unfortunately, the unfavorable descriptions that flooded the newspapers attracted the attention of more than just the Washington elite, it attracted the attention of the Priest who conducted their wedding.

And he wasn't happy.

Father Chappelle not only returned the $200 that had been paid to the church, for the privilege of conducting the wedding, but left a note for Mr. and Mrs. Tabor at the front desk of the Willard Hotel. In it he bitterly complained about the shameful deceit that had been thrust upon himself and The Saint Matthews Catholic Church and that he was declaring the marriage void in the eyes of God.

While Horace had no worries for his own soul, as he was a Protestant, he still had a slight understanding of what this meant for Elizabeth and her parents. He understood that they had all committed a mortal sin against God and that his new, little wife had just added another penance to her ever increasing list of abominations in the eyes of the Church.

A mortal sin is referred to as death to the soul and every act of a mortal sin effectively refuses God's grace. This type of sin, in the eyes of the Catholic faith, can be forgiven with confession and penance. It seemed that Elizabeth and her parents couldn't lie to God after all.

With the national newspapers filled with stories of Horace and Elizabeth's wedding and the lies told to a man of the cloth, the new Mr. and Mrs. Tabor needed a quick way to change their image. Luckily for them, an invitation to a party at the White House had just arrived.

Eager to present themselves to Washington as a respectable newlywed couple, they were thrilled with the chance to quiet the gossip that followed them like a dark cloud wherever they went. But unfortunately for them, the new Mrs. Tabor had a habit of grabbing the spot light in the most negative way possible.

On March 5th, the newly wedded Tabors headed to the White house to attend a party for the Presidents sister Mary Arthur McElroy. President Arthur had become a widower in 1880, after his wife Ellen died of pneumonia, which she contracted after sitting inside a carriage during a rainstorm. With no first lady by his side, President Arthur had chosen his sister to become the official hostess.

In his grief, the President had a portrait hung of his wife Ellen inside the White house and declared that she would still be referred to as the first lady. As a token of his eternal affection, he made sure fresh flowers were always in place on the table underneath her portrait.

As the guests greeted their hosts and listened to the beautiful music played by The Marine Band, they found themselves distracted. Instead of turning their attentions towards the portrait of former President Garfield or the Whites houses private collection of rare plants, they found themselves drawn to a small, figure draped in flowing black lace.

As they followed the ghostly figure through the White house corridors, they were surprised to find that the piles of black fabric covered the newly wedding Mrs. Elizabeth Tabor.

Deciding to resume her mourning, following her Brother James

Photo of Elizabeth Tabor in her black mourning outfit-89.451.4635 History Colorado

McCourt's death, Elizabeth chose to attend the Presidents party wearing a black dress and gloves, complete with floor length lace veil and mourning bonnet. Proper Catholic mourning dictates that faithful followers of the church not attend any social functions or dinners outside the family home for a period of 6 months and her appearance at this festive social function, as well as her recent wedding banquet, proved to high society that she was nothing more than a fraud.

The newspaper reporters, that attended the party, made sure to add the story of Elizabeth's unusual appearance and that of Horace Tabor, in the worse light possible.

> "...Tabor himself is a cross between an Arizona cowboy and Mollie Maguire. With his great dark eyes and features, he looks vindictive and hateful. His handsome nightshirts, his big diamonds and that ten million bank account were a great temptation to an obscure beauty like Miss McCourt..."

Heartbroken over the description, Elizabeth decided to add yet another confession and penance to her already lengthy list of sins, by setting aside her proper mourning outfit and attending her husband Horace's final day as Governor, in the most stylish outfit money could buy. She was confident that God wouldn't mind if she just extended her heavy mourning by a few more days.

With money to burn, Elizabeth walked into the Senate ladies gallery draped in a fabulous gown of brown silk with a tight fitting bodice that enhanced her every curve. Her necklace, earrings and bracelets were covered in diamonds, as was a unique piece of jewelry that she was sure would turn heads.

Around Elizabeth's waist she wore a jeweled waist-girdle shaped like a serpent, with diamond eyes, ruby tongue and a long tail covered in emeralds. As she slowly walked past the other wives and took her seat, she could feel their eyes watching her every move. With Elizabeth and Horace leaving on a train the next morning, she wanted this outfit to be the last image the gossiping residents of Washington D.C. had of Elizabeth Tabor.

With all the wives of Washington D.C.'s elite gaggling like hens over the shameful exhibition that Elizabeth Tabor had graced the

Senate chambers with, the women found that their husbands also had their feathers ruffled during the Horace's 30 day visit.

On March 8, 1883, just hours after Horace and Elizabeth boarded a train to New York City, the Secretary of the Interior Henry Teller began penning quite a scandalous letter. Waiting until the Tabors had left Washington D.C., he had it delivered to Senator Thomas M. Dawson from San Francisco, California, to help stop the gossip pertaining to his attendance of Horace Tabor's wedding just a week earlier.

> ". . . Tabor has gone home, I thank God he was not elected for 6 years. 30 days nearly killed us. I humiliated myself to attend his wedding because he was a Senator from Colorado (but Mrs. Teller would not) I felt as if I could not afford to say that the State had sent a man to represent her in the Senate, that I would not recognize socially, but I could not of kept it up.
>
> Tabor is an honest man in money affairs and I believe he is truthful, but he made a great fool of himself with reference to that woman and he ought now retire and attend to his private affairs."

The murdered Priest and a handful of gold coins

The newlyweds returned to Denver, following their honeymoon in New York City, with an air of confidence and pride. Horace had just finished his 36 day term as not only a Senator, but the Governor of Colorado and had made an honest woman out of his mistress Elizabeth. With a smile and an extra bounce in her step, she was eager to begin her new life as the second Mrs. Tabor.

Settling into her newly acquired role, Elizabeth spent her time between their suite at the Windsor Hotel and the Tabor Grand Opera house. Draped in lavish furs, diamonds and wonderful silk gowns, she felt that she finally had everything she had ever wanted, but fate has a way of changing even the best laid plans.

On May 10th Elizabeth heard a knock at the door of her suite and when she opened it, found the bell boy standing in the hallway holding a telegram. With a smile and a tip of his hat, he handed her the message and headed back towards the elevator. Curious, she opened the envelope to find the telegram had been sent, not by her family, but by a local doctor in Oshkosh, Wisconsin.

Sitting down, back inside her suite, Elizabeth read the urgent telegram numerous times, to make sure she had read it correctly. It appeared that her family's doctor had diagnosed her Father, Mother and younger brother Martin with Typhoid.

Upon hearing the news, Horace quickly obtained train tickets for himself, Elizabeth and her brother Peter, but the next train heading to Wisconsin didn't leave until the following night. Over whelmed with grief, Elizabeth pulled out her trunks and started to pack her black mourning gowns.

Despite finding the most direct route, the group didn't arrive in Oshkosh until 3:40am Monday morning. Desperately hoping they had made it in time, Elizabeth was relieved to see that her family was still alive when she walked through the front door of the house, but barely.

Seeing them enter, the doctor came to greet them and explained the situation, which was very grave. Where Elizabeth's mother was showing signs of improvement, her father and brother where sliding into delirium. Leading them into the sick room, they saw their loved ones ravaged by fever, while the family Priest stood off to the side issuing final rights.

For a few precious moments, their father's delirium broke just long enough for the family to say their final goodbyes, before he slipped from this world at 9:55am. As the priest said a final prayer, the family held their heads down low...

"I command you, my dear brother to almighty God to entrust you to your creator and may you return to him who formed you from the dust of the earth."

The Priest then leaned over the body and made the sign of the cross...

"...may you see your redeemer face to face and enjoy the vision of God forever. Amen."

As the tears flowed, Elizabeth realized that she might be watching two more family members cross over and be with God, before this nightmare passed. Glancing over at her little brother Martin, who moaned in pain, she said a silent prayer for him.

But it was no use.

Five days later, at 1:30pm, 20 year old Martin joined his father in Gods loving embrace.

The return to Colorado was a solemn one for Elizabeth. Dressed heavily in her mourning gown and veil, she spent the trip back to her luxurious suite in Denver reciting the rosary and praying for her mother's continued recovery.

With so much death and grief surrounding them, Horace was hoping they would find a good distraction once they got back to Colorado, but he wasn't expecting to lose money in the process.

Walking into the lobby of Denver's Windsor Hotel, Horace was handed a telegram from his partners that ran the stamping mill, which Horace had built in Leadville back in 1879. Hoping it was simply a progress report, he was shocked to learn that his mill had burned down while he was in Wisconsin. Despite knowing where he was, his partners saw no point in alerting him to the disaster until his return.

The mill had been built on a slope facing California gulch and treated low grade gold and silver ore, which the older smelters were not equipped to handle. But with his mill ranked at only 11 out of the 16 mills in Leadville, neither Horace nor his partners saw the point in rebuilding it.

Tired of the pattern of heart breaking situations, Horace and Elizabeth decided to enjoy being newlyweds and simply focus on each other. Elizabeth's 30 days of deep morning for her father would be ending soon and her 6 months of half morning would begin. Luckily the Catholic faith allows mourners to wear white outfits during half mourning, as long as they have black trim, which would help Elizabeth blend in while attending the theatre.

As Elizabeth entered her 4 month mark of mourning, on September 13, 1883, she discovered that she was pregnant. Overcome with joy, the couple was thrilled to have a child to share their love with.

But not everyone was happy with the news.

Horace's ex-wife Augusta had been afraid this would happen, as she feared that a new child would disrupt her son Maxcy's inheritance as his sole heir or possibly cause Horace to disown Maxcy completely. Desperate to keep her son in the spot light, Augusta had a letter delivered to her ex-husband, which announced their son Maxcy's engagement and upcoming wedding.

"Mr. Tabor, Sir:

OUR son is to be married on the 17th of January 1884. You have promised me that he should be well provided for financially. You also told Attorney Mr. Rockwell the same thing. Now something has to be done for him. You certainly cannot expect me to help him from the penurious mite that I received. So from your abundance, I entreat you to help him.

Your wife,
Augusta L. Tabor"

As 1883 ended and 1884 began, the upcoming wedding of Maxcy Tabor was found to not of attracted much attention and paled in comparison to his father's Washington wedding the year before.

```
"The Tabor-Babcock wedding will occur at
   noon today"
```

                                        - The Denver Republican

The day after the wedding, on January 18th, one newspaper did run a very short story, but hid it on page four.

> "The marriage of Mr. N.M. Tabor, son of the ex-Senator Tabor and Miss Lou Babcock, occurred at the home of the bride on Champa Street at 5 O'clock last evening .Rev. Dr. Reuben Jeffrey and Rev. Dr. A.M. weeks officiated. But a few of the immediate relatives of the families were present, and presents were of magnificent and costly character. After the bridal dinner the bride and groom left the city at 7 O'clock for a tour of the East"
>
> - The Rocky Mountain news

With the bitter cold of January settling into the Rocky Mountains and her son traveling with his new bride, Augusta decided that a vacation for herself was in order. Packing her trunks, she boarded a train for New Orleans, where she planned to embark on a health trip to Cuba. But leaving Colorado created a void in her whereabouts, which was quickly filled with outrageous speculations and rumors of a secret wedding of her own.

An acquaintance of Augusta's, a man named William Artman, had begun spreading a story that he and Augusta had secretly traveled to Saint Louis, Missouri and gotten married. With this fabrication in his pocket and Augusta out of the state, he was easily able to convince some people to lend him money, crying that he and his new wife were destitute.

With the story picking up steam, it caught the attention of Augusta's pastor and friend, Reverend A.M Weeks. The Reverend was the Spiritual leader of the Unitarian Church of Denver and had been boarding at Augusta's Mansion for quite a while. He was quick to point out that if Augusta were to of gotten married, he would have been the one chosen to conduct the ceremony and she wouldn't have run off to Saint Louis.

With the suspected groom continuing to spread the story of his false nuptials, the tall tale caught more light after the sudden death of Reverend Weeks only 12 days later. Found dead inside Augusta Tabor's home, on January 29th, his sudden passing caused outrageous speculation, since this wasn't the first death of a Unitarian Pastor in Denver.

The Unitarian Church had opened its doors, at 17th and California, on December 28, 1873. Built of wood and of a Gothic style, the beautiful stained glass windows shone down on a congregation of 225. On September 19, 1880, a Reverend named R.L. Herbert began to lead worship, to the small congregation, before his sudden death in August 1881.

The newly deceased Reverend Weeks had begun his turn at the pulpit on March 19, 1883, before passing at the age of 33, less than a year later. With speculation running at full speed, the people of Denver waited to hear the cause of the Priests death and if Mr. Artman was a suspected in quieting the young Priest.

Despite his young age, the doctor confirmed that Reverend Weeks had died of a condition called "Congestion of the brain." This is caused by the cerebral vessels of the brain filling with blood and can be caused by a sickness or a blow to the head. With no witnesses, the death was determined accidental, but suspicious.

But regardless of the decision, Denver's high society had already decided that the popular Reverend had been murdered, but before the torches and pitch forks could be set ablaze, William Artman quickly left town and vanished.

Arriving back in Denver on May 25, 1884, tanned, rested and relaxed, Augusta was shocked to hear about all the commotion that took place while she was gone. Despite being immediately saddened by the death of her Pastor, she was more shocked at how gullible the people of Denver had been, in regards to an obvious lie. To set the story straight, she quickly penned a letter and sent it out to the local newspapers.

"...I wouldn't certainly run away from home to get married. When I do get married, I will do so openly and above board. If I do marry you can be certain it will not be Mr. Artman. I will not marry a man whom I have to support, but will expect my husband to support me. It may be that Mr. Artman started the rumor himself. The dispatch says he borrowed money on the strength of the wedding. If there were any Denver people who were fools enough to be believe me so foolish, I'm glad they were duped."

As the stories faded, the people of Colorado began drawing their attention to the impending arrival of the newest little Tabor and on July 13, 1884, Elizabeth Bonduel Lillie Tabor was born.

With her parents intending on calling her Lily, the tiny baby girl also received her mother's middle name of Bonduel, which had special meaning for the McCourt family.

Originally, the new, little mother's middle name had been chosen to be Nellis, which was her own mother's maiden name, but was quickly changed to honor a visiting Catholic missionary.

Father Florimond Bonduel had been a missionary Priest who served the Menominee Indian's in the Oshkosh, Wisconsin area. Born in Belgian, he would stop by the McCourt house and bless them with mass, along with a dozen other families. He also started the local Saint Peters Parish in 1850, before returning to missionary work with the local Indians.

After Elisabeth and Horace enjoyed the arrival of their beautiful little daughter, Father Bonduel had surprised them with a letter from Naples, Italy, which included a blessing for their marriage. He talked about his service to Saint Peter's congregation, back in Oshkosh and about how he had been the one to baptize Elizabeth McCourt, but then ended his letter with an open hand.

"We are poor, but God is good and will assist us. Our Missionary in Italy could certainly use a bit of financial support."

Eager to please the Catholic Church, after all her transgressions, Elizabeth quickly sent him a donation.

Meanwhile, as Elizabeth was trying hard to buy her way into heaven, Horace was busy making little gold coins to hand out to his friends. Inscribed with "Baby Tabor July 13, 1884" on the front, and "Compliments of the Tabor Guards Boulder, Colorado" written on the back, he had them made to be about the size of a quarter. As Horace handed the newly minted tokens out like candy, one coin made it into the hands of Elizabeth's Priest at Denver's Church of the Sacred Heart.

Baby picture of Lily Tabor-The Oshkosh Public Museum-P2001.47.6

Holding the solid gold coin in his hand, Father John B. Guida smiled and knew the perfect gift for Horace Tabors new baby. And when Elizabeth and Horace brought the baby to the next church service, he handed Elizabeth a small, silver metal. "Here is a somewhat better badge of consecration for the baby. It is a silver medal, blessed by the Holy Father in Rome."

Elizabeth couldn't be happier.

In regards to little Lily's Christening, the Tabors boarded a train back to Oshkosh, Wisconsin so the baby could receive her blessings in the family's church. Her christening outfit, which had to be anything but ordinary, was a custom made $15,000 marvel, fit for the new little Princess.

Made of Honiton lace, the same type used in Queen Victoria's wedding dress, the base of the gown cost $1,000 alone and was combined with a matching cloak of white embroidered velvet. To finish off the gown, it was edged with point lace and fluffy, feathered marabou tips. The tiny baby also wore a French felt hat, with an abundance of additional marabou tips, each costing $10 apiece. She completed her outfit with custom made booties, gold diaper pins set with real diamonds and a miniature jeweled necklace complete with a locket.

Baby Lily was born the belle of the ball and lived the life of royalty. She was photographed every chance her parents had, with her photos selling not only in America, but throughout Europe. Once she became a toddler, Lilly attended the Opera with her parents and would sit on her Father's knee to the delight of the crowd below.

With a beautiful family and plans on more little ones, Horace decided that the suite at the Windsor Hotel wasn't fitting their growing family or his image. He was, after all, the former Governor of Colorado.

As Tabor had men scour every corner of Denver to find him and his Lady love the perfect home, one that oozed with sophistication and luxury, he discovered that a man who he greatly respected was dying. And the cause sent shock waves across the nation.

A STABLE FULL OF PEACOCK FEATHERS AND THE TWO BROTHERS

President Chester Alan Arthur was dead.

The man who had attended the Washington D.C. wedding of Horace and Elizabeth Tabor and gave them their first toast, in celebration of their union, had died.

Hidden from the public, during his Presidency, he had been diagnosed with Bright's disease, thought to of been caused by the Malaria he contracted during an 1882 trip to Florida.

The disease causes the victim to become extremely lethargic, which President Arthur chose to hide from his staff by faking a drinking problem, which he blamed on depression, caused by his wife's early death. Bright's disease is also known to cause hemorrhages, convulsions and blindness before the victim falls into a coma and dies.

Struggling with his condition, he finished his term labeled as a lazy, foppish President and on March 4, 1885, he welcomed Grover Cleveland as his Presidential successor. Being released from office and in a desperate attempt to treat his aliment, Arthur traveled the country before spending the summer of 1886 in New London, Connecticut.

Returning home to New York City, he became gravely ill and on November 16th ordered almost all of his personal and private papers burned.

The following morning, on November 17th, Chester Arthur suffered a cerebral hemorrhage and died the following day. He was 57.

Despite mourning the loss of the former President, Horace and Elizabeth continued searching for the perfect home to showcase Horace's wealth and to prove to the elite of Denver that his marriage to Elizabeth had been sincere.

And on December 15, 1886 they were handed the keys.

The mansion they chose had been built in 1880 by Joseph Watson, at the corner of Olive and Sherman Streets, which Horace purchased for $54,000. The stately home was surrounded by lavish grounds, with the front of the home framed by a brownstone wall.

The two story tall stone wonder included two separate driveways that led to the carriage house and stables, which contained three beautiful carriages for the family to choose from.

The first carriage was constructed of a brown stained wood and trimmed in red, while the second was constructed of wood which had been enameled in blue, with thin gold lines painted around the body. The third was a wooden carriage enameled in black, with white trim.

Sparing no expense, Horace employed five stable men, two drivers and two footmen. He also made sure his six horses where very well attended to and wore beautiful ornamental coverings and harnesses. As an added feature, the coachmen and footmen where to dress in uniforms, which matched the carriage that the Tabor's would chose when they traveled from the house.

The grounds of their home contained elegant fountains and nude statues that were replicas of Greek treasures, which caused a terrible scandal and complaints from prudish neighbors, despite the fact the statues were already on the property when the Tabors bought the house.

A few weeks after purchasing the home and with a sly smile,

Elizabeth collected a few old coats, hats and scarves and modestly dressed her statues for the chilly weather, in order to hush up her noisy neighbors. She wanted to ring in the New Year with confidence and for her new neighbors to know that 1887 was the year people were going to start respecting the name Tabor again.

As winter continued, Elizabeth spent the icy months playing inside with her daughter Lily and becoming accustomed to having servants in her new home. Finding free time, Elizabeth relaxed with the morning newspaper and discovered that a freak snowstorm in Montana was causing quite stir.

On January 28, 1887 the soldiers at Fort Keogh witnessed the largest snowflakes they had ever seen, falling all around the base. Measuring out at 15 inches wide and 8 inches thick, the freakishly large flakes were actually a phenomenon known as Giant flakes.

Giant flakes are formed when heavy, wet snow falls and is pushed around in the wind. If the conditions are just right and the regular size flakes already have a slight layer of condensation covering them, the wind can blow them together, which makes them stick and form extra-large snowflakes.

As winter ended and spring finally arrived in Colorado, Elizabeth removed the woolen coats, hats and scarves she had dressed her Greek statue in and replaced their attire with something more fitting for the warm weather.

Lingerie.

As her neighbors walked past her home and held their gloved hands to their mouths in artificial shock and disgust, Elizabeth smiled. A few months later she added to her rebellion by purchasing full grown peacocks to roam her grounds and laughed as the large birds called out their familiar Meow and flew around the neighborhood.

As summer came and went and fall reared its head, the peacocks were gathered up and made comfortable in the stables, so they could bother the horses until spring. And not to leave the Greek statues outside in the cold, their attire was once again changed to more winter appropriate apparel.

After the New Year, Elizabeth was elated to discover that she wasn't feeling well. Both she and Horace had been praying for more children and by the end of February 1888, she was positive she was pregnant. Elizabeth desperately wanted to give Tabor a son, which was the only thing his Ex-wife Augusta could hold over her head.

Elizabeth had just turned 33 the previous September, so she knew to get plenty of rest and the Denver Newspapers had just the stories to keep her entertained. Starting in March, the papers began printing stories about a string of violent murders in London, that the police felt was committed by the same man.

The first murder happened in the early morning of March 28th 1888, when a young dressmaker answered a knock at her door and was greeted by a stranger who demanded money. She refused to pay him, which resulted in him slashing her throat twice with a clasp knife before running off.

Stumbling into the road, holding her neck, she was spotted by two women who called the constables who bound up her throat and took her to the hospital.

Surprising to everyone, Ms. Ada Wilson recovered.

The second attack happened in the early morning hours on August 7th, when Martha Tabram Turner was found dead on the landing of a boarding house, by a man heading to work. Another man, who also lived at the boarding house, told police that the woman's body was not there when he returned from work at 2am.

The constable examined her body and pronounced life extinct, due to the 39 knife wounds the woman had suffered. She had lived just a short distance from Ms. Ada Wilson.

The third victim was discovered at 3:40am on August 31st, near where the first two victims had been attacked. Her name was Mary Anne "Polly" Nichols and she had worked at a local factory and was still wearing her workhouse clothes.

Like the first two victims, her throat had been cut, from ear to ear, but this time some of the woman's teeth had been knocked out and her hands were covered in bruises, which showed she had fought her attacker. Her abdomen had also been ripped open and her bowels were protruding, which was also different from the first two victims and the residents of London were scared.

The fourth victim was Annie Chapman, who was found on September 8th, but unlike the first three victims, Annie was a prostitute who favored the drink. She also had two regular customers, who witnesses say, wanted her for themselves and she also had made a lot of enemies at the boarding house she rented from, so her murder may have not been from the same killer.

It was recorded that her body had been found a little before 6am, by a boarding house resident walking up the front steps and then reeling back in horror. Two men walking down the street saw the man stumble and discovered Annie Chapman's body laying between the steps and the wooden fence.

Since the sting of murders in the area was common gossip, the story of a possible fifth victim spread like wildfire and by the time the Police surgeon arrived around 6:30am, he had to fight the crowd of several hundred bystanders just to examine the body.

Like the others, her throat had been cut, but unlike the other victims, her womb had been removed from her body. And with that last sentence, Elizabeth Tabor put down the newspaper.

With Elizabeth's summer spent reading stories of murder and mystery in London, she discovered that she could no longer sit for long periods of time and didn't feel like reading anymore. Her pregnancy with her third child, her second with Horace, was getting farther along and as October began, she was starting to have small contractions.

The baby would be here soon.

Finally, on October 17th, with Horace and their 4 year old daughter

Lily patiently waiting to hear the cry of a newborn, Horace Tabor was blessed with another son, who they named Horace Joseph Tabor.

But the baby didn't look right.

Frantic, a doctor was immediately called and the situation quickly began to look dire. The baby wasn't breathing deep enough to produce the expected howls and instead his cries were shallow and his color was ashy. As the midwife wrapped the baby up and placed him near the fireplace, in a desperate attempt to produce the desired pink skin tone, the call was also put out to find Father John B. Guida, to administer last rights.

After a quick search, Father John B. Guida was soon located and a carriage was sent for him. As the infant struggled to breathe, Elizabeth asked for her child back, cradled him against her body and began praying.

Hearing a carriage pull up in the drive, Horace quickly ran out to greet the Doctor and filled him in on the baby's condition, as he led him up the front steps of the house. Inside, the Doctor found the infant pressed up against his mother's bare breast, as Elizabeth desperately tried to get the baby to nurse.

"Please help him." Elizabeth begged, as she lifted up the limp infant and handed him to the Doctor. But the baby's grayish tone told the Doctor everything he didn't want to know.

The baby was dying.

Knowing he was under the watchful eye of one of the most powerful men in the State, the Doctor did a full examination on the struggling infant, in the hope he could find some ray of hope, but he couldn't.

Horace listened to the frantic screams of his young wife, as the Doctor gave his sincerest apologies to both of them, handed the baby back to Elizabeth and gave her instruction's to keep the baby warm. As Tabor's own eyes filled with tears, he would have given every dine he had, if it would just save his little boy.

Hearing a second carriage arrive in the driveway, Elizabeth pleaded for Horace to quickly bring the priest. The thought of her fragile infant dying without being baptized, terrified her more than the fact she was losing her son.

"Let me see the baby." Father Guida instructed, as he quickly set his bag on the table. As he peered down at the newborn, still cradled against Elizabeth's bare chest, he quickly kissed his Stole before placing it carefully around his neck.

Opening the bag, he pulled out a small bottle of holy water and a small bottle of an oil called Chrism, which was olive oil scented with Balsam. This would be used during the second anointing, as a symbol of being chosen.

"Do both you Horace and you Elizabeth agree to allow your child to be baptized in the Catholic faith?"

"We do."

Father Guida then gently removed the newborn from Elizabeth's grasp and held him against his own body. The infant's bluish color and labored breathing made the priest quicken the ceremony ,as he made the sign of the cross over little Horace Joseph's forehead.

"I claim you for Christ our Savior, by the sign of the cross."

As the priest continued to cradle the infant, he looked over at Elizabeth and Horace. It was so difficult to do baptisms on dying children and looking into the red, swollen eyes of distraught parents broke his heart every time.

"Horace and Elizabeth Tabor, do you both reject Satan?"

"Yes."

"Do you believe in God?"

"Yes"

"Do you believe in Jesus Christ, the Son of God?

"Yes"

"Do you believe in the Holy Spirit?"

"Yes"

With that, the Priest requested a basin for the Baptism and gently caressed the baby's cold hands as he waited. Luckily a small laundry tub

A STABLE FULL OF PEACOCK FEATHERS AND THE TWO BROTHERS 87

was found and placed next to the fire, as Horace helped his wife from the bed and led her over to a nearby chair.

"Horace Joseph Tabor, I baptize you in the name of the Father and the Son and of the Holy Spirit" the Priest announced as he poured holy water over the newborns forehead three separate times, once for each prayer.

He then used a cloth to dry the infant's forehead, before anointing him with oil.

"Mr. and Mrs. Tabor, I'm afraid your son doesn't' have very much time left before he meets our Lord and Savior and I think it best that he is taken outside to see the sun and feel the wind on his face, before he does." Father Guida instructed, as he gently handed the baby back to Horace.

"I'm sorry."

With the fall leaves blowing across the lawn and the sound of caged Peacocks singing their song in the stables, little Horace Joseph Tabor took his last breath.

He had lived for 10 hours.

With a private funeral held and a small white coffin placed into the cold, dark earth, Elizabeth spent her days in deep mourning. As she placed the black veil over her face and prayed the rosary, she knew in her heart, why her baby had died.

Because she had sinned.

Back when she was married to her first husband Harvey Doe, the newlyweds had moved to Central City to work the Fourth of July Mine, which had been a wedding gift from Harvey's father. But the small mining town had quickly grown boring and Elizabeth decided to slip on a pair of Miners overalls and help with their claim.

At first, Harvey welcomed his young wife's help and together they divided up the claim, with each taking a different side, in order to double their chances of striking Ore. But unfortunately for Elizabeth, the local Newspaper caught on and printed a story that caused her husband to have second thought.

> "I next reached the Fourth of July mine, which has not been worked for several years, but started back up some months ago under the supervision of the owner Mr. W.H. Doe and his wife. The young lady manages half of the property while her liege Lord manages the other.
>
> I found both at their separate shafts managing a number of workmen, Mr. Doe at his which is 70 feet and his wife who is full of ambition, in her new enterprise, at hers which is 60 feet."

The knowledge that a woman was wearing man's overalls and leading a team of miners sent shock waves through the prudish mining camp. A letter was even sent to Elizabeth's mother-in-law, explaining how her daughter-in-law was "A Hussy that needed to understand her rightful place"

The letter continued to smear Elizabeth's reputation by mentioning how the young woman "Dressed like a man all week and a princess on Sunday's, all the while cavorting around on spirited horse named Pet."

Furious, Elizabeth's in-laws, along with two of her husbands' sisters, packed their trunks and headed to Central City.

Soon Harvey and Elizabeth were faced with his angry parents, who demanded that Elizabeth act like a proper house wife and take care of their son. Desperate to get away from her In-laws, Elizabeth suggested that her husband's family move into her and Harvey's cabin, while they themselves moved to Black Hawk.

They accepted.

Renting an apartment, over top of a brick store on Gregory street, Elizabeth discovered that she was forbidden from working in the mine and getting tired of picking wildflowers for her scrapbook, desperately needed something to keep her occupied.

And his name was Jacob Sandelowsky.

Jacob was co-owner of the Sandelowsky, Pelton and Company Men's clothing store on Gregory Street, just a few doors down from Elizabeth and Harvey's apartment and he was the most beautiful man Elizabeth had ever seen.

With his deep, dark brown eyes, dark brown wavy hair and well-groomed mustache, he was well known around Black Hawk by the ladies, but that didn't bother Elizabeth one bit.

Elizabeth Doe, in her early 20's-The Oshkosh Public Museum-P2001.47.2

As they got to know each other, Elizabeth learned that Jacob had been born on December 25, 1852 and had emigrated from Poland, with his family when he was 15. A few years later, he opened up a clothing store with his partner Sam Pelton in Central City, before opening up a second store in Black Hawk when he was just 22.

Deeply smitten, but not wanting to ruffle any feathers, Elizabeth made sure to introduce Harvey to Jacob and Sam, even encouraging them to become friends, but she quickly became more than friends with Jacob.

A few months later, on November 18, 1878, Elizabeth's father-in-law decided that he didn't like how his son was running the Fourth of July mine and hired a new team and a new Forman to run it. Then, to add insult to injury, he got his son a job working at the new Forman's Mill, located in Nevadaville.

Needing to move back to Central City, to be closer to Harvey's new job, but wanting to stay close to her lover, Jacob offered Elizabeth a job at his Central City store. Happily excepting, she began working as the superintendent of the ladies Department, while finding an apartment nearby on Eureka Street.

And with Harvey working the night shift at the mill, Elizabeth and Jacob had every night together.

On March 11, 1879, Jacob gifted Elizabeth with her first pieces of real jewelry and made sure to leave the price tags on them, so Elizabeth would know they were Genuine. Jacob had bought her three diamonds, two solid gold puff bracelets and a solid gold cross for the combined total of $1,485.00.

Ironically, these were some of the Babbles her future husband Horace Tabor would have to rescue from debt collectors, after her brother's death years later.

But as Elizabeth continued spending her evenings with Jacob, while her husband worked nights, she soon discovered that she had something to tell then both.

She was pregnant.

Counting the days back on the calendar, Elizabeth knew the baby belonged to Harvey, but the residents of Central City began spreading the rumor that Jacob was the true father. Spending a night drinking, Harvey learned of the accusations and confronted his wife, who exploded in anger.

Filled with built up resentment, over discovering that the baby she was carrying didn't belong to her lover and then having her husband deny paternity, sent Elizabeth over the edge. Furious, she picked up an ore specimen and violently threw it at her husband's head, gashing it open. Seeing the blood, Harvey left.

Filled with emotion, Elizabeth wrote to her parents and explained Harvey's abandonment, but made sure to leave out the part about her acquiring a lover over a year before. Filled with parental worry, the

Drawing of Jacob Sands-Legends of America

McCourt's had Elizabeth come home to Oshkosh, Wisconsin to be with her family, in her time of need.

With Elizabeth back in Wisconsin, Harvey's parents learned that their daughter-in-law was pregnant and as far as they knew, carrying their grandchild, so they begged their son to put all matters aside and bring back Elizabeth. Despite knowing the child might not be his, but wanting his parent's approval, Harvey contacted Elizabeth and apologized.

Back in Central City, in a strange turn of events, both Harvey and Jacob began preparing for the birth of a child they felt might be theirs, but it was Jacob who took control when the baby was born.

On July 13, 1880, Elizabeth began having contractions and asked for the midwife to be brought up to the room. Frantic over the realization that he was going to be a father, Harvey panicked and ran out of the apartment, leaving Elizabeth alone with her lover. Furious at having to leave Elizabeth alone, while she was advancing in her labor, Jacob made her comfortable before going downstairs to fetch the midwife.

As the hour's passed and with the midwifes help, as well as Jacobs encouragement, Elizabeth gave birth to a blue eyed baby boy with a head full of dark brown wavy hair. But her joy soon turned to panic, when the baby wouldn't wake up. Despite all the efforts of both Jacob and the Midwife, the baby had been declared stillborn.

And now, 8 year later, she had once again given birth to a beautiful baby boy, who wouldn't live. She was thankful that her second son lived long enough to be baptized, something her first son never had the honor of receiving and she felt it was due to the sin of her affair with Jacob.

Her first son had been denied his baptism, by the local priest, since baptisms are meant to indicate the start of a lifelong effort to live out the Gospel. Some priests will perform a baptism if there is the slightest chance life is still remaining, but Elizabeth's child had never even taken a breath.

The only thing the Priest would allow, for her poor little son, was to recite the Blessing of parents after Miscarriage and make the sign of the cross on his cold little forehead.

"For those who trust in God, in the pain of sorrow there is consolation

In the face of despair there is hope, in the mist of death there is life.

Harvey and Elizabeth, as we mourn the death of your child, we place ourselves in the hands of God and ask for strength, for healing and for love"

Amen.

AND WHEN THE BOUGH BREAKS, SILVER WILL FALL

Her precious son was dead.

Just like with her first born, Elizabeth had to stand by and watch as her darling infant was placed into a wooden box and return to the earth.

Dressed in all black, with a long, shear veil covering her depression, Elizabeth began her six months of heavy mourning for the loss of the son she had with her husband Horace, as well as her first son, who was Horace Joseph Jr's big brother.

Maybe properly mourning both children would put her right with God.

Surprisingly, as Elizabeth neared the end of her six months of heavy mourning, she discovered that she was once again pregnant. Desperate for their son to be returned to them, both Horace and Elizabeth were over the moon and eagerly awaited the chance to see the face of their baby boy again.

And on December 17, 1889, just 14 months after their infant son had died, Horace and now 5 ½ year old Lily paced outside the bedroom door, while listening to the groans and agony of childbirth. Eventually the room was full of loud howls and Horace rushed in to meet his new son, but was taken back to discover it was another daughter.

As the midwife cleaned off the infant, Elizabeth and her husband suddenly realized that they had been so desperate for a boy, they never thought to choose a girl's name. Not wanting to rush, they decided to wait and just enjoy the newest addition to their family.

As well-wishers came to see the newest little Tabor and the house filled with fresh flowers, one guest brought something that he chose to give to the new father personally and out of the site of the fragile new mother.

A book.

"Chronicles of the builders of the common wealth-Historical character study", written by Hubert Howe Bancroft, had been in the works for years and Horace had been interviewed for the information it contained, but his friend warned him that the author hadn't done him justice.

In compiling the information for the short biography, Bancroft had also interviewed Horace's ex-wife Augusta, which had greatly irritated Horace Tabor at the time. Thinking it was just a casual conversation, Tabor had been very candid with the author about what Augusta may have added to the story and had now discovered that it had been added to the book.

"The data given by my wife Augusta must not be followed as she may be a little disgruntled and properly so. No doubt being displaced by a younger woman, with this question, we have nothing to do. So we steer clear of these things.

In regards to my matrimonial life, it has been very unsatisfactory and I wish you would omit that entirely. I think it would be better. As to my son, he is no son

> of mine and I would rather you would omit this, but I suppose you are compelled to do it. I suppose in history, it is necessary really"

As Horace read the paragraph's his friend pointed out to him, he found himself livid. As he scanned the rest of the page, he discovered that the author had added an additional, personal description of the Tabor family, which was completely uncalled for in a historical book.

> "The Tabor's are very bad eggs. He put away his wife for some cause and married a disreputable woman. The least said about them the better.
>
> "But as Horace Tabor paid a fee, to be included in this book, Senator Tabor should be made to appear, so far as the facts will sustain him, as being one of the most important factors in the development of Leadville.
>
> "He should appear as the man, above all men, not only in Colorado, but in that section of the country who created an intellectual atmosphere."

Horace thanked his friend for the book and placed it high up on a shelf.

As Christmas came and the New Year began, the Tabors welcomed a visit from William Jennings Bryan, who was a Nebraska Democrat running for the House of Representatives. Being in the Denver area, he felt it was fitting to meet the famous Horace Tabor.

After shaking hands with Horace, Elizabeth and little Lily, Bryan was brought over to the cradle to see the newest little Tabor. Seeing a friendly face, the tiny baby started to coo and squeal, which prompted William Bryan to make a historic announcement that, unknown to him, would forever link him to Horace and Elisabeth Tabor.

AND WHEN THE BOUGH BREAKS, SILVER WILL FALL   97

"Why Senator, that baby's laughter has the ring of a silver dollar!"

With a name finally chosen and dressed in an $800 lace and feathered gown, little Rosemary Silver Dollar Echo Honeymoon Tabor was christened and was given the nickname "Honey maid".

As the baby began her new life swaddled in embroidered diapers clasped with diamond studded pins, she had no idea that her lifestyle was the result of Congress or that it would soon come to an end.

In 1878 the United States Congress had voted through The Bland-Allison Act, which required the U.S. treasury to purchase between $2 million to $4 Million in silver each month from Western mines and mint them into silver Dollars.

This had been brought about following the Coinage act of 1873, which was put in effect after the German Empire stopped minting their own silver coins called Thaler's, which had been used throughout Europe for almost four hundred years. This in turn, caused a huge drop in demand and hit the United States silver mines hard.

In an attempt to return to bimetallism, which allows both gold and silver to be used as the standard method of currency, The Bland-Allison Act was presented to President Rutherford B. Hayes, who vetoed it, but his veto was overridden by Congress and passed on February 28, 1878. In response, Silver quickly jumped from .84 cents an ounce to $1.50 an ounce.

Which had made men, like Horace Tabor, very rich.

On July 14, 1890 a federal law called The Sherman Silver Purchase Act was put in place, which raised the amount of Silver the Government was required to purchase from 4 Million to 4.5 million ounces a month.

But President Grover Cleveland would change all that.

Convinced that The Sherman Silver Act was causing a drain on the gold reserves, he pressured Congress into repealing the Silver Act on August 8, 1893, which did nothing to protect the Gold reserve, but it did destroy the west.

In just a matter of four days Silver prices dropped from $1.50 an

Baby Silver Dollar-The Denver Public Library, Western History Collection-X-22004

ounce to .62 cents and by September 1893, just one month later, 377 businesses and 435 mines had closed. People quickly began swarming the banks and demanded that they be able to withdraw their money, which quickly caused the banks to shut their doors, leaving thousands of people penniless.

With nowhere to go and winter on the way, thousands of people headed to Denver in search of jobs. Combining all the mining camp residents, laundresses, saloon owners, miners and prostitutes, as well as all the now bankrupt shop owners, Colorado had 45,000 people out of work in one month.

Finding his Colorado silver mines closed and his investments quickly drying up, Horace took a desperate train ride to Morelia, Mexico to check on his Gold and silver mine.

Tabor had bought 7/10ths of the mine back in 1881 along with Benjamin F. Butler of Massachusetts, Thomas Jordan, the editor of "The mining record", Louis Janin, a mining engineer and Nevada Senator

John P. Jones. The mine was 40 miles from Morelia, which was the capital of Michoacan, in central Mexico.

This investment was actually a combination of 30 gold and silver mines, which were paying him and each of the other investors, around $5,000 a month. Unfortunately, this money wouldn't make a dent in the bills he was accumulating back in Colorado, with the market crash bringing all his mortgages due.

Before the 1893 silver crash, his Matchless mine in Leadville alone paid him over $80,000 a month, with the payout occasionally being as high as $10,000 a day.

$5,000 a month was chicken scratch.

He was losing everything.

But his ex-wife Augusta was doing just fine.

While Horace Tabor had been spending his money on lavish trips, poor investments and diamond studded diaper pins, Augusta had taken the money she earned from the apartments she had purchased during her divorce and invested it in real estate.

She purchased over 240 acres of land around Denver and its outlying suburbs, as well as investing in Senator Stephen Dorsey's resort in Springer, New Mexico. And when the Silver Market crashed in 1893, she chose to lease her mansion to the commercial club of Denver and moved in with her son Maxcy and his wife Luella at the Brown Palace, which he managed.

But as Augusta enjoyed spending the winter of 1893 basking in the sun of Southern California, her Ex-husband fought to keep hold of his ever crumbling fortune.

April 5th, 1894 saw Horace Tabor in a court room, listening to his creditors bark at the judge about how he needed to allow them to force the notes that had come due and sell the Tabor properties. Among the properties on the chopping block first, was Horace's beloved Tabor Grand Opera house.

His creditors informed the judge that the mortgage was running into the millions and needed paid, but luckily for Horace, the judge took pity on the former Governor and allowed the monthly profits from his Mexican mine to be accepted as payment.

For now.

With Horace frantically scrambling to find investors to save the building that was meant to be his legacy, he was introduced to a recent set of Gold filled millionaires, by his brother-in-law Peter McCourt.

Peter had taken an interest in the Florence and Cripple Creek railroad back in 1892, which traveled up an area known as Phantom Canyon, after the incorporation of a new mining camp called Cripple Creek.

Two years before, in 1890, a man named Bob Womack had discovered gold on his ranch after many, many years of searching, but unfortunately sold his claim the following year for $500, after a long day of drinking. The new owners of the claim were friends Horace

Bennett and Julias Myers.

After platting out their new 80 acre town, they decided to name it Cripple Creek, which is rumored to be from a story, told to them by an old miner, about a cow falling into a nearby creek and breaking its leg.

Desiring to add a personal stamp on their newly formed town, Bennett and Myers named their town's main thoroughfare after themselves, which ended up finding their own place in the history books.

Bennett Ave was chosen as the main street, which was four blocks long and lined with Department stores, dance schools, book shops, Photographers, specialty shops and the best Saloons and gambling halls in the area.

Myers Ave., on the other hand, held the towns Brothels, Cribs, dance halls, low class saloons and gambling halls. Its only reputable business was the Grand Opera house, but a tunnel had to be constructed under the street, which connected one block over to Bennett Ave., in order for the more refined residents of the town to attend the shows and avoid the painted ladies.

And now, two years after founding the town of Cripple Creek, Bennett and Myers met with Horace Tabor and Peter McCourt and with hardy handshakes all around, happily offered to help the former Governor.

May 15, 1894 found Horace Tabor in a much better mood. As he sat in the court room with his new business partners, he listened to the judge accept the past due mortgage payment of $250,000 from Horace Bennett and Julias Myers. He was also pleased to find that not only would litigation be dropped, but that his properties would remain in his name.

But as the year continued to look bright for Horace Tabor, it was beginning to look rather grim for his ex-wife Augusta.

At the age of 61, Augusta had suffered a devastating stroke and in turn developed a terrible cough she just couldn't shake. At the advice of

Older Augusta Tabor- The Denver Public Library, Western History Collection-X21985

her Doctor, she took the train to Pasadena, California with her friend Lizzie McClelland and checked into the Balmoral Hotel, hoping the weather would help.

It didn't.

Dr. Macomber, a well-known doctor in the area, diagnosed Augusta with Bronchitis and Pneumonia and was with her as she took her last breath, on January 30, 1895.

One day short of what would have been her and Horace's 38th wedding anniversary.

Upon hearing the devastating news, Augusta's son Maxcy took the train to California and brought home the body of his mother.

Crowded beyond capacity, Augusta's beloved Unitarian church conducted her funeral on February 8th, which was attended by all but Horace and Elizabeth Tabor. Standing by the coffin, in the front of the church, Maxy Tabor laid his hand on his wife's ever growing belly and promised to name his mother's future Grandchild after her.

A few months later, Persis Augusta Tabor was born.

But Horace Tabor had more things on his mind than a new grandchild.

With a dark cloud over his head, possibly caused by his lack of sympathy over Augusta's death, Horace Tabor once again found himself in a court room on November 9, 1895, fighting to save more of his properties.

Judge Rucker, in the states district court, issued an order to stop the sale of Tabors Mines and Mills Company, located in Ashcroft, Colorado. The claims in question were The Tam O'Shanter, Borealis, Montezuma, Halycon, Last chance, Green Lake and Ivanhoe.

Tabors attorney L.C. Rockwell presented his plea to the court, saying that "Injustice would be done to his famous client if the sale occurred at this time, whereas, if postponed a reasonable season, it might be possible for the owner to redeem."

With the strike of his gavel, the Judge agreed to postpone the sale until December 1896.

With this newest court battle over for now, Horace was pleased to see that the Denver Newspapers held a distraction for him, in the form of a story regarding Mystic and Clairvoyant Professor J. McIvor Tyndall. Horace and Elizabeth had watched one of his glorious performances almost 15 years earlier, inside the Tabor Grand Opera house and he was pleased to see that the man was still plying his trade.

On November 18, 1895, Professor Tyndall had decided to wow his audience by climbing into the driver's seat of an open carriage, while blind folded and drive a team of horses through the city.

Twice.

With the streets blocked off by nothing more than the bodies of curious onlookers, Mr. Tyndall invited the town's chief of police, the City Clerk and the mystic's own assistant Doctor Wise, to accompany him on his wild ride.

Sitting himself next to his assistant, Professor Tyndall placed a blind fold around his eyes, then using his right hand he grasped the hand of his assistant, leaving his left hand to hold the reins. Snapping them violently and with a loud, "Yah", he set the horse team in motion.

Missing street cars, trucks, carriages and terrified pedestrians by mere inches, he whirled up Fourth Street and turned onto Broadway to Second Street, where he pulled the carriage up to the side entrance of the Hollenbeck Hotel.

Still blindfolded. The Mystic was helped down from the carriage by his assistant and led over to the staircase of the Hotel. Letting go of his Assistants hand, Professor Tyndall began feeling the building's facade before quickly finding a feather duster, which had been placed up on a high hook and retrieving it. Pleased, he once again reached for his assistants hand and sat himself back in the carriages driver seat.

Repeating his harrowing ride from earlier, the Mystic led the team of horses back down the streets and pulled to a stop in front of the Hotel Ramona, holding the coveted feather duster high above his head to the pleasure of his captive audience.

But where Professor Tyndall was still at the top of his game, Horace Tabor's life was quickly falling apart.

As the months went by and winter turned back into Spring, Horace once again found himself fighting to protect his investments and to keep his head above water.

On May 19, 1896 Horace Tabor received a court order, issued by Judge Rucker, which contained a petition entered by Attorney Mike Johnson, on behalf of his client Thomas Wiswall. This suit was in regards to The Tabor Mines and Mills Co. and involved the Tam O'Shanter group of mines up at Ashcroft. Both Tabor and his book keeper were listed as witnesses in the case, with his book keeper being instructed to bring all books, papers and records in regards to the mining Company.

Reading farther down the petition, it mentioned that Thomas Wiswall was claiming that Horace Tabor had used $10,000 of the Companies profits to pay personal debts and that none of it went to benefit Tabor Mines and Mills Co. It further read that Mr. Tabor had recently acquired investors for loans, with the promise that it went towards the mine, but had in fact went into Horace Tabors personal account.

Frantic, and needing to stall, Horace had his book keeper file an extension with the court, claiming that he had been unexpectedly called to Phoenix, Arizona. But hiding wasn't going to help him, especially in regards to the mortgage being due on the Tabor block and his beloved Opera house.

The dominos were beginning to fall.

On June 8th, 1896, the court of appeals dismissed the motion of Horace Tabors attorney to stop the sale of The Tabor block and Opera house and gave him five days to prepare an appeal to the Supreme Court. If denied, it would only be a matter of months before the sale was finalized.

But Horace didn't have time to focus on a lost cause, as he was fighting to save one of his most profitable mines, which was also one of the first mines to make him rich all those years ago.

The Matchless mine in Leadville.

Dressed in their finest, Horace and Elizabeth climbed the steps of the court house at 10am on June 10, 1896 with their witnesses and Attorney Rockwell in tow, ready for a fight.

All rise. Judge Owers residing.

You may all be seated.

"Today we are hearing the case of J.W Newell, W.R Harp and W.F Page verses The Tabor Mines and Mills Company", the Judge announced, as he lowered his glasses. "The action is to recover the sum of $20,450.98, being the principal interest due upon a note given by the Tabor Mines and Mills Company in the summer of 1894 to W.A Everett."

"This note is secured by a mortgage upon certain mining properties, including the Matchless." The Judge continued. "The present plaintiffs became the owners of the note by purchase, from the Estate of W.A. Everett, who is now deceased."

Rising from his chair, Tabors attorney Rockwell addressed the judge." Your Honor, my client has stated that the company never received a cent of the money for which the said note was given, never authorized the borrowing of the money and cannot be held responsible for the same."

"Mr. Newell, Mr. Harp and Mr. Page, would your Attorney like to respond?" The judge inquired.

"Yes, your Honor", the Attorney began, as he straightened his suit jacket "The late Mr. Everett informed my clients that he had parted with $15,000, but said he had loaned the money to Mrs. Tabor, who said she needed the money to pay off claims against the Tabor investments."

"Your Honor, if I may." Attorney Rockwell asked, as he stood back up and faced the Judge. "My client's wife informed Mr. Everett on how she was going to use the money and therefore the Plaintiffs have no claim against The Tabor Mines and Mills Co., as the note was given to secure the loan."

"I would like to produce my first witness, your Honor, if it pleases the court." Attorney Rockwell inquired and after a quick wave of the Judges hand, the Attorney motioned for the man to approach the stand.

"State your name"

"Boyd Skelton"

"Do you swear to tell the truth, the whole truth and nothing but the truth, so help you God?"

"I do"

"Mr. Skelton, can you please state your relationship with Mr. Tabor, for the court." The Attorney asked.

"I'm a good friend of the Tabors."

"Could you please elaborate?" the Attorney instructed.

"Well, the Tabor's needed money badly in 1893, to meet the taxes and other pressing claims and July or August 1893, I overheard Mrs. Tabor and Mr. Everett talk about a loan of $15,000." He informed the court. "The loan was made in August 1893 when Mr. Tabor and Peter McCourt were in Mexico."

"Thank you, you may be seated."

"I would now like to call up Mrs. Elizabeth Bonduel Tabor to the stand." The Attorney announced, as a quiet hush filled the court room. Her tiny 5'2" frame was quickly swallowed up by the large, oak witness stand, which drew more attention to her petite size.

"Please state your name for the court."

" Elizabeth Bonduel Tabor".

"Do you promise to tell the truth, the whole truth and nothing but the truth, so help you God?"

"I do"

"Your Honor," The Tabors Attorney began. "As this is Mrs. Tabors first time testifying in a court room, I would like to ask that only the attorneys and interested parties be allowed to hear her testimony, if it pleases the court."

As the disappointed onlookers exited the court room and waited outside in the hall, Elizabeth patiently waited to be questioned.

After hearing the click of the court house door closing behind him and receiving a nod from the Judge, Attorney Rockwell approached the witness stand.

"Mrs. Tabor, I ask that you give the court the account of what happened between you and Mr. Everett, in regards to the money in question", he asked, as the room turned its attention towards her.

"I met Mr. Everett in the summer of 1893 and obtained a loan from him of $15,000, giving him a note signed by the Tabor Mines and Mills Company, as my husband Horace is the President and I am the Secretary." She began to explain, in a clear, calm tone.

"I gave him stock from the company to use as collateral, as security for the payment on the note. About a year later, I gave Mr. Everett a new note, secured by a trust deed upon the Matchless Mine in Leadville." She explained, as she turned to look at the Judge.

"Thank you Mrs. Tabor, you may step down." Attorney Rockwell instructed, as he called Horace Tabor to the stand.

With Elizabeth's statement complete, the people that had been sent out of the court room were allowed back in, as Horace took the stand.

"Please state your name for the court."

"Horace Austin Warner Tabor."

"Do you promise to tell the truth, the whole truth and nothing but the truth, so help you God?"

"I do."

"Mr. Tabor, can you please explain your meeting, in regards to Mr. Everett and the $15,000 loan?" his Attorney asked, as he approached the witness stand.

"Yes, of course, "Horace began, as he cleaned his throat and leaned forward in his chair. "In regards to the money, it did not go to the Mines and Mills Company. I was in Mexico and had left notes, signed in blank notes, with my wife Mrs. Tabor and she must have used them."

"Thank you, you may step down."

After attempting to call Elizabeth's brother Peter McCourt to the stand and the request rejected by the Plaintiffs Attorney, it was now their turn to call their witness.

"We call for Attorney Rockwell to take the stand."

A gasp echoed through the court room, as Horace Tabors own Attorney had been called up to the stand to testify.

"Do you promise to tell the truth, the whole truth and nothing but the truth, so help you God?"

"I do."

With a smile the Plaintiffs Attorney approached the former Judge, turned Attorney and pulled out his list of questions.

"Attorney Rockwell, would you please entertain the court, regarding your relationship with the now deceased Mr. Everett?"

"I was his Attorney."

As a shock ran through the court room and whispers began, the Judge asked for the room to remain quiet.

"Please continue"

"In regards to the loan made to my clients the Tabors, I was Mr. Everett's Attorney when the loan in dispute was made." He explained, as he looked over at Horace and Elizabeth Tabor. "I was surprised that Mr. Everett had made the loan to Mrs. Tabor, but the loan was made and The Matchless stock put up as security with 3% interest per month, payable monthly."

"The note was left with me for safe keeping by Mr. Everett, but neither the interest nor the principal were paid when due. I wrote to my client, who was in California at the time, and informed him that Mr. Tabor refused to pay." Attorney Rockwell continued. "Mr. Everett then came to Denver, had a meeting with Mr. Tabor and the new deal was drawn up on the $15,000 note with 1% interest per month and the deed was given on The Matchless mine to secure the new note."

The Attorney for the Plaintiff approached the Witness stand and asked Attorney Rockwell if the note had ever been paid, in which Attorney Rockwell replied it hadn't.

As everyone returned to their seats, Judge Owers read back over his notes and decided to rule in favor of the Tabor's. He explained that the loan and the note had been a contract between the Tabor's and the now deceased Mr. Everett, not the Plaintiffs J.W. Newell, W.R. Harp or W.F. Page.

Case dismissed.

A STACK OF FIREWOOD AND THE SHOVEL FULL OF GOLD

With the first court hearing finished and another one scheduled for the next morning, Horace and Elizabeth made arrangements to stay at Aspen's Hotel Jerome, which charged a hefty $3 a night. Despite being broke, Horace didn't want to be seen leaving a lower prices Hotel and have it used against him in the Newspapers.

The Hotel Jerome was a newer Hotel, built in 1889, by the Co-Owner of the Macy's Department store Jerome B. Wheeler. The Hotel had the distinguished honor of not only being one of the first fully electrified Hotel's in Colorado, but for also being haunted.

One of the Hotel's famous ghostly residents was a silver prospector named Henry O'Callister, who moved into the Hotel after striking it rich, which is where he met his lady love. She was the daughter of a wealthy Boston family who defiently did not approve of a match with a lowly miner, regardless of how much money he had.

Devastated that his love had been sent back to Boston, O'Callister drank himself to death inside the Hotel. The Hotel staff and many of the guests have reported seeing the ghostly figure of O'Callister walking the halls at night and hearing the cries of a heartbroken man.

Another one of the famous Ghostly residents involves a beautiful 16 year old girl named Katie Kerrigan, who was a maid at the Hotel. Her beauty caused her to attract a lot of attention from the wealthy guests, but resulted in terrible jealousy among her co-workers.

One freezing winter night Katie's co-workers teased her and said they had thrown her prized kitten into an ice cold pond, which caused the frantic teenager to jump into the lake in search of her pet. It is not known if the poor kitty really met an icy fate that night, but poor Katie Kerrigan caught pneumonia and died three days later.

Since her death she has become a prankster, possibly as her way of seeking revenge against the Hotel Staff who caused her early demise. She is blamed for messing up freshly made-up Hotel rooms, pulls down bed sheets and fills sinks with soapy water.

But the Tabor's had other things to think about, besides ghost stories and broken hearted miners.

Horace was trying to keep his head above water.

Walking back up the steps of the court house the next morning, the Tabor's had to find more ways to stall, as this hearing was yet another sad attempt to stop the sale of The Tabor Mines and Mills Company.

The year before, on November 9, 1895, Horace and his lawyer L.C. Rockwell were able to postpone the sale of the company until December 1896, which was now just six months away. In the meantime, Horace had been asked to send copies of all his records and bills of sale for the company to the Plaintiffs' Lawyer, which he did.

"All rise, the honorable Judge Rucker's residing."

"You may be seated."

As the court room remained quiet, Judge Rucker reviewed the transcripts from the last hearing, in regards to Byron J. Smith's claim that The Tabor Mines and Mill Company owned him a note for $10,000, and his request that the company be sold to pay the note.

"Mr. Rockwell, I see that we last spoke in November of 1895 in regards to this matter and it is now June 12, 1896, has your client Mr. Tabor paid the money due Mr. Smith?" the Judge asked, as he laid down his paper.

"No your honor."

Turning towards Byron Smith's Attorney Mr. Thomas, Judge Rucker asked if anything had been received at all from opposing council.

"Your honor, in November of 1895 we requested a record of the company's minutes and detailed records and we received blank papers." Attorney Thomas replied, as he glared over at Mr. Tabor.

"I knew we were served with something, but I don't know what, so I just gave it all to Attorney Rockwell to attend to." Horace Tabor shrugged, as he attempted to put all the blame onto his lawyer.

Filled with anger over Tabors nonchalant attitude, Attorney Rockwell exploded. "You're crazy! That wasn't a subpoena at all from this court!"

As Horace laughed at the outburst, Attorney Thomas looked at the Judge and said "For the good of Mr. Tabor, I hope Attorney Rockwell is crazy… and who is paying for the expenses of Mr. Smith's suit? I'm sure Mr. Tabor isn't and his wife isn't."

Standing up to face the Judge, Horace stated his position on the whole hearing. "Look, I don't want to lose 1/4th of a million dollars' worth of property for a $10,000 debt."

"So, Mr. Tabor." Attorney Thomas interjected, "Your only reason for attacking the vitality of this debt is because you didn't want to lose security?

"Yes" replied Horace. "The Tam O' Shanter mine is worth about $400,000 alone."

"Mr. Tabor, is it true that you had at least two opportunities to pay off Mr. Smith's note, but chose not to." Attorney Thomas asked, as he sent a glace over towards the Judge.

"Yes"

"Why didn't you, Mr. Tabor?"

With a shrug of his shoulders, Horace Tabor simply replied, "It was too hard."

Straightening his suit jacket, Attorney Thomas asked Judge Rucker if he could address the court, which was quickly granted with a nod of the Judges head.

"If this sort of juggling is to be permitted, if it shall be held that the real plaintiff in this case, H.A.W Tabor, can borrow money here, there and everywhere and then laugh at the men who accommodate, I suggest that the figure of justice that adorns the front of this court house be taken down and in its place a huge, bronze statue of H.A.W Tabor be erected! And above it, inscribed in large letters, "I can borrow money and don't pay it back!"

Regaining his composure, Attorney Rockwell slowly stood back up and made one last attempt to save his clients property. "Your Honor, while I don't represent Horace Tabor, but the company itself, I cannot let the remarks of Attorney Thomas be used to attack one of Colorado's most prominent citizens. A man who has done more than any one man, towards the advancement of the state and for it to go unnoticed."

"Thank you Attorney Rockwell, for your heavy hearted speech, but I have decided to allow the sale of The Tabor Mills and Mines, in order to settle the $10,000 note to Mr. Smith." Judge Rucker announced, with the crash of his gavel.

Stunned and desperate, the Tabor's quietly headed back to the Hotel Jerome, where Horace was deep in thought. In a last ditch effort to save his property, he contacted G.C. Schleier, a wealthy real estate developer in Denver and pleaded for his help.

He agreed.

On June 15th, just three days after Judge Rucker allowed the sale of the company, Horace Tabor, Attorney Rockwell and Mr. Schleier entered the Aspen court house and filed for a 10 day extension on the sale. Upon receiving the signed document, Judge Rucker noted that

G.C. Schleier was offering to advance Mr. Tabor the $10,000 owed on the note to Mr. Smith, but only after he had the opportunity to examine the titles and check on the condition of the mines involved.

The Judge allowed the extension.

But as the Tabor's boarded the train back to Denver, their happiness was short lived, as Horace now had to watch his beloved Tabor block and Opera house be auctioned off to the highest bidder.

On June 23, 1896 the Tabor block, which contained the Tabor Grand Opera House, was auctioned off to pay the past due mortgage, held by the Northern Mutual Life insurance Co. of Milwaukee. Represented by Colonel Dennison, the highest bid was offered by Mrs. Laura B. Smith, in the amount of $488,143.59.

Wishing to meet with Mr. Tabor, Mrs. Smith respectably informed him that she would be willing to hold the property for him, for a period of 9 months, but he politely refused.

Horace had more to worry about.

He was losing his home.

Mortgaged to the hilt and unable to pay back any of his loans, Horace began a frantic attempt to save at least one piece of property and spare his children the grief of becoming homeless. He grudgingly allowed his furniture, beautiful carriages and fabulous pieces of art work to be auctioned off, but as the year continued and the families many possessions dwindled down to bare scraps, he watched his bank account continue to drain.

Which drew the attention of his mortgage holder.

Hardware mogul Mr. Trinch, sporting a heart as cold as any winter freeze, knocked on the front door of the Tabor's mansion and announced that they either paid their past due mortgage or be out by December 23rd.

Two days before Christmas.

Knowing he couldn't come up with the funds to save his home, Horace scrambled to find housing for his family, but when Elizabeth discovered that both the electric and water had been shut off for non-payment, he became all the more desperate.

With winter quickly approaching, Elizabeth and the children gathered firewood, hauled water from the pitcher head pump inside the carriage house and even made a game out of lighting the candles, when night fell onto the cold, dark mansion.

On December 17th, little Rosemary Echo Silver Dollar Honeymoon Tabor, celebrated her 7th birthday, but for the first time in her opulent life, little Silver Dollar experienced a birthday without the glow of a festive Christmas tree, a fabulous party or a mountain of gifts.

Being young and not able to truly understand what was going on, Silver Dollar thought it was her fault that the family was losing their home and chose to write a heartfelt apology to her beloved fairy friends, in hopes they would forgive her and save her house.

My own darling fairies,

Well darlings, I will hope for the best and the best is presents from Santa Claus on Xmas, which I am unworthy to receive, on the account that I have talked and thought so badly of Momma to Lillian.

How badly I feel and how ashamed I am of myself. My heart is breaking because of fear that I will be left out of this Xmas, which I could not stand . . .

But just when Horace Tabor felt all hope was lost, he answered a knock on the front door of their home from an unexpected visitor.

Mrs. Laura B. Smith

Welcoming her into their cold, bare mansion, Mrs. Smith talked privately with Horace and Elizabeth and offered them a free apartment, inside Mr. Tabor's former Tabor Block, which she had purchased at auction just a few months before.

And they could stay as long as they wished.

Shocked and ecstatic, the look on the faces of the couple was one of pure joy. Pleased that the Tabor's had accepted, Mrs. Smith immediately made arrangement for the Tabor's remaining belonging to be delivered to their new residence.

But this didn't mean all was well.

As the sun rose on December 23rd, the last day in their now former home, Horace threw a few more logs on the fire while Elizabeth got the children dressed. It was a frigid 23 degrees outside, but there was no snow on the ground to even hint that it was almost Christmas Eve, which made the entire experience feel even more surreal.

But as Horace took one last walk around his home, he began to feel an intense anger building up inside him. His hard work and immense fortune had helped turn Denver into a shining metropolis, that rivaled even New York City and this is how they thank him!

By kicking his family out of their home right before Christmas!

Elizabeth Tabor's Mansion- The Denver Public Library, Western History Collection-X-27094

Hearing a carriage pull up along the side of the house, Horace peaked out the window and saw his mortgage holder's coachman open the door for Mr. Tritch , who appeared to have a satisfied smile on his face.

Inside Elizabeth Tabor's Mansion- 89.451.2063 History Colorado

He was laughing!

You son of a Bitch!

With an added bounce in his step, Mr. Tritch walked around to the front of the house and knocked on the door. But instead of being greeted by a solemn and defeated H.A.W Tabor, he was instead greeted by cold steel pressed against his forehead.

Watching the commotion from across the street, little Margaret Jane ran to get her father. "Daddy! Daddy! Come see! Silver's daddy is going to shoot a man!"

Jumping up from his chair, Mr. Hunter quickly grabbed his jacket and followed his young daughter outside. Hearing the sounds of a very angry Horace Tabor and the pleading of a man, who he assumed was the dreaded mortgage holder, he sent his daughter back inside the house.

He was afraid something like this would happen.

Running across the street, Mr. Hunter kept his eyes on Mr. Tabor, but wasn't able to see the true fear in the mortgage holders eyes, until he got closer to the front door.

"Governor please, it's not worth it!" Mr. Hunter pleaded, as he quickly ran up the twelve stone steps that ascended from the sidewalk. "Think of your children! Governor, please! He isnt worth it! He isn't worth it Governor!"

"It's Christmas! You don't foreclose a family's home on Christmas!" Horace hissed through clenched teeth, as he clicked back the barrel and pressed the gun tighter against Mr. Tritch's forehead.

Desperate to escape the situation the mortgage holder had egotistically put himself into, he slowly began backing away from H.A.W Tabor, but soon found himself trapped due to the homes six foot high stone wall that framed the front lawn. If he stepped back any further, he would fall almost seven feet onto the sidewalk below.

But every step the man took, Horace followed. Never once allowing the gun to stray from its predetermined spot between the mortgage holder's eyes.

"It's not worth going to prison Governor. He isn't worth losing your family. Think of Elizabeth and the children. Governor, please", Mr. Hunter pleaded with Horace, as he gently placed his right hand over the gun and slowly began lowering it towards the ground. As emotion overwhelmed him, Horace Tabor allowed his neighbor to remove the gun from his shaking hand.

Un-cocking the gun, Mr. Hunter looked down at the heartless mortgage holder with a stern gaze and added a menacing growl to his voice. "The Tabor's own this property until sundown, I suggest you leave."

With no pressure and with his pride partially intact, Horace headed back into the house, packed up the last of his families belongings and headed to their new apartment inside Horace's beloved Tabor Grand.

As Christmas came and ushered in 1897, Horace was able to find a job working at a Leadville Smelter for three dollars a day. But heading off to Leadville unfortunately drew a crowd, as photographers and newspaper reporters swarmed the area, in their desire to document the fall of Colorado's silver king.

Knowing that his pride would recover, Horace was just relieved that his family had food to eat and a warm place to live.

Horace Tabor at the smelter- The Denver Public Library, Western History Collection-X-1989

But things change.

Returning back to Denver on March 24, 1897, Horace and Elizabeth were pulled aside by Mrs. Laura B. Smith and informed of more bad news. The North Western Insurance Company had taken the title of the Tabor Block away from her and the Tabor's would soon need to find a new place to live.

When Mrs. Smith had originally purchased Horace Tabor's former property at auction the year before, she received a

A STACK OF FIREWOOD AND THE SHOVEL FULL OF GOLD   121

mortgage for $400,000, but had also purchased a second property that had a mortgage of $330,000, neither of which she was able to pay.

But Horace didn't want to just find a new place for his family to live, he wanted to find a new mining claim.

With his free days off, from dumping slag over in Leadville, Horace spent his time digging around Boulder County, in a newly incorporated mining camp called Ward. And with all his digging and picking, he eventually found what he was looking for, staked a claim and with Elizabeth's blessing, decided to put all their belongings in storage and dig themselves out of poverty.

Literally.

Finding an a abandoned cabin with a small lean-to off the side, Horace, Elizabeth and their daughters settled into their new life and together dug for gold using nothing but picks, drills and shovels. They made progress, but they desperately needed better equipment and unknown to the Tabor's, word was traveling fast in regards to their families "Never give up" attitude.

And it was this attitude that attracted the attention, of none other, than Winfield Scott Stratton.

Stratton was born in 1848, in the town of Jefferson, Indiana, but found himself in Iowa at the age of twenty, after shooting at his father with a rifle. He missed, but he felt so ashamed, that he never returned home.

He did odd jobs and a lot of prospecting, before finally striking it rich on July 4, 1891, in the newly formed town of Cripple creek, Colorado. He was 18 days shy of his 43rd birthday.

And with a bank full of money and a mine of never ending gold, Winfield Stratton headed over to Ward, Colorado to help out the famous H.A.W. Tabor.

The mining town of Ward, so named after miner Calvin Ward who discovered ore there in 1860, had developed into a mining camp of around 5,000 residents by the 1890's. But when it was finally incorporated into a town in 1896, a rule was passed that any lots not already claimed would be sold, for a very small amount, to anyone found living on the lot.

And with an old cabin already near his new claim, which he named The Eclipse mine, Horace Tabor fell into this new loop hole and once again became a property owner.

Which is where Winfield Stratton found him on October 20, 1897.

With a big friendly smile and round of firm hand shakes, Horace proudly showed Mr. Stratton around his new mine and shared his plans for the future. "You know Governor, you really need some better equipment, if you plan on making anything out of this new mine of yours." Stratton added, as he kicked a few pieces of ore with his shoe. "Why don't we head down to the bank and make that happen, shall we?"

Transferring $15,000 into Horace Tabor's bank account, Winfield Stratton smiled over at the former Governor. "No need to pay me back Horace. Just consider it a gift, but contact me if you need anymore."

Word quickly spread, as Stratton's generous donation to the former Governor began making headlines. Desperate to see if the story of the Tabor's digging

Winfield Stratton-Z-8875 History Colorado

themselves out of poverty were true, reporters were stunned to see that Elizabeth had indeed stayed with her much older husband, even after the money dried up and all the diamonds were gone.

But just weeks shy of Horace Tabor's 67th birthday, he discovered that his days of swinging a mining pick could be coming to an end, if Colorado Senator Edward Oliver Wolcott had anything to say about it.

Edward Wolcott had started his political career in 1879, as a Colorado Senator and in 1889 he was chosen to represent Colorado in the U.S. Senate. Impressed with his work, President McKinley also named him the chairman of the committee for Post offices and Postal roads.

And it seemed that Denver had an opening for a new Post master.

Sending a man over to Ward, Colorado to find Horace Tabor among the dirt and rocks, the nomination papers were delivered and Horace happily agreed to throw his hat into the ring for Post Master. And with the stroke of a pen, his nomination join the pile of other hopeful candidates and was soon discussed on the Senate floor.

Horace Tabor won by a landslide.

Personally traveling to Ward, to deliver the good news, Senator Wolcott watched as Horace dusted off his miner's overalls, so he could give the Senator a proper handshake. "Horace, every miner in Colorado has a feeling of love and admiration for you, as do I, which is why I nominated you for this position. We will see you in Denver on Feburary 1st, Governor Tabor."

With winter winds blowing in and the mines in Ward quickly becoming covered in unmanageable snow drifts, the Tabor's boarded up their cabin and left the 9,450 ft. elevation town for an apartment inside Denver's Windsor Hotel.

It appeared that their life had gone full circle and had brought them right back to the Windsor, where their life together had begun.

And with their little cabin up in Ward buried in deep snow drifts, the Tabor's felt truly blessed to spend Christmas inside their warm, Denver apartment.

But despite having a dependable income, Horace was still scouting out new mining claims up in Ward, which is how he started his new partnership with J.W. Newell and W.F. page.

On Feburary 14, 1898, Horace Tabor became 1/3rd owner of the former John Rice Mine, for $11,660, which was his part of the total amount of $35,000. The mine was considered one of the most valuable properties in the area, but bad management had prevented the shaft from going past 165 feet, but the smelter returns looked very promising.

With the snow and cold preventing any real mining until spring, men were hired to repair the existing machinery so that the shaft could be extended by another 100 ft., once the ground thawed. And when spring finally arrived, Elizabeth and the girls headed back up to their little cabin at Ward to continue mining their Eclipse mine, while Horace joined them on his days off.

And it was on one of these weekend trips that he found it.

A human bone.

Thinking it could be the bone of an Indian and possibly worth money, Horace made arrangements for Elizabeth and the girls to travel to New York, in an attempt to sell it to a Museum. And hopefully, while they were there, both 14 year old Lily and 44 year old Elizabeth could be diagnosed and cured of their recurring ailments.

Elizabeth, Lily and 9 year old Silver Dollar boarded a train for New York City on December 27, 1898, with a possible Indian bone carefully wrapped up inside one of their trunks.

After renting a small apartment for $20 a month, Elizabeth and the girls traveled to the American Museum of Natural History, in Manhattan and eagerly awaited the results of the bone that Horace had dug out of their Eclipse Mine.

But it wasn't Indian.

Disappointed but not discouraged, they brought the bone back to the apartment and turned their focus on finding a Doctor for Lily and

Elizabeth. Horace had been afraid that his daughter was suffering from Catarrh, which appeared to get worse when she traveled up to Ward from Denver. Poor Lily would develop a pressure in her head and ears, as well as develop excess mucus in her nose and throat, which their New York Doctor diagnosed as Sinusitis.

Turning his attention to Elizabeth, he found her to be suffering from a condition called Neuralgia, which causes the sufferer to experience constant migraine headaches, aching teeth, ear aches and occasional electric shock like stabs in the back of the scalp and neck. Luckily a treatment was available to help her and she was prescribed Marijuana to reduce her neuropathic pain.

Never out of his thoughts. Horace and his girls exchanged letters while they were apart and he would send money to keep his girls happy and healthy.

> "My own darling Papa, I love you so much. Your registered letter came today with $20 in it. I'm so glad, because Lily had left her blue ring in the Baker store last night for bread. We will get it today. I want to live here, but you must come and live with me. Cannot live away from you. My dear sweet Papa..."
>
> —Silver Dollar

Horace smiled when he read the letter he received from Silver, but grimaced at the dull pain he was feeling on his lower right side. Gently rubbing the area, he vowed to take it easy at the mine tomorrow, as he was sure it was simply a strained muscle and nothing serious.

A Cup Full of Leeches and the Ring of Flowers

Arriving back in Denver on March 31, 1899, rested and ready to take on the Eclipse mine, Elizabeth and her daughters took a carriage from Union Train station and enjoyed their ride back to the Windsor Hotel.

Within hours, Horace arrived back at the apartment and was immediately met with hugs and kisses from his girls, but the tight hugs made him quickly pull away. Seeing that her husband was favoring his right side, Elizabeth shooed the girls away and had Horace sit down in a nearby chair.

Worried for her 68 year old husband, Elizabeth took a serious look at Horace and noticed that he had lost a bit of weight and would wince when she pressed his abdomen. Reassuring her that he had just pulled a muscle, he excused all his symptoms and laughed off her concerns.

With spring in the air and the snow melting up in Boulder County, Horace traveled back up to Ward the next day and helped Elizabeth and the girls open up their tiny cabin. Walking around and taking easy steps, Horace examined his Eclipse mine, as well as the John Rice mine, in which he had a third ownership.

With an arm full of hugs, Horace left his family in Ward to manage their mining claims, while he climbed back onto the train headed towards Denver. He again reassured his nervous wife that he just needed some time to rest and looked forward to a well-deserved nap in their Windsor apartment.

But on April 3rd Horace finally had to admit something was terribly wrong and summoned Elizabeth and the girls to come back to Denver immediately. The pain on his right side had evolved into a sharp, stabbing sensation, which had started to cause extreme discomfort when he urinated and with his loss of appetite getting worse, he was sure this wasn't a pulled muscle.

Arriving at the Windsor Hotel at 5pm that night, Elizabeth found her husband curled up in bed with a raging fever and clutching his side, which prompted her to quickly summon not only one Doctor, but two.

Within the hour, Dr. C.A. Powers and Dr. P.V. Carlin arrived to find a very sick Horace Tabor and an extremely worried family. Setting down his black, leather doctor bag on a nearby table, Dr. Carlin quickly turned his attention to Governor Tabor. Pulling back the bed covers and finding them wet with perspiration, he immediately knew that Horace's body was fighting off some sort of infection. Raising Horace's night shirt and pressing hard onto his lower abdomen, his patient let out a loud, pain induced moan which was quickly followed by vomiting.

Looking over at Dr. Powers, Dr. Carlin shook his head before lowering Horace Tabors night shirt. Waiting until his patient's nausea had passed and his mouth had been wiped with a damp cloth, Dr. Carlin gave the family bad news.

"Governor, I'm sure you already suspected this, but you have appendicitis." The Doctor explained, as he looked first at Horace, then over at Elizabeth, who let out a heart wrenching gasp. "With your advanced age, any type of operation would be unquestionably fatal, but we will do everything possible to keep you comfortable."

Pulling up a chair, Dr. Powers began asking Horace about his other symptoms and discovered that his patient was also suffering from chronic constipation and had seen some blood in his urine. To help

Newspaper drawing of Horace Tabor's death
- History Colorado

with the constipation, which was possibly adding to his stomach pain, the Doctor administered fractional doses of Calomel with soda and Pepsin (one tenth of a grain every hour until five doses were taken) and ordered quinine grains to be taken 12 times a day. When Tabor finally had a movement, he was also found to have small blood clots in his feces.

To help with his pain, Horace was given Morphine Sulfate in ½ grain doses every two hours until his pain was relieved, at which point leeches were ordered.

As his abdomen continued to swell, 10 leeches were places on the area, in an attempt to remove the inflammation underneath the skin, since the Doctors still didn't believed surgery was possible.

Neither Dr. Powers, nor Dr. Carlin wanted to risk performing surgery and forever be known as the men who killed Horace Austin Warner Tabor, the Silver King.

Historic treatments for Appendicitis had previously included bloodletting, forceful vomiting and repeated enemas, while having the patient swallow small, lead balls, the more the better. It was believed that the weight of the lead would force their way through the obstruction and cause it to be released from the body in a bowel movement.

Luckily for Horace, these practice's were stopped in the 1830's, as it was very obvious that the Doctor's, at the time, didn't' fully understand where the appendix actually was.

With Horace sedated and resting comfortably, the Doctor's allowed extended family to be contacted and that evening Tabor's son Maxcy and Elizabeth's brother Phillip McCourt arrived to sit with him. But by Sunday morning Horace's health was beginning to fail and he requested to be baptized in the Catholic faith.

Unknown to Horace's family, he had been in talks with Father Guidosa, of Denver's Sacred Heart Catholic Church and had already arranged a baptism for the end of April. But it appeared he wasn't going to live that long.

With the priest called to his bedside and surrounded by his family, Horace Tabor was finally the recipient of the Sacrament.

"Horace Austin Warner Tabor, you have asked to be baptized,

because you wish to have eternal life. Do you acknowledge this?"

"I do"

"As well as professing your faith in Jesus Christ, you must also be willing to follow his commands, as Christians do. Are you willing to accept this?"

"I am"

"And are you prepared to live as Christians do?"

"I am"

"Therefore you will now be baptized into eternal life, in accordance with the command of our Lord Jesus."

As Father Guidosa removed the vessel of Holy water from his bag, Horace was helped into a sitting position on his bed and with a clean basin set in front of him, he received his baptism.

"I now baptize you in the name of the father and of the son and of the Holy Spirit." The priest commanded, as he poured water over Tabor's head, the required three times.

As Horace's head and face were dried off, Father Guidosa asked him if he would like to confess his sins, in which he eagerly accepted. After he was laid back against his pillows and made comfortable, the priest asked everyone to leave the room, while he heard Tabor's confession. Giving out a light penance, the priest them brought the family and the Doctors back into the room.

With Horace also wishing to receive Holy Communion, but suffering from nausea, the Priest dissolved the host in a small glass of wine, which Horace was able to slowly drink.

Laying back against his pillows again, Horace Tabor smiled at his wife Elizabeth. "This is the happiest moment of my life. I am at peace and resigned to the will of God."

As the two doctors continued their frantic attempts at saving Horace's life, which included applying plasters to his abdomen, Horace began fading away. Holding tightly to her husband's hand, Elizabeth asked him if he was in any pain.

Turning towards her, he replied weakly to her question and said the last words he would ever say on this earth.

"I'm in some pain."

And then, he was gone.

Time of death was a little after 9:30am, on April 10th, 1899.

Father Guidosa stayed by Elizabeth's side, while her brother Phillip began closing all the windows, drawing the curtains and covering all the mirrors. Seeing that her Uncle needed help, Lily quickly went over and stopped the clock above the fireplace and made sure to lay all the family photos face down, before returning to her father's side.

In Victorian times, there were many superstitions in place to help protect not only the recently deceased, but the living as well.

Mirrors were covered to prevent the spirit of the deceased from becoming trapped inside the glass and the pictures of family were placed face down, to prevent those family members from becoming possessed by the spirit of the dead. The ritual of the clock being stopped and the curtains drawn, was to not only signify the moment of death, but to prevent back luck from falling onto the living.

As word quickly spread, in regards to Horace Tabors passing, Colorado fell into a deep mourning over their lost Silver King. Flag were lowered to half-mast, as telegrams full of condolences and elaborate floral bouquets began to fill the Tabors Windsor Hotel Apartment.

One of the condolences graciously included a wreath of boxwood, tied with black ribbons, which was a customary gift that was to be hung on the apartment's front door, to inform passersby that there had been a death.

With the help of the Priest, the family began cleaning Horace's body, while they waited for the casket to arrive. Removing his soiled clothing and changing the bedding, his body was first washed with soapy water mixed with vinegar and then rinsed with water scented with lavender, before being dried with a towel.

Going through his clothing, a fine suit was chosen and he was fully dressed by the time the dreaded knock was heard on the door. Set on top of a wheeled cart and chilled with ice, the wooden casket was brought into the front room and the wheels of the cart locked in place. With help, the long, lanky body of H.A.W Tabor was respectably lowered inside, with a small pillow placed under his head.

For the next few days, the family took turns watching the body during a period called a "Wake" or "Death Vigil". This period was set aside to allow family and friends to say their goodbyes and adjust to the loss of their loved one, but more importantly, this time was used to confirm that the person was actually deceased.

The term "Wake", originally meant "Awake", as the death vigil was used to confirm if the deceased person was actually dead, or could possibly be woken back up. By having friends and family visit the deceased, it was felt that their presence would rouse the dead back to life.

During Horace Tabor's Death Vigil, the ever arriving floral arrangements were positioned around the casket, while clusters of single flowers were placed inside, against his body, to keep down any smell that might emanate

At noon, on Thursday April 13th, a knock was heard at the door of the apartment, which revealed a coachman dressed in proper mourning attire. With solemn and sincere condolences for the loss of her husband, the man asked Elizabeth if he could remove the casket, bearing the body of Horace Austin Warner Tabor, so it could be put on display inside the State Capital building.

Following one last kiss for her sweet husband, Elizabeth lowered her veil and allowed his body to be removed from their apartment.

Traveling inside an elegant, black, horse drawn hearse, the body of the Silver King was respectfully and quietly followed by mourners for a little over a mile, until it reached the State Capital Building, located on 15th and Sherman Street.

Following closely behind the hearse, the First Regiment Band began playing the death march as the National Guard and Employees of the

A CUP FULL OF LEECHES AND THE RING OF FLOWERS 133

United States Post Office followed in respectful silence.

Upon reaching the Capital, the hearse was surrounded by the State Military, as the casket was carefully unloaded and brought inside the building. Placed inside the reception room of the Governor's office, a large framed portrait, made when Horace Tabor was Lietendent Governor, was placed on a stand and draped with an American flag. Alongside the ever growing mountain of fragrant flowers, guards quickly took up post around the casket and kept their rifles positioned across their left shoulder.

And at 2:30pm the doors were opened.

As a show of love, respect or just out of shear curiosity, thousands of people began filing into the Capital building to view the remains of the Silver King. Newspaper reporters stood just outside the doors, to interview anyone who was willing, in an attempt to fill tomorrows headlines.

"The Governor was surrounded by a vast horde of human parasites and his nature was free and confiding. He was easily imposed upon and he lost greats amounts of money by indorsing paper and loans to people who pretended to be his friends, only because the money he had. I noticed later these very people turned a cold shoulder and shunned him"

- Colorado Governor Charles Thomas

"H.A.W Tabor was not a good man in the best sense, he was not a great man in hardly any sense, but he was a type of the rugged, sturdy American citizen who pioneered the great west."

- The Ouray Herald

"Tabor was an American and not a damn fool dude or book varmint who was pregnant with theory and void of experience"

-The Durango Democrat

"He was a genial, uncultured, good hearted citizen and his funeral promises to be the greatest ever known in this city or state"

- Colorado Senator Edward O. Wolcott

At 6pm the doors were shut and the last of the mourners ushered out. While people continued their vain attempts to enter the Capital building to view the body, guards were posted at the casket for what would be an all-night vigil. With the lid of the casket remaining open, the pale light of the room shone on Horace Tabors face, while guards stood watch with drawn sabers.

The next morning, as the sun began to rise the eager public began lining up outside the Capital's doors and begging for a final chance to gaze upon the face of Horace Tabor. By 7:30am the streets outside were overflowing with thousands of people, who began pressing against the doors, screaming to be let inside to view the body.

While the National Guard began pushing people back, their cries found the ears of Governor Charles Spalding Thomas, who threw open the doors of the Capital building. "Let the people see him", he commanded.

At 8:45 am the Governor announced that the parade was ready to begin and the Hearse was brought to the side door of the Capital building. As eager mourners pressed forward to witness the casket being brought out, the National Guard once again found themselves pushing back the throngs of curious citizens, in order to get the casket to its destination.

Dressed in their mourning suits of black, the eight pall bearers walked up to the casket and assumed their positions. Governor Thomas, Mayor Henry V. Johnson, M.J. Macnamara, William N. Byers, John H.

Poole and J.M Berkey each grabbed a handle and delivered the body of Horace Tabor to his waiting hearse.

As the horses where set into motion, the parade participants followed lead, as they traveled the 1 ½ miles to the Church of the Sacred Heart at 28th and Larimer street.

A squad of mounted police led the parade, followed by the first Regiment band playing the death march, which marked the time for the soldiers who followed. As the mounted officers led the parade onto Sherman Street and started down 17th, a platoon of Police officers, all on foot, moved out of a small archway and were quickly joined by a company of Firemen, headed by Chief Roberts.

Behind the men were black carriages, which contained the pall bearers, the hearse and its military escort of eight uniformed soldiers and their Lieutenant. The head of the mail carriers and postal clerks followed next, 100 strong, in full uniform, as well as the heads of various departments and clerks.

Following close behind were 60 civilian Postal carriers who bore American flags, draped in black crape and held at half mass, with almost 70 carriages full of mourner's taking up the rear.

Arriving at the Church, the Calvary cleared a path through the packed street, which allowed the hearse to arrive at the front steps. The carriage containing the pall bearers was then led up to the church, with the men quickly exiting their carriage and resuming their positions at Horace Tabors side, with a strong grasp of the Caskets handles.

Opening the door to the church, Father Gubitosi looked around

Horace Tabor's funeral parade-Ph.Prop.165 History Colorado

at the large group of mourners outside the church, as well as the chaos being caused by the tightly gathered carriages and agitated horses. With a motion towards the pall bearers, he signaled for them to bring the casket inside.

Led to the altar by ten Acolyte's bearing crosses, the procession slowly made its way down the aisle of the church, with the casket and its pall bearers escorted by eight members of the National Guard, in full dress uniform.

Elizabeth sat in the front pew, with her daughter's and watched in numb silence as her husband's casket was brought towards the altar.

Joining her, in her time of need, was her mother, her brother Phillip and her sister Claudia. Horace's son Maxcy had chosen to sit off to the side, apart from his father's second family.

As the casket was placed on the bier and the room silenced, Father Barry addressed the congregation.

"What of life have we before us? Father, miner. Millionaire, Governor, Senator of the United States, Post Master. The memory of this man will live to be handed down from sire to son, in this city and state."

With the church service continuing behind the closed and guarded doors, mayhem was quickly beginning to brew among the mourners waiting outside.

In order to back the hearse into position and have it ready to receive the casket, the National Guard had to move a few carriages out of the way, which maddened a nearby horse, who had no desire to be touched. Already panicked over the tight knit situation, the horse violently pulled its small buggy into the street and ran though the dense crowd for nearly a block. Thankfully, the buggy's driver was able to steer the frightened animal in a way that spared both human and neighboring vehicles.

Unfortunately, the commotion panicked the horses ridden by the Chaffee Light Artillery, who then took off running down 28th street. Turning the corner, the momentum threw the riders off and scattered them along the street, while fellow mourners attempted to grab the bridles as the horses ran past, to no avail.

The horses were later found standing next to a tree, far from the congestion of the crowd.

As the Church service ended and the pall bearers had returned H.A.W Tabor's casket to the hearse, the announcement was made that only the Chaffee Light Artillery and immediate family were invited to attend the final service at Calvary Cemetery.

But as the invited began following the hearse to Horace Tabor's final destination, they discovered that some people were refusing to show the respect asked of them and continued to follow the procession regardless.

And as the mourners arrived at the cemetery and the pall bearers carried Horace's casket to its set location, the uninvited parked their carriages nearby and found seats on top of nearby tombstones and grieving benches.

The Chaffee Light Artillery, prepared for their final salute, stood ready to receive the signal. The squad of eight men, under the command of Captain George Grear, patiently waited as flowers were placed on the lid of the casket.

But seeing his husband's final resting place was too much for Elizabeth. As she walked over and lovingly touched the wooden container that held her Horace, she broke down and fell to her knees, draping her head among the decorative flowers covering the lid. In an effort to comfort her mother, Lily knelt down beside her, while Silver Dollar stood sobbing near the head of the closed casket.

In an attempt to console Elizabeth, Father Guida approached her, which simply caused her to faint. With the help of her brother Phillip, Father Guida was able to administer smelling salts to rouse her back to the land of the living and help her back to her seat.

> **"Because God has chosen to call our brother Horace Austin Warner Tabor from this life to himself, we commit his body to the earth, for we are dust and unto dust we shall return. But the Lord Jesus Christ will change our mortal bodies to be like his in glory, for he is risen, the first born from the dead…"**

But as the casket began to lower, Elizabeth collapsed to the ground and crawled over to her husband's grave. Raising herself unto her knees and burying her face in her veil, she was inconsolable in her grief, but her agony only drew in the curious.

As Elizabeth screamed in response to the sounds of dirt hitting her husband's casket, the uninvited mourners began leaving the tombstones they had sat on earlier and drew closer, despite the loud cracks of the Chaffee light artillery firing off their final salute.

Perhaps they wanted some of the dirt being used to cover the Silver Kings grave as a morbid souvenir or perhaps they sincerely wanted to console the grieving Mrs. Tabor, but the onlookers were removed before their intentions were revealed.

Soon the void in the earth was filled in and then topped with two large, flat stones, which compacted the soil enough to allow more dirt

Newspaper drawing of Elizabeth Tabor on her husband's casket -History Colorado

to be added on top.

But Elizabeth refused to leave.

Seeing that she was staying, the mourners entered their carriages and were waved off, containing all but Elizabeth and her brother Phillip.

As the sunset on this somber day, Elizabeth remained planted at her husband's grave and spent hours gently running her hands over the fresh soil. Feeling pity for the new widow, the grave keeper handed Elizabeth's brother Phillip a lantern, before tipping his hat and turning in for the night.

As the midnight train whistle sounded at Union Station, Elizabeth became aware of the late hour and began gathering flowers from the beautiful floral arrangements, to set into the freshly laid dirt. Carefully choosing only the most fragrant, she pulled pink roses, hyacinths and lilies out of the multiple arrangements and used them to lovingly outline the grave that held her beloved.

And near the center of the grave, the area Elizabeth felt would be over his heart, she arranged violets to spell out one word.

Father.

A Queen's Diamond and a Tin of Chewing Tobacco

It was almost 2am when Elizabeth was escorted back to her Windsor Hotel apartment, by her brother Phillip and she was relieved to see that her daughters were sound asleep. They all desperately needed their rest, as the last week had been exhausting for everyone.

On the afternoon of April 16th, just two days after Horace's funeral, Elizabeth received an unexpected visitor to her apartment, who wanted to discuss a surprising business proposition. Removing his hat and with sincere condolences for the loss of her husband, Senator Edward Wolcott asked if he could discuss a business matter with her.

Heavily veiled in mourning black, Elizabeth invited the Senator into the sitting room and was almost in tears when he made his offer.

"Mrs. Tabor, it is my understanding that your husband has left you practically without an estate and I would like to offer you your husband's position as Post Master General. "Senator Wolcott informed her, as he held his hat in his hands. "But please understand it is only a nomination, as it still needs to be voted on and approved."

With her brother Phillip at her side, Elizabeth eagerly accepted the

Senator's nomination.

The position of Post master had been handled by Assistant Post master Joseph Vick Roy, since Horace Tabor had been stuck down with appendicitis and Roy himself had also been nominated for the coveted position.

So the cards were already stacked against her.

But 22 days later, as Elizabeth continued to mourn her husband's death, she found herself called into another court hearing. Surprisingly, this hearing wasn't in regards to another of her husband's mines, but instead involved her fabulous Queen Isabella diamond necklace.

Queen Isabella of Castile was born in 1451 and with her marriage to Ferdinand of Aragon, fought to unify Spain under one religion, which cost countless lives. Known as The Spanish Inquisition, Queen Isabella's desire to promote the Catholic faith resulted in the expulsion of more than 160,000 Jews and Moor's from Spain, as well as almost 5,000 people being burned alive at the stake.

In 1492 Queen Isabella had a strong desire to finance a voyage across the Atlantic, to spread Christianity and informed her court "I will assume the undertaking for my own crown of Castile and I am ready to pawn my jewels to defray the expense of it, if the funds in the treasury should be found inadequate." But fortunately, Christopher Columbus's voyage was funded instead from private investors and funds found available in the royal coffers and the jewels didn't need to be sold.

When Queen Isabella's only surviving son Price Juan married Archduchess Margaret of Austria in 1497, she was so delighted that she gifted her new daughter-in-law with a large collection on jewels, including what would one day be referred to as "The Queen Isabella diamond".

After Prince Juan's death three years later, Archduchess Margaret of Austria married Philibert the 2nd, Duke of Savoy who also died three years after their marriage. Heart broken, Margaret threw herself out of a window, but survived the fall and later had her deceased husbands heart embalmed, so she could keep it forever.

As the years passed, her jewels were bought and sold to royalty all around Europe, until a gold necklace containing the Queen Isabella Diamond found its way to England, where it was purchased by Horace Tabor as a wedding gift for his new bride Elizabeth McCourt.

And now it sat inside a safe deposit box in Denver, Colorado.

On May 8, 1899 Elizabeth and her Attorney listened as Judge LeFevre granted a decree of sale for one share of stock in the Tabor Amusement Company and one share of stock in the Tabor real estate and Investment Company, in order to pay back a 1894 loan of $15,000 from a Mr. Herman Powell.

Horace and Elizabeth had used $40,000 worth of diamond and gold jewelry to secure the loan, which they hadn't been able to pay back, but now with Horace gone, Elizabeth was trying hard to regain her property.

Mr. Powell and his attorneys had two weeks to decide if they were willing to except the offer.

Unfortunately, as Elizabeth frantically tried to piece together a life for her two daughters, she discovered that Senator Wolcott had pulled his recommendation for her to become Post master and had instead recommended Commissioner John C. Twombly to the position.

And on May 27th, 1899, Elizabeth discovered that she had not only lost the potential job as Post Master, but Mr. Herman Powell had refused to accept Mrs. Tabor's worthless stock, in exchange for the return of her jewelry.

With no source of income and only meager payouts from the Gold mines in Ward, Colorado, Elizabeth and her girls were forced to move out of their Apartment in the Windsor Hotel and into a small, brick, 3 room cottage at 833 Broadway in Denver.

Feeling like she couldn't stoop any lower, the newspapers seemed to be enjoying her downfall and printed heart breaking stories about her to fill their pages.

> "Only a few weeks after her husband was laid to rest, widow had to move out. Now living in a bleak one story brick, next to a blacksmith's shop and her two children are sick. A great many people never forgave Tabor for leaving his first wife and a relentless fate has followed the Tabor's and retribution is exacting a heavy reward."-Julesburg Grit June 22, 1899

As Elizabeth struggled to feed her children, she was informed that the Tabor block, which contained the Tabor grand Opera house, had been purchased from The Northwestern Trust Company by a Corporation composed of Colorado's finest.

When Horace Tabor originally lost his beloved Tabor block and Tabor Grand Opera house, it was sold to Mrs. Laura D. Smith on June 23, 1896, but she lost it due to non-payment of her mortgage on March 24, 1897 and it was returned to the Mortgage Company.

Now, after sitting empty for almost two years, it was not only being purchased by one investor, but six.

David Moffat, John P. Campion, William Byrd Page, George W. Baxter, Horace W. Bennett and Julius F. Myers had come together, forming The Bimetallic Company and planned on spending $250,000 to re-model their new joint investment.

Ironically, back on May 15, 1894 both Horace Bennett and Julias Myers had paid Horace Tabor's past due mortgage of $250,000, so the bank wouldn't repossess the building and now they had gone in on a group venture to not only buy the entire property, but remodel it.

As June came to pass, Elizabeth discovered a letter from an Attorney in regards to her husband's Last Will and Testament and it asked if she could arrive on July 8th so it could be reviewed and filed. Hopeful that the Will contained something that could help her feed her children, she instead found it empty and with a request she couldn't fulfill.

The document , drawn up on March 14, 1884, read that Elizabeth Tabor was the sole legatee and executor to his estate and that upon Horace Tabor's death, she should not only make just provision's for their children, if any were born, but that she should place a monument, to cost no less than $1,000 on his grave. The rest was left to her discretion.

As Elizabeth signed the document and handed it back to the Attorney, she was reminded that her beloved's grave was marked with a $12 grave stone that simply bore the name Tabor, which had been paid for by her family.

Desperate to keep her head above water, Elizabeth and the girls spent the next few months traveling between Denver and their mining claims in Ward, in order to dig up enough ore to pay their rent and put food on the table. When winter arrived, they unexpectedly found themselves spending Christmas in Leadville to attend to business, which is where Elizabeth first read the Newspaper story that made her stomach drop.

The gold and silver mine in Morelia, Mexico, of which Horace had bought 7/10th interest of back in 1881, was now pouring out $40,000 a month in ore, but her husband had sold his share in the mine to keep food on their table in 1894, after the Silver crash happened. If he would have kept his share, Elizabeth and her daughters would have been rich again.

Horace had sunk thousands of dollars into that mine after the Sherman Silver act was passed, in hopes that the Mexican mine would revive his fortune, but it had run dry. And with no money left to drill any deeper, he had abandoned it and then later sold his share.

But two Mexican boys, who had been employees in the mines store room, had begun working the abandoned mine and continued to dig the shaft deeper, by hand. And they only had to extend the shaft six feet deeper before they hit ore.

And to add to her misery, Elizabeth found a strange letter from California in her mailbox, once she and the girls returned to Denver. It was from a Spiritualist who claimed to of conducted a séance on her behalf, and the results were nauseating.

> "Latest advice from a Spiritual Séance are to the effect that you are now upon the verge of great misfortune and continued failure in every way. That you treacherously meditate evil in your heart towards one who was sent to you to be your deliveror in time of your greatest need and some distress, but whose counsel you now rejected for that of another, which shall not prosper you, but result in confusion and final ruin.
>
> Dirty friendships and personal interests implies me to give the above message and warning with my sincere regrets, also at the unfortunate outlook for the future which will entail such bitter disappointments and loss for all concerned and for which you have only yourself, yourself alone to blame."

As the New Year turned from 1899 to 1900 and their first Christmas without Horace was passed, Elizabeth found herself busy trying to save any of her husband's properties that she could. As she flipped through files full of legal documents and deeds, she stumbled upon the file on the Tabor Mines and Mills Company in Leadville, up on Fryer Hill, which contained a mine called The Matchless.

Named after Matchless Chewing Tobacco, the mine was one of her husband's most profitable, when it wasn't filling up with water and flooding. The file showed that Horace had lost the property about a year and a half before and it was ordered sold, but maybe since silver wasn't very profitable right now, the new owner wouldn't mind if she took it off his hands.

On February 14, 1900 Elizabeth Bonduel Tabor walked into the court house, dressed in her full mourning costume and asked Judge Owers to dissolve the injunction, as she wished to have the property returned to her.

With baited breath she silently waited for his response and was relieved to see a smile cross his face, as he agreed to pospone the sale and to hear her plea. A court date was set for June 7, 1900.

"All rise, the honorable Judge Owers residing"

"You may be seated"

Taking her seat, Elisabeth straightened her black mourning gown with its white trim and sat up straight, as the Judge began discussing the case. In her Catholic faith, Elizabeth had been required to dress in a full mourning costume, which was all black, for a period of one year, before she could begin adding white to her costume. It would be almost October before she could return to wearing any type of color in her clothing.

"Mrs. Tabor, you have shown interest in reacquiring the silver mine referred to as The Matchless. Is this correct?"

"Yes, your Honor."

"As this mine has a debt of $24,896.99, I will grant you six months to raise the money needed to save the property. After which time, the mine will be auctioned off."

"Dismissed."

Elizabeth left the court room with her head held high, but unfortunately on January 27th, 1901 she had to watch the mine slip out of her hands, as it was purchased by Herman Powell at a Sheriffs sale.

But Mr. Howell was quickly regretting his new purchase.

Going into a partnership with James W. Newell and Warren F. Page, the men soon discovered that Mrs. Tabor's desire to reacquire her husband's former property may have been purely sentimental, as the promised Silver deposits were drowning in a mine shaft full of water.

Bringing in experts to examine their new purchase, the men discovered that it would cost almost $30,000 in pumps, riggings and machinery, before the existing shafts could even be reached and even then, there was no guarantee that a rich vein of silver lay underneath all that water.

Not wanting to invest any more money, Mr. Herman Powell handed the reigns over to S.W. Belford, made him the trustee of his regretful purchase and washed his hands of it. Unfortunately, this left his business partners with the task of investing their own money into the Matchless mine.

As they contemplated investing the possible $30,000 needed to get the mine up and running, they couldn't help put stare down the water filled shaft and question the possible profit that might lay beneath.

They needed to pump out this mine.

Contacting their now missing partner Mr. Powell, they were surprised to find that he had quietly passed the title of the property to his trustee James B. Belford, who in turn handed it over to his son Samuel Belford, who wanted it gone. And on June 1st, 1901, J.W. Newell and W.F. Page, along with their newly acquired partners Mr. Messrs and Mr. Harp were offered the chance to become the sole owners of the Matchless mine for $14,500.

But before they could decide if they were willing to except the offer, the Matchless mine was sold out from under them for $15,000.

When they angrily inquired who the mines new owner was, Samuel Belford simply said "The man who purchased the mine is the noblest man in the state and with a modesty which is characteristic of him, he wishes to conceal his identity from the public.

This man plans on sinking the shaft 2,000 feet if necessary and believes he will uncover bodies of Ore which will rival in richness anything worked by Senator Tabor."

With the fight over the Matchless finished, in regards to Elizabeth Tabor, she once again took her daughters up to their mines in Ward, Colorado to dig for ore, which is where Winfield Stratton found her.

After a look around the Eclipse Mine, Winfield Stratton revealed the true purpose of his visit and invited Elizabeth and her daughters to Leadville on July 3rd, as he had something he wanted to show them.

A QUEEN'S DIAMOND AND A TIN OF CHEWING TOBACCO 149

But unknown to him, his well-planned out intentions were quickly being pulled out from under him.

On June 9th Mr. Stratton had purchased the Matchless mine for $15,000 and had arranged to pay any liens against the property, with his sole intention of gifting it to Elizabeth Tabor. He also planned on giving her a large sum of money to work the mine, as a final farewell gift to Mrs. Tabor and the children, as Mr. Stratton's own alcoholism was quickly destroying his health. His thin body was growing weaker by the day, as he discovered that his overabundance of drink had diseased his liver and he was putting his affairs in order.

He had also purchased land outside Colorado Springs for a home meant for Widows and Orphans, which he had already named after his father Myron Stratton. Winfield Stratton regretted his decision to shoot at his father all those years ago and had decided to dedicate his future institution not to himself, but to his father.

His Will assigned $6,000,000 towards the future Myron Stratton home for widows and orphans, as he knew his death would cause every parasite in Colorado to beg for a piece of his estate. And helping out Mrs. Tabor put his heart at ease.

His only request to the mortgage holder of the Matchless Mine, due to Stratton's own superstitions, was that the money wouldn't be paid until July 4th, 1901, which was only less than a month away.

On July 4th 1891, Winfield Stratton had struck it rich in the newly found town site of Cripple Creek and it made him a millionaire almost overnight, with the mine he named The Independence.

And his desire was to pay for the deed to Leadville's Matchless mine on July 4th, was not only a gift to Mrs. Tabor, but also a gift of good luck on her future mining endeavors.

And he would not change his mind.

But with the knowledge leaked that Winfield Stratton had purchased the Matchless mine, people began filing liens against the property and on June 27th Judge Johnson allowed a judgement against the property for $24,896.99, by none other than Herman Powell.

Powell had purchased the Matchless mine at a Sheriff's auction on January 27th, just six months earlier, for $24,896.99, but had given the property to his trustee Samuel Belford after discovering that he would have to sink a possible $30,000 more into the mine to reach ore.

But now that Winfield Stratton wanted it, Herman Powell wanted it back.

The judgement authorized by Judge Johnson not only allowed the lien, but empowered Mr. Powell to become the Mine's creditor, which gave him the right to not only pay off any prior judgements, but to take back the property from his trustee Mr. Belford and keep it for himself.

And to add more fuel to the fire, Mr. Powell demanded that the mine be offered for sale on June 25th, after learning of Mr. Stratton's superstition of wanting to buy the Mining property on July 4th, in order to mirror his highly successful Independence Mine.

Heading to Leadville on June 24th, Elizabeth and her daughters stood by helplessly as they waited for the sale to begin. With an evil laugh, Mr. Powell teased Mr. Stratton about his good luck superstitions, without realizing his desire to purchase the mine was purely a sentimental gesture to Mrs. Tabor from a dying millionaire and nothing more.

Infuriated over Mr. Powell's treatment of both Mrs. Tabor and Mr. Stratton, the former trustee of the mine, Mr. Samuel Belford met with Sheriff Daniels before the auction began and paid the original lien of $13,847 plus the $1,008 in added interest.

This made Mr. Herman Powell and himself legal business partners.

And with a firm hand, Mr. Belford insisted that Mr. Powell lend the $25,000 needed to purchase the mine, to Mrs. Elizabeth Tabor, which infuriated him. Seeing that he was backed into a corner, Herman Powell eventually agreed to the proposal, but added unachievable stipulations.

In a malicious tone, Mr. Powell informed Mrs. Tabor that before he would secure the loan of $25,000, she would have to put up her own deposit of $10,000, which could not be gifted to her by Mr. Stratton.

And she only had until August 2nd to come up with the money.

Luckily, for Elizabeth, a little Winfield Stratton luck was floating in the air, as the Sheriff pulled her aside to show her a pile of papers that listed Horace Tabor as the owner of a few old mining claims in Leadville, that could possibly still belong to her.

Maybe Winfield Stratton's good luck was going to bless her after all.

Stolen Mining Stock and the Dead Millionaire

Looking over the deeds to the newly discovered mining claims, Elizabeth quickly recognized them from the boxes of her husband's paperwork she had sifted through, just a few months earlier. Horace hadn't paid the taxes on any of these properties in years, as he deemed them worthless, but the Sherriff explained to her that her husband's assumption wasn't quite accurate.

"Mrs. Tabor, I know for a fact that someone shipped over $1,500 worth of ore from at least one of them." The Sherriff explained with a smile.

"What can I do?" Elizabeth asked, as she flipped though the small stack of paperwork. "Can I have the man who is stealing the ore arrested?"

With a laugh, the Sherriff tipped his hat up a little and gave her a goofy grin. "Mrs. Tabor, did you ever hear of your husband having anyone arrested?"

"No." she admitted, with a defeated tone." If my Horace wouldn't have done it, then I won't either." With the deeds in hand, she then headed over to the mining claims to see if they were workable and if so, she would attempt to pay the overdue taxes and work the mines herself.

But with no money to pay Herman Powell his $10,000 deposit on the loan for The Matchless, Elizabeth had to just sit back and watch The Matchless mine slip from her fingers on August 2, 1901. With the strike of a judge's gavel, Mr. Powell was free to begin working the mine, without the intrusion of Horace Tabor's widow getting in the way.

Walking away from the court house with a smile on his face, he was eager to get to work on a mine that he was sure would be a bonanza. Why else would Winfield Stratton want to go into a partnership with Mrs. Tabor, if he wasn't hiding the knowledge of a huge vein of silver ore?

With his engineers at his side he traveled up to The Matchless, stared down the huge shaft full of ice water and listened to his engineers explain his options. He already knew that the upper layers had been thoroughly exhausted and that they would have to sink a shaft possibly a thousand feet deeper just to hit ore, but his main concern was how they were going to pump out all this water and keep the shaft from constantly filling back up.

He was starting to think this investment might not have been such a good idea.

Returning to Denver and still sore from her failed attempt to purchase The Matchless Mine, Elizabeth discovered more bad news in the form of a certified letter, sent to her from the State Capital building.

When Horace Tabor died, Colorado Governor Charles Thomas had insisted that he get a funeral fit for a king, but despite knowing that Tabor had left his family destitute, the state of Colorado was still insisting that his widow pay for it.

With the price of his casket at $325 and the overly elaborate funeral priced at $652.50, Elizabeth was overwhelmed with the burden of paying for something she was forced to have and angry that she was being put into this situation.

She voiced her concerns to undertaker McGovern, who respectfully approached the Legislature on her behalf, making her plea of poverty and asked if the Senate could cover the funeral costs. Unfortunately, he was met with cold stares by all but Senator Buckley, who did address the Senate further on the matter.

"Senator Tabor's funeral was really a State funeral, as the body lay in state at the State Capital building and if Mrs. Tabor had managed the funeral, it would not have amounted to $600, therefore she should not have to pay the bill" the Senator explained, as he addressed the room.

"What about Senator Tabor's son Maxcy Tabor? Is he willing to pay for his father's funeral?" Governor Orman questioned, as the other members of the Senate began to whisper in agreement.

"No Governor, Maxcy Tabor has refused on the grounds that his father secured a divorce from his mother, in order to marry the present Widow." Senator Buckley answered, as the whispers in the room became louder.

The request for payment was denied.

A ray of hope did appear in Leadville, as the local newspaper The Herald Democrat had held a fund raiser and was able to raise $625 towards the bill, but after reading the story printed about it in the newspaper, Elizabeth politely declined the much needed donation.

The newspaper had run a heartwarming story showcasing all the hard work that Marshal Lomeis and the Elks Lodge had done to raise the money for Horace Tabor's burial expenses, as he was one of their own and the former Mayor of Leadville, but then bashed Elizabeth as a home wrecker who now found herself begging for handouts.

With no acknowledgment of their catty behavior towards the second Mrs. Tabor, the Herald Democrat then ran a story shaming Elizabeth for not excepting their wonderful gift, after all the hard work they had done to acquire the money.

With a heavy heart, Elizabeth went through the boxes of her

husband's mining claims and gave the undertaker a stock certificate as payment in August 1901, which he graciously accepted.

And as newspapers all around Colorado continued to print stories of the ungrateful Mrs. Tabor and all the hard work that Leadville had done to help her in her time of need, Elizabeth realized that she would need to sell one of her husband's mines if she was going to keep her children fed.

After contacting numerous interested parties and investors, a deal was finally reached on December 18th 1901 with the Earl Mining Company of Colorado Springs, to purchase the Eclipse mine in Ward, Colorado. She received $15,000 in cash, as well as $100,000 worth of stock in the company, which gave her enough money to move her and her daughters to Leadville to work her newly found mines, on which she had quickly paid the back taxes.

With money in the bank, Elizabeth moved her children up to Leadville and rented a little cottage on west 7th street, in January 1902 and began looking for men to help her work her mines. But a surprise visit from her youngest sister Claudia McCabe would change everything.

Her sister Claudia, who was Baptized Clotilda and married Ralph McCabe 10 years her senior, had done very well for herself and her surprise visit to Leadville instantly put a smile on her sister Elizabeth's face.

As the siblings talked, Claudia informed her sister of a strange turn of events, in which Mr. Herman Powell had once again decided he no longer wanted The Matchless Mine, but this time it was due to a shocking discovery underneath the flooded shaft.

No high grade silver Ore.

Under the false belief that Winfield Stratton wanted to purchase the mine for Elizabeth Tabor, because the mine was rich in ore, Powell had invested money into drilling down past the flooded depths, but was sickened by what he found. Sample and after sample showed nothing but low grade ore and no indication of the desired silver vein below the icy water.

With Herman Powell putting The Matchless Mine back up for sale, the news of the available property reached the ears of Elizabeth Tabor's brother Phillip, who traveled the news throughout their family, until the information was dropped on the desk of Ralph McCabe. Seeing an investment and being familiar with his sister-in-law's strong work ethic, he purchased The Matchless Mine and put the deed in her name on February 13, 1902. The purchase price was $30,000, which was only $5,104 more than Herman Powell had paid for it, which showed he added the price he spend to drill under the water filled shaft and broke even.

Thrilled with finally owning The Matchless, Elizabeth moved her and her daughters out of their little rented cottage on west 7th street and up to small house near the mine, originally meant as a home for the Forman and began advertising for people to work on removing the ore come spring.

The first men to apply to work the mine were Mr. McGarry and Mr. Raney, who were set to work one section, while Mr. P. Kelly and Mr. Jack Cunningham, known as Sailor, would work another. Needing to wait for the first sign of spring and the ground to begin to thaw, they would have to wait a bit before they could start working the shaft.

But as the snow began to melt and small, green shoots of grass began to dot the Matchless, Elizabeth found herself filing not one, but two lawsuits, after coming across more of her husband's mining documents, this time located inside a forgotten safe deposit box.

But to her surprise, in regards to the first lawsuit, she was able to team up with another widow.

On April 8, 1902 Mrs. Elizabeth Tabor and Mrs. Timothy Foley filed a suit against George W. Trimble, A.V. Hunter and John F. Campion for a combined total of 870,000 shares in the Iroquois mining Company and $100,000 in damages.

Elizabeth claimed that at or around July 1, 1897 the stock was put with Mr. Trimble and Mr. Hunter with the belief that it was to be transferred to Mr. Campion upon the payment of $50,000. Mr. Campion never paid for the stock and it was never returned to Mr. Tabor or Mr. Foley.

Elizabeth's second lawsuit was going to be a hard one to fight, as this one involved going against one of the most powerful men in Colorado, David Halliday Moffat.

David Moffat owned over one hundred mines, nine railroads and had served as president and treasurer for numerous banks and government positions all around Colorado, but that was no excuse when it came to stealing her husband's stock.

She charged that Moffat had never paid her husband for his 71,250 shares of stock in the Maid of Erin Silver Mining Company of America, valued at $498,750 and 1,168 shares in the Gold and Silver Mining Company of America, valued at $45,840.

Her claim was that her husband Horace Tabor had placed the stock into Mr. Moffat's hands as trustee, pending negotiations of a sale, but that the sale was never made and that the stocks had never been returned to her husband, despite repeated demands.

But as she reviewed her husband's old bank records, for the upcoming lawsuit against Mr. Moffat, Elizabeth then found that a Leadville banker might have stolen $55,000 from her husband's account years before his death. Shocked, she picked up the bank records and headed straight over to the Bank Managers desk.

Sitting down with the manager and showing him the paper trail, she pointed to evidence that a Mr. George W. Trimble had been the one in charge of her husband's account. In a shocking twist, the man in question admitted to garnishing her husband's accounts, but voiced his option that Mrs. Tabor was simply a widow and that he was under no legal obligation to refund her the money.

But with a quick trip to the court house, the Judge changed the bankers mind and the money was returned to her.

Ironically, only a year after Leadville's local newspaper bashed Elizabeth Tabor and described her as a "Home wreaker begging for scraps", the paper surprisingly changed their view of her and added it to a story about a local legend.

On May 25, 1902 the wife of Mr. George H. Fryer, who lived in Chicago, checked into the Vendome Hotel in Leadville in order to assess her husband's mining interests. Mr. Fryer had made one of the first discoveries in the Leadville area, which was named Fryer Hill in his honor, which prompted the Newspaper to write a gossip piece regarding his wife's visit.

> "Like the brave little woman Mrs. Tabor, she has come to look after her interests, although only a woman."

With Elizabeth's Leadville mines being worked and money in her pocket, she packed up her girls and began checking out a few more mining claims she had found in those old, dusty storage boxes, in hopes of discovering another bonanza.

On June 28th Elizabeth took her daughters over to Silverton to investigate The Alaska Mine, located between Poughkeepsie Creek and Cement Creek, after finding out her husband had a small amount of stock in it. She also was looking into The Red Rogers claim near the top of the divide, between the two creeks, to see if they were worth purchasing. They had both been closed after the Silver Panic, but they had a good streak and were quite prominent shippers in their time.

As Elizabeth and her daughters continued working their many mining interests, Elizabeth learned on July 18th that the new owners of her husband's beloved Leadville Opera house were planning on reopening the doors.

The Leadville Elks had purchased the building just the year before and had been busy remodeling the stage area and had even spent several thousand dollars on new painted back drops. By dividing the building in half, on the ground floor, they were able to add two store rooms that totaled 60 feet, as well as

Elks club meeting rooms on the second floor and a fine lounge room on the third, for a grand total of $30,000.

As work at The Matchless Mine continued and more ore was removed, Elizabeth and her lessee's decided to extend the road from the mine to a nearby road, known simply as Road 3. As this road got closer to town, the name changed to the more recognized East 7th street. As her men continued working on extending the road from the Matchless, Elizabeth received wonderful news that Leadville was going to be extending "The Blow Tunnel" into the Fryer Hill basin, in order to drain the water from the lower workings of the local mines.

The tunnel was created by The Silver Cord Mine and Mill, which itself was spread over 60 acres and included its own reservoir, which ran their hydro powered impulse turbines, but like most mines they also needed a way to drain their excess water.

A.A. Blow was the manager of The Silver Cord Mine and was the brainchild behind the drainage tunnel, which emptied first into a mill styled crusher and then finally into the nearby Arkansas river. With the tunnel being extended over four miles into Leadville's mining district and reaching the top of Fryer Hill, the highest point was drilled at a depth of 1,200 feet and finished at 800 feet, which successfully drained even the lowest points of the area's mines, including The Matchless.

But with a new use for the tunnel, a fresh name was chosen by mining man John F. Campion, who had a love of hoofed animals. And with his own mines previously being named The Elk shaft and The Ibex, after the Alpine Ibex from the European Alps, the Blow Tunnel became known as the Yak Tunnel.

With the new road up to The Matchless nearly complete and the drainage tunnel under construction, Elizabeth and her daughters headed over to Breckenridge to check on a few interesting mining claims and the local paper gave her a sparkling review.

> ```
> "Wednesday evening the Journal was
> favored with a call from that plucky little
> lady Mrs. Senator Tabor, with a remarkably
> bright view of life and seems happy. Her
> mission in Breckenridge was to confer with
> Hiram Johnson, with whom she is interested
> in a couple of mining claims"
> ```

On September 13, 1902 Elizabeth Tabor purchased a ¾ interest in the Hunkidori mine near Breckenridge from Giuseppe Cuneo, which she quickly transferred into her younger sister's Claudia McCourt's name, as a thank you for believing in her.

But as Elizabeth and her daughter's continued with their Breckinridge visit the next day, they overheard the terrible news that Colorado legend Winfield Scott Stratton had died the night before, at only 54 years of age.

After a lifelong obsession with hard liquor and a grossly infected liver, coupled with diabetes, he slipped into a painless coma and died at 9:35pm, with his friend Bob Schwarz by his side.

The root cause of his alcoholism was the result of his greatest gift, which was also his greatest curse. His Cripple Creek gold mine, The Independence.

On July 4th, 1891 Winfield Stratton and a man named Leslie Popejoy staked two mining claims near Victor, Colorado, naming one The Independence and the other The Washington, in honor of the holiday. While working the claim, Winfield Stratton discovered ore samples that showed high amounts of gold, which prompted Stratton to sell his house and buy out his partner.

And within a year he became a millionaire.

As his money poured in, he poured it back out all over Colorado Springs. He gave money for a 13 year old violin player to study in Germany, he donated land, he built a five story building for the

Colorado Springs mining exchange, he spent $1,500,000 to install a state of the art Street car system, he built band stands and paid for musicians to play, he bailed out Denver's Brown Palace Hotel when it faced bankruptcy…but it wasn't enough.

It seemed the more he gave, the more people wanted. In one four month period alone he spent over $4,500,000 to help improve Colorado, but the hands kept asking. With his charity well known, he quickly discovered that if he said a simple "Hi" or tipped his hat in greeting on the street, he would find himself in a court room, facing breach of contract charges from the greedy masses.

He defended himself against woman who claimed he had backed out of marriage proposals or had gotten them pregnant and against men who would insist that Stratton had promised them money and then never paid them. Disgusted with society, Winfield Stratton eventually locked himself inside his home and found safety inside quart sized bottles of whiskey. When he did leave his home , it was only to attend to private matters and he made sure to keep his head down and avoid eye contact or conversation with anyone he passed by.

But his death quickly brought out the leaches from every corner of Colorado.

As his body laid in state, inside his beloved Mining exchange building, over 9,000 people came through to pay their respects. But while the street cars stopped at 2pm, as a silent show of appreciation for the man who purchased them, the money hungry throngs of Colorado residents were waiting on the sidelines to pounce.

When Winfield Stratton's Will was read a week later, it revealed that he had left millions to his close Nieces, Nephews and to the son of his friend Zeurah Stewart, while the remaining $6,000,000 had been placed in a trust for the future home he had envisioned for widows and orphans, which he christened The Myron Stratton Home.

In total, over 100 people tried to claim the money Stratton had set aside for his institution, including the State of Colorado, 12 women who claimed to be his widows and even his old mining partner Leslie Popejoy.

In regards to Popejoy, the fact he had already accepted a smaller payout only two years earlier ,voided any future attempts at a piece of Stratton's pie and he left the court house empty handed.

In 1900 Winfield Stratton had sold The Independence to a London Corporation called Venture, for $10 Million. This prompted his old business partner Popejoy to sue Stratton for half the money, by claiming that he had defrauded him back in 1891, by lying about the amount of gold inside The Independence. Winfield Stratton and his Lawyers eventually won their case, but understanding that his former business partner was still sore, Stratton kindly offered Leslie Popejoy $40,000 as a small token of their former friendship, which he accepted.

After Winfield Stratton's death, it took seven years for his estate to finally become settled and construction on the Myron Stratton home for Widows and Orphans finally began in 1909, as soon as the last court hearing was complete.

It still proudly stands to this day and continues to serve the people it was intended for.

Missing Silver ore and the man who owns the Earth

With everything going so well for Elizabeth Tabor, she knew something had to give.

As she stood in the doorway of her rented Denver home, Elizabeth quietly held the letter to her chest and took a deep breath before bringing herself to read it out loud to her daughters. With all the death they had faced, she desperately wanted to shield her children from any more heartbreak, but within the pages she learned that her own mother might soon leave this world.

Elizabeth Anderson Nellis had been a widow for 19 years, after losing her husband to Typhoid Fever in May 1883 and now, at 76 years old she had suffered a massive stroke that left her unable to speak or move.

Quickly boarding the next train to Oshkosh, Wisconsin, 48 year old Elizabeth, 18 year old Lily and 12 year old Silver Dollar were relieved to find that not only was the family matriarch still very much alive , but sitting up in bed when they arrived on October 10th, 1902.

But as they stayed for what would now be a short and pleasant visit, the family pleaded with Elizabeth to allow Lily to stay and take care of her Grandmother, as they yammered on about being too busy with their own lives and children. Eager to help her mother recover and seeing the excitement in her daughter's eyes, Elizabeth grudgingly agreed.

With kisses for her family and eyes full of tears, Elizabeth left Wisconsin with only her youngest daughter in tow and returned to Colorado to continue fighting for what was rightfully hers.

On November 7, 1902, Elizabeth found herself, once again, in a Denver court room, this time attempting to collect a past due insurance claim. With her head held high, she presented an insurance policy on a building called The Peoples Theater, which had burned down 10 years before and demanded payment.

The Peoples Theater had been discovered engulfed in flames at 12:15am on June 11, 1892, after a patron left an unattended cigar burning, after what would unfortunately become the theatres last performance.

The beautiful stone building had been constructed in 1889 and had been partially funded by Horace Tabor, which is why he had taken out an insurance policy on what was thought to be a fire proof building. Her husband had spent years trying to collect the $22,000 he was owed, but had run into so much red tape and excuses, that he had just thrown the insurance claim in a box.

But now Elizabeth was determined to get at least a partial payment for the loss of the building.

As the Lawyers in the case argued back and forth, the Judge suggested that Elizabeth should receive a fractional reimbursement of only $5,000, which was quickly refused by the Insurance Company who asked for an extension on the matter.

Leaving the court room with her lawyers, Elizabeth discussed another upcoming court hearing, this one scheduled for January 17, 1903 in Denver, against David H. Moffat, one of the richest men in the state. And while she finished the year with a quiet Christmas, with only her now 13 year old daughter Silver by her side, Elizabeth spent her holiday going over all of her husband's papers and preparing herself for her battle against Mr. Moffat.

"All rise, Judge Carpenter residing"

"You may all be seated"

As the Judge began to discuss the case before him, the story unfolded concerning the $552,090.00 that Horace Tabor's widow, Mrs. Elizabeth Tabor, claimed that David Moffat still owed the Tabor estate. Yet it appeared that Mr. Moffat couldn't be bothered to attend the court hearing.

"Mrs. Tabor is suing for the restoration of her dead husbands stocks and moneys alleged to have been put into the hands of Mr. Moffat in trust." Mr. Moffat's Lawyer Charles Hughes explained, as he glanced over at the Judge. "Which have long since been fulfilled"

As Mr. Moffat's lawyer finished his bold statement and sat back down, Elizabeth Tabor's attorney began enlightening the Judge on the real reason they were all in the court room, which quickly wiped the smug look off the face of Moffat's lawyer.

"Your honor, when Horace Tabor was riding high before the Silver strike, he had put his faith in David Moffat to be his trustee and secure his stocks, bonds, deeds and other properties, but when the Silver crash occurred all of Mr. Tabor's properties instantly vanished and his widow is simply demanding that her family's rightful property be returned." Elizabeth's Lawyer explained, as he walked towards the Judge. "I have here the deeds and stocks in question for you honor to review."

As Moffat's lawyer sat up a little straighter, the Judge slipped on his glasses and began entertaining the courtroom with the documents placed in front of him.

"Stock in the Maid of Erin mine valued at $356,250, stock in the Gold and Silver extraction Company of America valued at $45,840 and personal holdings valued at $150,000." Judge Carpenter read aloud, before lowering his glasses and addressing Mrs. Tabor. "And I understand you are also asking for all Attorney fees to be paid as well?"

"Yes, your honor" Elizabeth answered, standing as tall and proud as her tiny frame would allow. "I am asking for a judgement of the money's alleged to be in the trust, for an accounting of those money's and for damage sufficient to cover the prosecution of this suit"

"Thank you Mrs. Tabor, I will take this claim under advisement and make my decision on whether or not there is enough proof to proceed."

Dismissed.

As Elizabeth and her lawyer waited to hear back from the courts, she took a trip up to Leadville to check on the Matchless, Robert E. Lee and the Dunkin Mines, since she had decided to spend the winter in Denver with her youngest daughter. But as she approached the Matchless, she discovered a horrifying truth regarding the men who she allowed to work her claims.

They had destroyed her buildings.

Shocked, she walking the properties and saw that her mining structures were in shambles and the area surrounding it in ruins. The Robert E. Lee and the Dunkin, which were adjacent to the Matchless, also had large piles of tailings, which appeared to have been removed from the Matchless by the way of an underground shaft.

Furious, she walked around her claims until she spotted J.W. Newell and W.F. Page, two of the men who leased The Robert E. Lee and The Dunkin mines from her and confronted them on the ore she felt they had removed from the Matchless, which they were not allowed to touch.

After a heated exchange of words, the leases were removed from the site and Elizabeth filed a claim against J.W. Newell, Mr. Harp, W.F. Page, Herman Powell and Mr. Messer's who owned the Ransome leasing company, on February 3, 1904.

With her Attorney's J. Warner Mills and L.J. Stark at her side,

MISSING SILVER ORE AND THE MAN WHO OWNS THE EARTH 167

Elizabeth walked into the Leadville court house and filed suit for $3,200,000 in damages, claiming that the company and their employee's wrecked her mines, destroyed buildings and other properties and removed large amounts of ore from The Matchless through a shaft she felt was located inside the Robert E. Lee and the Dunkin mines.

As she left the court house and said goodbye to her lawyers, Elizabeth boarded the train back to Denver and spent the ride praying that she would hear back from her Denver Lawyers soon and that they would give her good news in regards to her court hearing against David Moffat.

But unfortunately when she returned to Denver, all she found was an upsetting letter from her older daughter Lily, who was still living in Oshkosh, Wisconsin and caring for her Grandmother.

She wasn't coming back to Colorado.

Settling into a nearby chair, Elizabeth re-read the letter from her now 19 year old daughter and despite the wonderful news that her mother was recovering well from her stroke, she was disappointed in her daughter's decision to remain in Wisconsin.

Her family was slipping away from her.

As she lay the letter, scrawled in her daughter Lily's familiar handwriting, onto her lap, she gave a silent prayer that her youngest daughter Silver would retain her love of the mountains and never chose to leave her alone in Colorado.

All the mining claims in the world don't amount to much, if you don't have anybody to share them with.

Luckily for Elizabeth, good news did come in the form of a letter dated February 9th 1903, that stated she had been awarded payment from her lawsuit against David Moffat. Judge Carpenter had adjusted the amount she had originally asked for, based on what the stocks were currently worth and had awarded her $750,000, which was $191,910.00 more than she had asked for!

Reading through the court papers, she read that Mr. Moffat's attorneys had 20 days to respond to the Judges verdict and the final court hearing on the matter would be March 8, 1903.

Unfortunately, to add to her stress, a new lawsuit had been filed in Leadville, this time by the Ransome leasing company, in response to Elizabeth Tabor's lawsuit against them. It appeared that they were denying any theft of silver ore from the Matchless and were asking the court to grant them $40,000 in damages and loss wages, since she had broken their lease.

The Ransome leasing company had a contract with Elizabeth Tabor to work her Robert E Lee and Dunkin mines in Leadville, but not the Matchless, which she was working herself in the warm months with her daughter Silver. The two mines were in very close proximity to the Matchless and they claimed that they hadn't touched any of the silver ore located inside the Matchless or had dug a connecting shaft in order to retrieve it.

The hearing was scheduled for June 8th 1903 and if she couldn't prove, without a reasonable doubt, that The Ransome Company had connected a shaft through to The Matchless and stole her silver ore, she was going to have to pay out a lot of money. And she wouldn't have the money, unless her case against Mr. David Moffat goes through.

Her accusations could lose her The Matchless.

Taking a deep breath, Elizabeth tried to focus on her upcoming March 8th court hearing against Mr. David Moffat and prayed that she would be granted the $750,000 that Judge Carpenter decided on in her favor, back on February 9th.

"All rise the honorable Judge Carpenter residing"

"You may be seated"

"We are here today to review Mrs. Tabor's complaint that Mr. David Moffat holds in his possession funds that rightfully belong to the Tabor estate and which were committed to his custody during Mr. Tabor's life." The judge explained, as he read from his notes. "I was informed, during our last hearing, that these funds were held in a trust and were to be delivered upon the performance of certain conditions that I understand have long since been fulfilled."

"Furthermore, neither Mr. David Moffat nor his council responded to my February 9th decision to grant Mrs. Tabor the $750,000 she requested, despite having 20 days to do so." Judge Carpenter informed the court. "But I see that J. Hughes, Mr. Moffat's attorney is present today to oppose my decision and once again I see that Mr. Moffat could not find the time to enlighten us with his presence. Mr. Hughes, you may address the court."

With a smile, Mr. Moffat's attorney explained to the Judge that neither he nor his client received any notice from the court that a decision had been made on the matter and begged that they be given a continuance.

"You're Honor, I was not apprised on this matter and in consequence of my ignorance, I allowed the period in which to answer to expire without taking advantage of it." Attorney J. Hughes asked, as he held his head down in false sorrow.

Flipping back through his papers and questioning the possibility that neither Mr. Moffat nor his Attorney received the previous court decision, he granted them a 15 day extension.

"Dismissed."

Furious, Elizabeth Tabor and her lawyer J. Warner Mills confronted J. Hughes outside the court room and tempers flared, to the entertainment of the local newspapers.

"I know you Charley Hughes!" Elizabeth angrily stated, as she followed him down the hallway of the court house.

"Yes, and I know you too!" Mr. Hughes responded, as he quickened his step in avoidance. "And poor Senator Tabor. I knew both of you and Dave Moffat, to his sorrow."

"You and David Moffat robbed Senator Tabor of his entire fortune!" Elizabeth Tabor accused him, as she kept up with his hasty pace. "You know it and Moffat knows it!"

Seeing that the newspapers were still writing down their every word, Mr. Hughes abruptly stopped and turned to face Elizabeth.

"When it comes to this matter of personal acquaintanceship, let me inform you madam." He added, with a disgusted lift of his nose. "I knew your husband to the tune of $100,000,000 in a note which I now hold. And if a man spoke to me in the matter in which you are speaking to me, I would attend to him!"

"Good day, Madam."

As Attorney Hughes stormed out of the court house and down to his waiting carriage, Elizabeth glanced at the eager newspaper reporters and holding her head high, took the arm of her attorney and followed Hughes lead.

But despite Moffat's arrogance and proof that he was at fault, the Judge sided against Elizabeth Tabor and she lost her case.

The letter she received from the Denver court on March 25th 1903 held the Judges verdict, but she just didn't have the money to fight David Moffat anymore. Laying down the letter that stated that she had lost her case, she was reminded of a newspaper article she had read about Mr. Moffat in the Aspen Democrat entitled "Moffat owns the Earth!" and realized it was true.

The article, which came out on April 21, 1903, was titled "Moffat owns the Earth! At least he owns all of Colorado, which really amounts to the same thing." The story talked about how the same lawyer David Moffat had hired to rob Elizabeth Tabor of $750,000, had secured sweeping injunctions against the New Century power and Light Company, the Hydro Elevator power Company and all their officers for interfering with The Denver Northwestern and Pacific railroad, of which Moffat was part owner.

And if David Moffat's attorney could cause major companies to kneel down and bend to his will, then there was no use for her to continue fighting a losing battle, in regards to her husband's stolen mining deeds.

But bad news comes in three's.

During her June 8th hearing in Leadville, against the Ransome leasing Company which she claimed stole ore from her Matchless mine through an underground shaft and destroyed her buildings, the leasing Company was found not guilty.

As she feared, the judge in her case decided in favor or the Ransome Leasing Company, after Elizabeth could not prove, beyond a reasonable doubt, that they had removed any ore from the Matchless Mine. Unfortunately, the companies owners had filed a counter suit for lost wages and profit to the tune of $40,000, which the Judge was now granting them and giving them the Matchless as collateral.

But before her lawyer could stand up to object, Mr. Herman Powell, one of the owners of the Ransome Leasing Company, stood up and asked if he could address the court. With a smile, he turned towards Elizabeth Tabor and her Attorney and informed them that they had no desire to steal the Matchless mine from Mrs. Tabor and instead wished to offer her a deal that would satisfy both parties.

If Elizabeth agreed to allow the leasing company to return to work on her Robert E. Lee and Dunkin mining claims, then they would allow her to make payments on the $40,000 from ore she removes from the Matchless or any of her other mining claims and to sweeten the deal, they would give her three years to pay them back.

"And if Mrs. Tabor is unable to remove enough ore during the three years, we will agreed to accept the payment in diamonds." Mr. Powell added, as he glanced over at the Judge.

With a nod of approval and the strike of a gavel, the deal was made and Elizabeth Tabor was relieved to discover she still owned The Matchless mine, at least for the next three years.

Eager to pay off the $40,000 as fast as possible, Elizabeth headed up to Silverton to check on her Red Rogers claims in the Poughkeepsie gulch area and began plans to open the mine back up. The last person to work the mine was Chas Carlstrom who had removed so much high grade lead and silver ore, that he took a large chunk of it to the 1893 Chicago World's fair, where it mesmerized fair goers with the riches of the Colorado mines.

The fair opened on May 1st and show cased not only mineral specimens, inside over 200 buildings, but new products such as Cream of wheat, Juicy fruit gum, Pabst Blue Ribbon beer, Dish washers and early prototypes of the fluorescent light bulbs.

But despite the Red Rogers historic display at the Chicago World's fair, Elizabeth's real draw to the mine was the fact it had not been worked since the 1893 silver crash, so all that high grade ore was just sitting inside waiting for her.

And with all her mining ventures, she knew it was time to stop spending her winters in Denver and move to Leadville permanently. So on August 30, 1903, with her 13 year old daughter Silver's help, Elizabeth packing up her rented house in Denver and once again moved them into the modest sized foreman's house on the Matchless Mines property and began preparing for the frosty Leadville winter.

Unfortunately, Elizabeth wouldn't be able to end her year on a high note, as she received a letter from the Denver courts in regards to her insurance policy claim for the People's theater.

"In regards to your letter of November 21, 1903 asking for a option on the part of the supervisor Uzzell upon the resolution of the November 7, 1902-the Tabor Amusement Company- on a unpaid insurance claim, due to the Chief of the Fire Department ordering part of the wall of the Peoples Theater torn down, as it was deemed unsafe after the burning of the old Fifteenth street theater.

This case has been pending and never came to trial. The Tabor Amusement Company went out of existence and was absorbed by a new company and Mrs. Tabor has no rights to this case."

With a heavy sigh, Elizabeth returned the notice to its envelope, paper clipped it to the original insurance policy and added it to her box of lost court cases.

A DEADLY SNOWBALL FIGHT AND THE LOVING HAND OF GOD

A New Year is supposto be a type of fresh start and a time for new beginnings, but for Elizabeth Tabor, 1904 was starting out with broken promises and more lawsuits.

The first man's name was Max Dogenal, an Italian immigrant who said he was interested in leasing the Matchless mine and helping Elizabeth to remove the silver ore, but when he refused to do the work, he decided to sue her for his $600 deposit back instead.

And Elizabeth said no.

Dogenal's had originally filed suit back on November 29, 1903, but the judge had chosen to give the man more time to prove his claim, so it was pushed back until May 4, 1904.

The second man was a lessee named James McMordie who was suing The Matchless mines main Lessee J.O Collarette and his personal lessee N.E. Williamson for $1,200. He was also suing The Coin Mining and Leasing Company, which Williamson had incorporated and which had hired McMordie in the first place.

And since the real owner of The Matchless mine was Elizabeth

Tabor's sister Claudia McCourt McCabe, who was still making payments to Herman Powell, who sublet the mine to J.O Collarette, who was in violation of his contact by leasing the mine to N.E. Willamson, the local newspaper was anxious to write about the circus that would be filling the court room on March 6, 1904.

"All rise, court is now in session"

Held inside the Leadville County court house, the first one to speak was Mrs. Claudia McCourt McCabe, who rightfully owned The Matchless Mine, but had put it into her sister Elizabeth's name as a gift.

Claudia McCabe explained to the Judge that the $1,200 should not be returned to Mr. McMordie, but to her, as the money garnished was really her property.

"Your honor, prior to February 13, 1902, Herman Powell was the owner of The Matchless Mine and I entered into an agreement with him on February 13, 1902 to purchase the property for $30,000." She began explaining to the Judge. "We agreed that I would pay him $7,000 in cash upon the delivery of the contract, $5,000 in two years and $18,000 in three years at the rate of 6% per annum."

"Furthermore, our contract stated that both myself and my sister Mrs. Elizabeth Tabor had the privilege of extracting ore from the mine and that a certain percent would be applied to the purchase price. After I made the contract with Mr. Powell, a lease was made with J.O Collarette on a portion of The Matchless and he understood he was not to sublet the ground without written consent of either myself or my sister, but he still chose to lease it to Mr. N.E. Williamson in December 1903." She informed the court, while staring disapprovingly over at Mr. Collarette.

As the details of the case unfolded, it was revealed that Mr. Williamson then incorporated a company he named the Coin Mining Company, took Mr. McMordie on a lessee and secured a payment from him of $1,200, which he was told would be used for coal and timbers.

Mr. Williamson also removed ore worth $1,588.59 from The

Matchless, which was being held at the American Smelting Company and Mrs. McCabe also felt was rightfully hers.

And the Judge agreed.

Reaching a verdict, the amount of $2,788.59, minus the sum due to the miners, was awarded to Mrs. Claudia McCourt McCabe.

"Dismissed."

With their heads held high, Elizabeth Tabor and her sister walked out of the court room triumphant and as they approached their waiting carriage, Elizabeth hoped this was a sign of good things to come in regards to her upcoming May 4th court hearing.

And it was.

On May 4th, inside a Denver court house the judge heard the claim against Mrs. Elizabeth Tabor, on the grounds that she refused to return Mr. Max Dagenal's $600 deposit. Standing tall and straightening her suit jacket, Elizabeth enlightened the Judge on the reason she had chosen not to return then money, while holding the original signed receipt in her gloved hand.

"On July 9th, 1903 Mr. Dagenal's agreed to become a lessee of my Matchless Mine and gave me a deposit of $600 towards the full amount of $1,000, which was to be used to build a railroad switch and I gave him 60 days to complete it." Elizabeth explained, as she laid the receipt on the table in front of her for the bailiff to retrieve. "But instead he asked me to extend the time frame, which I did, and gave him until September 1, 1903 to complete the work."

"Did he complete the work?" The Judge inquired.

"No, you're Honor."

"I find in favor of Mrs. Tabor for the amount of $1,000."

"Dismissed."

As the year continued, Elizabeth began relaxing and her daughter Silver spent the warm summer months outside in the mountains picking wild flowers and playing with her friends. And when winter approached, Elizabeth Tabor felt confident enough in her hired help

A DEADLY SNOWBALL FIGHT AND THE LOVING HAND OF GOD

to take her daughter back to Denver for the winter, but sometimes the best laid plans don't turn out how you expected them to.

On the evening of December 10, 1904, while Elizabeth and Silver were preparing for their Christmas holiday, she received the call that the Matchless Mine had caught on fire.

Desperate to check on the condition of her Mine, both her and Silver boarded the next train to Leadville to assess the damage, which luckily hadn't spread. Meeting them at the train station on December 12th, her employees enlightened her on the condition of the mine and how they thought a simple spark had set the engine house ablaze.

Arriving at her mine, she was taken to the charred remains of the #5 shaft and it's engine house and saw that the cage, which originally was at the top of the shaft, had crashed to the bottom, as the engines burned. With nobody working the night shift, as Leadville's winter temperatures had dipped to frigid lows, the men were not alerted to the flames until around 8:30pm and by then it was too late to save the building.

Luckily for Elizabeth, the fire was contained inside the engine house and didn't affect any other structures, but she was still facing over $2,000 in damages.

As she packed her daughter back into the carriage and headed towards the warmth of the Vendome Hotel, she reconsidered her decision to spend the winter in Denver and wondered if she could have prevented the fire if only she had been close by.

But as she pulled her carriage blanket tighter around herself and her daughter, while watching the ice slowly spread across the windows, she remembered why she spent her winters in Denver and was looking forward to returning to her rented home.

Arriving at the Hotel, Elizabeth grabbed a newspaper to entertain herself with up in their room and saw a terrible story of a senseless death, on the same pages that held the story about the fire at the Matchless.

"BOYS THREW SNOWBALLS OLD MAN FELL DEAD "

Six school boys, none more than 14 years old were held up at the stockyards police station all night waiting the coroner's verdict on the sudden death of Rabbi Abraham Glick.

Glick was killing chickens for David Levy in the rear of his store when a crowd of boys made him the target of a volley of snowballs, some of which contained stones to give weight and accuracy. One snow ball hit Glick in the back of the head, killing him. The arrest of the boys followed."

-Chicago Dec.9, 1904

Reading that the boys were close in age to her own daughter Silver Dollar, who would be turning 15 on December 17th, caused her to quickly cross herself and say a small prayer of protection for her soul. The thought of her precious daughter throwing her life away so carelessly, like these boys had just done, sent shivers down her spine.

Elizabeth was also thankful that, unlike her older daughter, her youngest daughter was still a strong warrior in regards to the Catholic faith.

As Elizabeth and Silver celebrated the Christmas holiday back up in Denver and welcomed in 1905, Elizabeth started to hear rumors of a possible dedication in her beloved husband's honor, which was confirmed on January 24th to her delight.

The State capital had entered a proposition regarding a commemorative statue of Horace Tabor in one of Denver's city parks that included a $5,000 price tag, but as the months continued the stories in the local newspapers, regarding the statue, became smaller and smaller until they vanished all together.

But despite her disappointment over the loss of a possible statue of her husband, she knew he was smiling down on her in regards to the large quantities of silver ore coming out of her numerous mining claims.

And as spring turned into summer, Elizabeth was graced with a visit from her little brother Mark, who lived in Chicago. Hearing the gossip throughout the family, regarding his older sister's success, he thought he would pay her a visit and see if all the rumors were true and he was happy to see they were.

As September rolled around, Elizabeth began hiring Fin's to work her mine dumps and look for any discarded silver ore, of which they found plenty. The Finnish people turned out to be wonderful workers and would find several carloads a week of discarded silver ore, to send to the smelters.

With Shaft #5 back up and running, after the disastrous December 10th fire, her workers Ira Johnson, A. Jorstad and Marvin Hollister were removing on average 10 car loads a month of siliceous silver ore from just The Matchless alone, at the 360 foot level and Elizabeth planned on opening up more shafts, once she found willing workers.

And in October she found a team of Denver Capitalists to lease Shafts #1-3 at the Matchless and was delighted to hear they were planning on starting the following month. With so many people working her mines, she knew that bother her and her daughter Silver Dollar would be spending this winter in their modest little house up at the Matchless.

With the year coming to an end, Elizabeth and her now 16 year old daughter Silver celebrated the holidays with the noise of mining machinery grinding and squealing away outside their front door. To most people, the noise would quickly become a nuisance, but to Elizabeth it was the sound of money.

As the year 1906 reared its head and spring finally began peaking around the corner, Elizabeth had a set of unexpected visitors up at The Matchless that wished to talk money…a lot of money.

The men were eastern Capitalists who invested in mines all around Colorado and their interest today was Elizabeth's seven mining claims up in the San Juan Mountains, which included the Red Rogers mine that she had let sit idle.

She had heard rumors that the San Juan area was beginning to boom again and that a few of the mines were being re-opened, but with her Leadville claims occupying most of her time, she hadn't been able to work The Red Roger, but she would be willing to sell it.

Inviting the men into the office and being joined by a few of her workers as a safety measure, the work of negotiating began. And when the Easterner's offered her $1,000,000.00 for the properties, she quickly held out her hand and with a shake of good faith, accepted their offer.

The only thing left was to draw up the contracts and make sure that Mrs. Elizabeth Tabor was not only the rightful owner, but was caught up on her taxes.

The Red Roger mine, which was named after a miner named Roger's who sported a set of red whiskers, had been left untouched since H.A.W Tabor had purchased it back in 1893 for a song, after the Silver crash. But luckily, when Tabor lost his fortune, his friend Winfield Scott Stratton had picked up the tab and paid all of its back taxes until his death in 1902, which is where the problems started.

Elizabeth had managed to find friends and family to cover the tax burdens she wasn't able too, but now as the men from the East coast walked out the door of her mining office and headed down to the tax assessors to check on the status of the payments, she felt a chill run through her spine.

What if the taxes were delinquent?

Climbing into her carriage, Elizabeth followed the men down into town and sat quietly in the tax assessor's office, as the results revealed the mines real owner, which unfortunately wasn't Elizabeth

A DEADLY SNOWBALL FIGHT AND THE LOVING HAND OF GOD 181

Tabor. The records revealed that the taxes on the property had been delinquent for so long, that the title had already changed hands.

As Elizabeth Tabor sat down on a nearby chair to steady herself, an employee walked over to her and inquired about her name. "Yes, I'm Mrs. Tabor." Elizabeth replied in a quiet whisper, as the woman handed her an envelope and with a smile, walked back to her desk.

Confused, she opened the envelope and pulled out a delinquent tax paper that stated that The Matchless was also in default for the year 1905, to the tune of $37.44.

After recovering from her shock, Elizabeth stood up, brushed herself off, thanked the woman behind the desk and headed back to The Matchless. There was no sense in mopping around about lost money or delinquent taxes, when she had silver ore to find.

And she was going to find it, if it killed her.

And it almost did.

On November 28th, 52 year old Elizabeth Tabor was busy working down a shaft at The Matchless, in her usual denim overalls and favorite cap, when she fell and she fell hard.

Elizabeth was working with a man named Atkins, 245 feet underground and together they were cranking the mines windlass, as it took two people to operate it. A windlass consists of a horizontal cylinder, which is rotated by the turn of a crank and on either end of this cylinder a winch is attached, which holds a rope. And on the end of this rope hung a large bucket, which they lowered down the shaft to the miners below.

The shaft which was 65 feet below where Elizabeth and Atkins were standing, was occupied by a man named Wilbur Simmons, whose job it was to load silver ore into the bucket, which they would then pull back up to their level and transfer into another bucket, to be pulled up to the surface.

With the ore bucket empty, Elizabeth began helping Atkins pick up stray pieces of ore, from around the opening of the lower shaft, when something caught his eye. "Hey, Mrs. Tabor! I think this is the stuff you're looking for! Come see this!" he cried out.

Walking over towards the man, Elizabeth suddenly recieved a terrible blow to her forehead, which knocked her off her feet and caused her to fall backwards down the 65 foot shaft. Fearful that she would land on Mr. Simmons, Elizabeth quickly began grabbing at the sides of the shaft for anything that would slow her down, while screaming for Saint Anthony to give her strength and to spare the man below her.

Luckily, she caught onto one of the timbers and landed on a board, while listening to the screams of Mr. Atkins above her. Regaining her wits, she slowly sat up, balanced herself on the ledge she had landed on and rubbed her gloved hand across her forehead expecting blood, but not finding any.

Letting her eyes adjust to the dim light of the shaft, she spotted a ladder and slowly made her way over to it. Finding her footing, she made her way up to the windlass and after only a short break, resumed helping Mr. Atkins turn the crank.

Silver Dollar didn't hear about her mother's harrowing brush with death until she came back up out of the shaft hours later. As they ate dinner, Elizabeth explained to her daughter how it must have been Satan that struck her head, because if anything else had hit her, there would be a mark to show for it.

"But, Mama." Silver asked, as she intently listened to the story. "Why does Satan want to hurt you?"

"Because Satan knows we are going to save this mine and he wants to kill me." Elizabeth replied, as she reached over and lovingly picked up her bible. "But God in his mercy has attended to me with his mighty angels all through this battle."

But despite all of her prayers and praises to the angels, Elizabeth found herself traumatized for weeks and plagued with horrible nightmares of falling down an endless shaft, unable to stop herself.

But nothing was going to stop her from working this mine.

A DEADLY SNOWBALL FIGHT AND THE LOVING HAND OF GOD

As 1906 turned into 1907, Elizabeth continued to toil away deep in the bowels of the earth, digging through rock and creating new shafts, while her now 17 year old daughter finished her education at the local high school. And when Silver Dollar had time, she would join her mother on her quest to find that next rich vein of Silver ore, which she proudly knew was her name sake.

As spring arrived and the sun began to warm up the frosty mining town, Elizabeth was pleased to find that she could once again sit in the sunshine, read the paper and enjoy her tea. Flipping through a copy of the Eagle County Blade, on May 2, she stumbled upon an odd little story which contained her beloved husband's name and unfortunately reminded her of his untimely death.

The story, out of Boston, talked about a man named William F. Fernald who owned a disturbing scrapbook full of newspaper stories involving victims of appendicitis.

"My first experience in a hospital was when I had my appendicitis and after I left the hospital, my interest in the subject grew, so I started to collect clippings." Mr. Fernald explained to the reporter. The story continued by mentioning that the man's scrap book contained clippings from anyone, big or small, who has ever had a story written about their appendicitis in the newspaper, such as Colorado Senator Horace Tabor. On a further disturbing note, the collector Mr. Fernald will even show people his own appendix, which he keeps preserved in a small vial of alcohol.

But before Elizabeth could spend too much time thinking about her beloved Horace, she hear a loud commotion coming from the shaft house. Running towards the sound, she discovered that shaft #3 had just collapsed and unfortunately buried a newly found vein of rich Silver ore deep inside of it.

Pushing her aggravation aside, she focused her energy on making sure all of her men were safe and accounted for.

As she looked down the collapsed shaft, she knew it would take all the money she had to dig out her mine and as she watched her men pack up their gear and head into town, it was obvious she would also need to find a new group to work it, but luckily she didn't have to wait long.

Word travels fast.

Within days of the collapse, Elizabeth was besieged with offers from men willing to work her mine and if needed, drill a new shaft, which eased her mind and gave her the energy she needed to begin digging through the rubble. But after a few weeks of back breaking work, she heard about a newspaper reporter, who didn't seem to understand the dynamics of Horace Tabors marriages and had thought Elizabeth was Horace's first wife Augusta and his description of her made her smile.

> "Mrs. Tabor, widow of Colorado's Spectacular Senator, is reported to be in a fair way to retrieve the fortune of her ungrateful husband, who in his days of prosperity, set her aside for a younger, handsomer woman. She was never known to speak harshly of the man who treated her so cruelly."
>
> -Telluride Journal May 30, 1907

Getting back to work, Elizabeth discussed the options involving the #3 shaft with her men and it was decided to abandon it, in favor of sinking a new shaft nearby and attempt to hit the vein from a different angle. But just as work was getting underway, the entire mine was placed under quarantine.

Elizabeth's daughter Silver Dollar was sick.

Thinking she had Small Pox, members of the local health board came to the mine on June 27th to check over Silver and determine if she was truly suffering from the dreaded disease. But luckily, once their examination was complete, she was found to simply have a bad cold, but was still confined to the house. When Elizabeth inquired on how the health department even knew Silver Dollar was sick, they explained that her neighbors had attempted to visit with both her and her daughter earlier in the week, but when they were unable to gain admission to their house, they assumed that the worst had happened and that perhaps Silver was seriously ill.

Thanking them for their concern, she returned to her daughter and tried to distract herself from the most recent court papers she had received, which informed her that she could possibly lose The Matchless Mine.

Again.

July 1907 marked the three year anniversary of the agreement between Elizabeth's Sister Claudia McCourt McCabe and Mr. Herman Powell, to purchase The Matchless mine. To obtain the original $17,500 deposit, Claudia had borrowed the money from a Mr. George Douglas of California, who held the deed of trust for the mine until he was paid back, but unfortunately not enough ore had been removed from The Matchless to pay off the loan and he was putting the mine on the auction block. The paperwork showed that it would be sold at the court house steps on August 26th, if the remainder of the loan was not paid to him in full.

Frantic, Elizabeth contacted Mr. Douglas and offered him what remained of her jewelry, to pay off the loan, which he quickly accepted and asked that the pieces be placed with the Continental Trust Company in Denver for safe keeping. With a payment agreement in place and the auction scheduled for the mine on hold, the date for the auction of her jewelry was scheduled for December 17th.

Elizabeth's daughter Silver's birthday 18th birthday.

Heart broken and immediately regretting her decision, Elizabeth arrived at the Leadville bank, lovingly removed her jewelry out of her private safe deposit box and inspected each piece one more time.

Her beautiful Isabella diamond necklace, which was meant to be a surprise wedding gift from her husband, but arrived too late from England to be worn on her wedding day, still glimmered and sparkled as much as it had the day Horace placed it around her neck.

Her 14 carat diamond earrings she used to wear to the Tabor Grand Opera house, as well as a bracelet set that contained three large diamonds, that beckoned her to wear them once more.

As she picked up the velvet bag that held her loose diamonds, she untied the satin draw string and slowly poured the stones into her gloved hand. As she watched them sparkle under the light of the banks vault, she picked up an 8 carat diamond that had originally been inset in her engagement ring. The unadorned gold ring still sat safe inside one of her trunks, back at a Denver storage unit, but seeing the diamond again reminded of her of the day Horace placed it on her tiny little fingers.

Pouring the diamonds back into the bag and tightening the draw sting, she was faced with a piece of jewelry she had purchased for herself, back when Horace spent his 36 days as the Senator of Colorado. Lifting the beautiful, gem encrusted golden girdle out of its box, she carefully laid it out on a nearby table to appreciate its craftsmanship just one more time.

When Horace and Elizabeth exchanged vows, across the street from the State Capital building in Washington D.C., they were shunned by many people, including the wives of the elite, which treated her like she was a vile, disgusting creature. But on her husband's final day in office, she shocked the Senator's wives by wearing a silk gown and encasing her hour glass figure in a tight fitting girdle, which had been formed into a gem encrusted serpent.

Admiring the girdle in the light of the bank's vault, Elizabeth smiled as she remembered the looks of shock and displease on the faces of the judgmental, jealous women. She had chosen the serpent shaped girdle as a statement, with his ruby tongue, emerald tail and diamond eyes and she just hoped it would be purchased for a woman who would flaunt its original purpose.

With a final peak at her jewelry, Elizabeth slowly closed the case and nodded to the man who would now help sell them all to the highest bidder.

She had already decided not to take the train to Denver to watch her jewelry be auctioned off to strangers, so she straightened herself up, wiped the tears from her eyes and instead spent the day celebrating her daughter's birthday inside their small house up at the Matchless.

The jewelry, which she had fought to keep after her husband's death, was purchased by one man, for $8,750. Mr. Mason bought the entire lot and was planning on splitting the jewelry between his wife and some private investors.

Minus one stone.

Days after the auction and right before Christmas, Elizabeth and Silver Dollar heard a knock on the door of their little house. Assuming it was one of her employees, Elizabeth was surprised to see her friend Mrs. Nugent from Denver, standing outside in the Leadville snow holding gifts.

Happy to see her friend, she quickly invited her inside and after a bit of chit chat, Mrs. Nugent handed Elizabeth a small box. Curious, she opened it up and discovered her engagement diamond staring back at her.

Merry Christmas Mrs. Elizabeth Tabor.

The Presidents hunt and the Scientific Method

Your children can't stay little forever.

Elizabeth's older daughter Lily had moved to Wisconsin years ago and now her precious 18 year old daughter Silver Dollar was getting that itch. She had been spending more time away from the mine and making a lot of new friends, so Elizabeth knew it was just a matter of time before Silver spread her wings and left the nest.

And on May 6, 1908 she made that leap.

Boarding a train to Denver, Silver Dollar kissed her mom goodbye and left to see what the big city of Denver held for her. Elizabeth had been dreading this day and gave a prayer for the safety of her yougest daughter, who wasn't nearly as worldly as she thought she was.

But just days after Silver Dollar left the nest, Elizabeth received a letter from her oldest daughter Lily on May 15, which informed her mother that she had just started building a nest of her own, by getting married!

"Dear ones,

I was married yesterday to the best man in the world and I cannot tell you how happy I am. If you knew how good he is you would be happy with me and I want you to love him, not only for my sake, but because he is so fine and I tell you darlings-I would never have been happy without him. We both send you heaps of love,

Your loving daughter, Lily."

Looking at the return envelope, Elizabeth noticed the name of her new Son-in-law and felt a cold chill run though her body.

She married John Last the 3rd!

John was Lily's first cousin!

John Last the 3rd was Elizabeth's nephew from her sister Cornelia Teressa McCourt, who they called Neilly. Lily was two months shy of being 24 years old, where Elizabeth's nephew John was 33 years old, which was plenty old enough to get married and she knew he was a good man, but he was Lily's first cousin!

Trying to shake off the shock, Elizabeth tried to focus instead on her new employees, who would be leasing one of the shafts at The Matchless, starting in June. The lease allowed the men to work the shaft and pay her a profit from the ore they brought up, without her paying them a salary, so it was really a great deal for both of them.

The man's name was Thos M. Raney and he not only brought his own team of men to work the shaft, they were also installing new equipment, since the hoist and the engine, inside the shaft building, were both in pretty bad shape.

Another man who arranged to lease one of the shafts at The Matchless was Henry J. Stevens of Denver, who also brought in his own crew of men, which kept the mine pretty busy.

As the summer continued, Elizabeth was thrilled with the return of her daughter Silver Dollar, who wasn't able to find the kind of work she wanted in Denver and returned home. Silver had been showing a passion for writing and singing during the last few years and had been promised an unpaid internship at Leadville's local newspaper, so she could work on her writing skills.

As Silver told her mother about everything she experienced in Denver, she filled her in on a little secret she had kept from her. "Mama, I wrote a song for President Roosevelt!" she informed her, with an excited bounce to her step "And I'd like to get it published."

Silver explained that while she was in Denver she had contacted her old middle school music teacher, Professor A.S. Lohmann and he helped her compose the music for her song. The song, which she dedicated to her father H.A.W Tabor, was called "Our President Roosevelts Colorado hunt" and she had already sent a letter concerning it to the President himself.

"I sent Mr. Roosevelt a letter in January, addressed to the White House and told him about the song." Silver happily explained to her mother. "And if I get it published, I can send it to him!"

Handing her mother the song, Elizabeth sat down and began reading the lyrics. She was impressed that her daughter had put so much time into the song and had even gone the extra mile to contact her old teacher to compose the music for it.

Elizabeth Tabor had the song published in August 1908, with the cover showing a drawing of the President

Teenage picture of Silver Dollar-Legends of America

himself, surrounded by the words "To the memory of the late U.S. Senator H.A.W Tabor", on either side. Silver chose to shorten her given name of Rosemary Echo Silver Dollar Honeymoon Tabor and listed herself as only as Silver Echo Tabor.

Silver Dollar meets President Roosevelt- The Denver Public Library, Western History Collection-X-21998

She also listed the names of her three unpublished songs "Spirts", "Love and lilies" and "In a dream I loved you" in small print on the bottom of the cover, as a teaser for possible future publications.

As the summer turned into fall, Elizabeth was starting to get a little suspicious over the amount her lessee Thos M. Raney was paying her, as she was watching his men send out a freight car load of ore every day. But when she talked to Mr. Raney about her concerns, he would simply repeat the same reason over and over to her. *"Mrs. Tabor, I am paying you your share of the profits after I deduct the freight charges, like we originally agreed on back in June."*

But Elizabeth still felt she was being short changed.

And on November 25th 1908 she walked right over to Thos Raney and told him to pack up and get his men off the property, stating that she was tired of being lied too and would just start working the shaft herself.

With a sigh and a tip of his hat, Mr. Raney grabbed the contact paper he had signed back in June, packed up his men and headed down to the court house to file an injunction against Mrs. Tabor.

On November 27th 1908 an injunction was issued by Judge Harrison, of the Leadville County courts to temporarily restrain Mrs. Elizabeth Tabor form interfering with or operating the Matchless Mine.

"All rise, court is now in session."

"It's been brought to the courts attention that Mrs. Elizabeth Tabor is prohibiting her lessee Mr. Raney from working her mine, The Matchless, despite having a signed contract from Mrs. Tabor to do so." The Judge explained, as he looked over at Elizabeth. "I would like to hear your reasons, Mrs. Tabor."

Standing before the judge, the now 54 year old Elizabeth Tabor explained why she was so bothered by her lessee's actions. "Your Honor, I was told that I would be paid my royalties based on the gross smelter returns, but instead I discovered that they are instead paying me the gross amount, minus the hauling and switching charges."

Looking over at Mr. Raney, the Judge asked him if he would like to respond to Mrs. Tabor's allegations, which he quickly agreed to. "Your Honor, last week Mrs. Tabor informed both me and my men that she was dissatisfied with us and handed me a notice that our lease had expired, due to my failure to comply with the terms. Mrs. Tabor was informed, back in June that she would be paid the gross amount minus the hauling and switching charges and we have kept to that agreement."

Looking back over at Elizabeth, the Judge inquired on a matter that had been mentioned in the original court filing. "Mrs. Tabor, it is my understanding that until November 25th, you had been residing in

Denver with your youngest daughter. Is this true?"

"Yes your Honor."

"And when did you return to your cabin at The Matchless?"

"I returned on November 25th."

"And Mr. Raney, when did you realize that Mrs. Tabor had returned to her cabin?" The judge asked, as he read through the court documents.

"One of my men noticed smoke rising from her cabin, which is over next to shaft #5. It's a pretty good ways' from the shaft we recently sunk, which is shaft #7." He replied as he looked over at Henry E. Steven's, who he was partners with in this venture. "Our men, who are also working shaft #5, had gone into town for a bit and when they came back they saw that Mrs. Tabor had returned, but we don't knew the time."

Lowering his glasses, the Judge informed the court that he was allowing Mr. Raney and all other lessees to resume their work at The Matchless Mine, until the next court hearing scheduled for December 7th, which would give Judge Harrison time to interpret the terms of the lease.

"I am putting in place a temporary restraining order in place for Mrs. Elizabeth Tabor, which states she cannot work any of the shafts on the property, live on the property or harass any of her lessees. The money due to Mrs. Tabor will still be paid as per the lease agreement, but will be paid to the clerk of court until this matter can be resolved." The Judge explained, as Elizabeth held her head in defeat.

"Court is adjourned."

Leaving the court house, Elizabeth was met by her lessee's, who agreed to let her follow them back to the mine to retrieve her clothes from the cabin, before she headed down to the train station and back to her rented house in Denver.

Arriving back to 1613 Court place, Elizabeth thought her attention would be solely focused on her upcoming court hearing, but a letter from her older daughter Lily on December 4th quickly changed all that.

Elizabeth Tabor had just become a Grandmother.

The letter, that happily mentioned the six pound little baby girl, who they named Caroline M. Last, also listed her birth date as the beginning of December, which sent Elizabeth into a shock. Sitting down on a nearby chair, Elizabeth handed the letter to Silver, who realized the problem right away.

Not only had Lily married her first cousin, but their new baby had been conceived out of wedlock.

Reading farther down the letter, Lily had also mentioned that she had chosen to raise her new daughter scientifically, instead of naturally, as she had quickly discovered that her body wasn't producing enough milk for the baby to thrive.

But if Lily didn't breast feed her infant, then she faced the possibly of quickly become pregnant again, which could cause both her and her next baby to become too weak to survive.

Overcome with grief, Elizabeth was afraid she would lose her daughter Lily, like she had lost her older sister Neilly to a premature death, only three years after giving birth to her 6th child.

Cornelia Teresa McCourt, who everyone called Nealia or Neilly, was only 35 years old when she died and the family felt it was caused by impoverished blood, from birthing her children so close together

With Elizabeth full of grief and confining herself to her bed, Silver Dollar wrote a letter back to her sister and reminded her that their Aunt Neilly had spent her remaining years with a child in her womb, one nursing at her breast, one on her lap, one at her dress, one at her feet and one barely able to walk and had gone to a premature grave because of it.

She further reminded Lily that her husband John, who was their Aunt Neilly's second child, watched his mother die and that if Lily won't take care to space her children, then it was his responsibility to protect his wife from the same fate.

Glancing away from her letter, Silver looked towards her mother's bedroom and listened to the heart wrenching sobs coming from inside. Unknown to Lily or the rest of the extended family, Elizabeth had just been diagnosed with a dripping heart that past May, by a Swedish Doctor, who had told Silver that very few people suffer from this condition and that the family Priest should be informed of her condition, which he was.

A dripping heart, which is also known as a leaky heart, is caused by a faulty heart valve that allows blood to leak backwards when the heart beats. This sound can be heard with a stethoscope and is sometimes referred to as a heart murmur.

But unfortunately for Elizabeth, stress and high blood pressure can aggravate the condition, which can lead to congestive heart failure and death.

Returning to her letter, Silver chose to turn her caring tone into a righteous one, as she accused her sister Lily of going against the word of God himself, by refusing to nurse her infant daughter.

"Don't ever tell a stranger that you have raised your poor little baby scientifically, it only sounds cruel and coarse. Grandma raised fourteen and never lost a baby in her life, raised by common sense and love.

And what do you mean by science? Do you mean that you are denying our Lord Jesus Christ and his sufferings?"

Changing her tone back to more personal matters, Silver chose to inform her sister that she was practicing her writing, by using the typewriters at the local newspaper and had many manuscripts ready to publish, once the money was available. She also informed her sister that she was also being taught how to not only work The Matchless Mine, but how to one day be the superintendent.

But despite her calm tone, Silver quickly turned back to her religious beliefs and how Lily needed to keep her sins in the shadows, until they regained The Matchless.

"Momma is the most wonderful woman in the world, the most magnificent intellect, fearless and with powerful strength of character that she risks all, to do the right thing. She is perfectly fearless, but alas she is nothing but love Lily, her clinging to the cross and religious life, our Lord Jesus blesses her with visons and interpretations of such. I too have been blessed through her holy teachings and gentle influences.

We are about to close the last deal on The Matchless and she is praying every minute that you will not leave Chicago until this Matchless deal is closed and at an end, because if a newspaper reporter prints a piece about Senator Tabor's daughter marrying her cousin, it will be heralded all over the U.S. and Mamma will never rise to dictate and sign the last papers on The Matchless."

But despite keeping her sins in the shadows, Lily's distance didn't change the Judges mind, in regards to Elizabeth Tabor accusing her lessees of not paying her a fair share and questioning the amount of ore they were bring up from the surface.

"All rise, court is now in session."

The December 7th hearing was conducted in Leadville's district court by Judge Cavender, who after reading the minutes of the last hearing, quickly upheld Judge Harrison's original decision.

"Due to Mrs. Tabor's decision to cancel the lease she had signed with Mr. Thomas M Raney and his associate Mr. Henry E. Steven's, I give temporary possession of The Matchless Mine over to the current lessees, who will continue to pay Mrs. Tabor based on the pay scale originally set back in June, until a final royalty amount can be agreed upon." The Judge informed the court, with a crash of his gavel.

"Dismissed."

Disappointed over the judge's decision to turn her mine over to her lessee's, Elizabeth was nonetheless pleased that her mine was being well looked after and that she was still getting payments from the ore being removed. Boarding the train, Elizabeth and her soon to be 19 year old daughter Silver Dollar headed back to their apartment in Denver, to enjoy the holidays and watch the year change once again.

Flipping their calendar over, to welcome in January 1909, Elizabeth and Silver Dollar found they had become quite comfortable in their third floor Denver apartment. In the heart of the city, Silver searched for possible jobs to expand her love of writing and in May, Elizabeth had surprised her daughter with a new kitten.

But their apartment building held a surprise of its own.

In the evening hours of June 11th, the smell of smoke began seeping under the door and into the family's apartment. Carefully peeking out into the central hallway, Elizabeth noticed that the other tenants were scrabbling towards the main stair case, as smoke filled the building.

Closing the door to her apartment, she soaked a bath towel in water, placed in across the threshold of their door and locked it. Feeling it was safer to stay in the apartment, then attempt the fire escape from the 3rd floor, the pair moved into the corner of the apartment and waited.

As the fire began to engulf the building, Chief Terrance Owen's instructed the firemen to scan the building for any trapped tenants and it was Edward Schoninger who headed to the third floor to do his sweep, who found them.

Opening up every door he could and kicking open the locked ones, Mr. Schoninger found Elizabeth and her daughter still sitting in their apartment. "You have to get out right now!" he commanded, as he ran to the windows, looking for the fire escape.

"We are not going out. We feel it's safer to stay in our rooms here." Elizabeth announced, as she held her daughters hand.

Finding the window he was looking for, the muscular fireman opened it and peaked down to the first floor roof, where he saw his waiting crew. "I've got two! We're coming down!"

Without another word, Edward Schoninger grabbed Elizabeth, tossed her across his shoulders, headed down the fire escape and planted her feet firmly on the first floor roof. But when the fireman headed back up the fire escape, to retrieve Silver Dollar, Elizabeth climbed right back up behind him!

Reaching the third floor apartment, Mr. Schoninger went inside to grab Silver, but with all the smoke, he didn't notice Elizabeth squeeze back into the apartment. With Silver Dollar thrown over his sturdy shoulders, the fireman happily reached the first floor roof, only to have his crew point back up into the apartment.

"She followed you back up. You must have just missed her." Chief Terrance Owen's informed him, as the smoke continued to bellow out of the window.

But before anyone could head back up the fire escape, the crew head a faint Meow sound coming through the smoke and watched as Mrs. Tabor appeared at the bottom of the ladder, with a small kitten in her arms.

Seeing that Silver had already been moved to the adjoining building's roof, Elizabeth walked over and quickly jump over to the next building, to join her daughter, but instantly discovered that it was farther away than she was expecting.

As she lost her footing, Elizabeth held the kitten tighter, as she felt herself catch on something she couldn't see. Looking up, she saw the face of two men who had seen her fall and discovered that they had grabbed the only thing they could reach.

Her dress.

As the men helped her back up onto the roof, Silver dollar ran over to her mother, who handed her the kitten. "And who do I have to thank for catching me? "Elizabeth asked, as she attempted to brush the smoke and soot off her dress.

"My names Robert Sullivan Mam and this here is Henry McCabe." The first man answered, with the tip of his hat. "We were just busy watching all the commotion, when we saw you start to fall. Just glad you're ok."

With their apartment building in ruins, Elizabeth and Silver spent the next few months getting their affairs in order, which is when Silver stumbled upon a possible way to reclaim some of her father's old mining claims for herself.

The Bureau of abandoned mines reclamation act.

On December 9, 1909, Silver Dollar Tabor, who was eight days shy of turning 20 years old, filed three reclamation notices for mining claims her father originally owned, but had been sold due to unpaid taxes. The reclamation act allows minor heirs to claim a treasures deed on properties, which Silver filed under the name R.E.S. Tabor, which was short for Rosemary Echo Silver Tabor.

She filed on The Big Chief mine #835, The Oolyte mine #1,201 and The Tabor claim #1202, all located in the California mining district of Leadville and stayed at the Vendome Hotel in Leadville, to make sure all the paperwork was filed correctly, before heading back to Denver.

With a silent prayer, Silver hoped that 1910 would be a productive year, but as the New Year began it was looking more like it would be starting off with a bang.

On January 6th, 1910 a bomb was discovered at the Tabors former mansion, as children played among the marble statues and unkept gardens, that originally had been pranced upon by flamboyant peacocks. As the foreclosed home stood empty and forgotten, it had become a target for the more sinister types, as the police admitted this was the third time a bomb had been discovered on the property.

But unfortunately for the police, this time the bomb was missing.

Discovered by a resident of the fashionable housing district, the nearby home owner picked up the bomb, carried it away from the house and placed it inside a nearby bush, which was then covered over with leaves. But when the police arrived, the bomb was nowhere to be found, as nobody had thought to guard it.

Luckily, a pleasant story about the Tabor family made headlines on February 16th, as the Real Estate Exchange held a luncheon to discuss funding a possible monument over the grave of H.A.W Tabor in the Catholic cemetery, to mark his final resting place. D.C. Burns had proposed that not only $1,000 be spent on a grave marker, like Horace stated in his Will, but that a statue be erected of Governor Tabor in one of Denver's City parks.

But Elizabeth would allow no such thing.

After contacting Mrs. Elizabeth Tabor on the matter, she informed the group that her husband had left detailed instructions on the condition of his grave, as he lay dying and he had no desire for an elaborate grave marker. He had instructed his wife to leave his grave bare, with no flowers or grass to cover his remains, but Mrs. Tabor felt that her husband would be fine with a commemorative statue.

But unfortunately for Elizabeth, the talk of death wasn't over, as she received a telegram on March 17, that her mother, her name sake, had passed away at the age of 85.

Mrs. Elizabeth Anderson Nellis McCourt had been living in Chicago, to be near her granddaughter Lily and her Grandson-in-law/Nephew when she had died. Taking out their black morning clothes, both Elizabeth and Silver Dollar boarded a train, along with Mrs. Tabor's siblings Peter, Phillip and William who also lived in Denver.

But arriving in Chicago for the funeral also allowed Elizabeth to meet her granddaughter Caroline for the first time, as well as witnessing the birth of her second Grandchild, a baby boy her daughter named John Beauchamp Last the 4th.

One life ends, as a new life begins.

And as 1910 turned from summer and then into fall, Elizabeth discovered that she might actually receive some of the money from the Maid of Erin's stock certificates she had fought David H. Moffat so hard for in court, back on January 17, 1903.

David H. Moffat, who had won his court battle against Mrs. Elizabeth Tabor once before, was now facing a court battle between not only Mrs. Tabor and her daughter Silver Dollar, but the First National bank of Denver as well.

As history would record, the stock certificates in question were placed in the hands of David H. Moffat by Mr. H.A.W Tabor in 1893, with the full power to sell them if the First national bank of Denver was ever to default, but were not to be kept by Mr. Moffat indefinitely.

At the time of the 1903 court hearing against Mrs. Tabor, the stocks were thought to be practically worthless, but Mr. Moffat still fought to keep possession on them, in case the stock increased in value, which it now had.

On November 7, 1910 the First National bank of Denver made a formal demand of Mr. Moffat for the stock certificates, after The Maid of Erin Mine went back into production and discovered a rich vein of zinc carbonate, but Mr. Moffat refused.

Instead he decided to arrange an auction of the 71,250 shares of stock in the Maid of Erin Silver mine to help finance his dream of building a 6 mile train tunnel through the Continental divide and planned to use the funds from the sale of the stock to do so.

Mr. Moffat, knowing he would be contested, had already passed the auction request through the Colorado Supreme court, which granted permission for the auction to proceed. They explained that the mining stock certificate placed with Mr. Moffat, by Mr. Tabor, can be disposed of if sold at a private sale, outside of court.

Once again greed and power is King.

Stolen Virtue and the Taxidermied Lion

Greed and power.

It can be used for good or, if in the hands of the wrong person, it can tear apart families and cause a life time of resentment, which is why Elizabeth Tabor felt no sorrow when David H. Moffat died.

Inside a fabulous Hotel suite in New York City, the man who stole H.A.W Tabor's 71,250 shares of stock from The Maid of Erin Mine died of the Spanish Flu, also known as La Grippe, at the age of 72.

He had suffered through not only the flu, but pneumonia 10 days before his death before suddenly being struck by a severe chill at 10am, the morning of March 18, 1911.

Less than 2 hours later he was dead.

But all the money in the world doesn't buy you the love of your fellow man.

Unlike the public viewings and elaborate funerals held for both Horace Tabor and Winfield Stratton, Moffat's funeral was a solemn family affair, attended only by people who faked their sorrow until his Will could be read.

On March 30th the state of Colorado expressed their disapproval of what they now understood was a narcissistic, self-indulgent man, as David Halliday Moffat's Will was made public. His estate was listed with a worth of $20,000,000 and not a penny was set aside for a single charity, library, public institution or even a public water fountain with his name engraved on a plaque.

But despite the fortune left behind by the dead millionaire, his estate still asked the State of Colorado to donate $5 million towards his unfinished Moffat train tunnel, which would allow passage of Moffat's own train to travel through the Rocky Mountains and bring yet more money to his heirs.

> "David Moffat was a very differently constituted man from H.A.W Tabor. Tabor made millions and lost them trying to make more for himself and all he wanted it for was to distribute them among his fellow man.

> Where Moffat left a fortune, his life is accounted a success. He could of retired years ago, but his only pleasure and comfort was the accumulation of more money"- Telluride Journal March 23, 1911

As the year continued, Elizabeth watched her youngest daughter Silver get the itch to leave home again and this time she had rented a small room inside a cheap boarding house, just down the street from the Winsor Hotel in Denver.

But despite her best intentions, Silver had been unable to secure a paying job at any of the Denver Newspapers, so her Uncle Peter offered to pay her bills for her, until his niece's desired writing career took off.

Desperate for a way to encourage her daughter's love of writing, Elizabeth brought Silver Dollar to Chicago with her, after receiving the news that her older daughter Lily just had her third child, a little girl they named Jane, on August 6th.

Excited with the possibly of getting a writing job close to her sister, Silver packed up her best articles and attempted to find a job at one of the cities newspaper's, while her mom spend time with the new baby.

The newest addition to the Tabor legacy, little Jane Last, was a combination of both her Grandfather and Grandmother Tabor, with Elizabeth's big beautiful eyes but unfortunately Horace's tall forehead, that could become more pronounced as she got older.

Her brother, John Last the 4th, had inherited both his Grandfather Horace's gangly stance and his tall forehead, but as a male child, it wouldn't hinder his looks much, as he got older. It was only Lily's first born daughter Caroline that inherited both her Grandmother Tabors dainty heart shaped face and big beautiful eyes.

As the week went by, Silver Dollar quickly discovered that her dreams of writing for a big Chicago newspaper just wasn't meant to be and returned to Denver with her mother. But always the writer, Silver made sure to pen a story about her experience in Chicago, for the local Colorado newspapers.

But instead of just publishing her story, one Colorado Newspaper chose to bash Silver Dollar for her description of the windy city and made her out to look like an unsophisticated fool.

"I feel that the restraints and conventionalities of the city and freedom and naturalness of the country are as antipodean as the east and west of Kipling" Silver wrote of her experience in Chicago. But seeing a way to pick fun, at Silver Dollars expense, The Kiowa County Press chose to translate her original story and give their own spin on it, for the entertainment of their readers.

> "This is the experience of Silver dollar who was accustomed to wearing men's' clothes and handling a pistol. She found Chicago big and ugly and the air was impure, so

```
she returned to the west where she feels
people are natural and not hypocrites."
```

Brushing off the comment, Silver decided to inquire about a new pet from the Priscilla Ranch in Glen Eyrie, Colorado, which might be slightly hard to find and even harder to raise inside a Denver boarding house.

Miss S.D. Tabor-Denver, Colo.,

Your letter of inquiry of recent date relative to baby wild cat received and contents noted. In reply I would say that in the spring of next year I will try and locate a den of kittens and if successful will advise you.

Yours very truly,
A. DeV Baldwin

As Silver Dollar waited for a possible kitten to bring home to her rented room, she continued doing freelance work with both the Denver Post and the Pueblo Chieftain, but soon got a heart breaking critique from the editor of the Chieftain.

Bringing her into his office, Silver was informed that she wasn't showing enough progress with her writing and would need to improve her technique. Insulted, Silver instead quit and informed the Editor that her writing was wonderful and that she would just start her own newspaper.

And she did.

"The Silver Dollar Weekly" ran for only a few months, before going under. It seemed that perhaps it would take more than the name Tabor to make her writing a success.

But Silver Dollar had another idea up her sleeve.

A Novel.

Disgusted with her failed attempts at publication in Colorado, Silver moved up to Chicago and rented a room within a cheap boarding

Silver Dollar posing with a lion-89.451.3936 History Colorado

house and happily began typing. As an added bonus, Silver's uncle Peter continued to pay all her bills, so she could focus on her manuscript.

Titled "The Star of Blood", Silver's novel was a story about a criminal named Allen Hench Downen and Artie Dallas, the woman who loved him. The 74 page manuscript ended with the poor girl dead in an unmarked grave and her lover sentenced to life in prison, but unfortunately for Silver, nobody wanted to publish her novel.

And despite sending out letters to every publishing house, Silver received only rejections and alternate ideas for how she could promote her manuscript, such as its use in a magazine or a newspaper story instead, but that's not what she wanted to hear. Discouraged and home sick, she returned to Denver defeated.

But Elizabeth loved her daughter and wanted her child to be happy, so with some digging, she found a man in Denver who would print Silver's book, based on her last name alone and not her writing abilities. With a regained sense of accomplishment, Silver Dollar eagerly looked through the cover choices the man had in his print shop and chose a stiff, grey cover with bold red lettering.

Under the title "Star of blood", Silver had the man print a large red star and then place her name underneath, but the inside cover picture was the real eye catcher.

The conservative and proper hair style for a young lady over 17 was the pompadour, which was a large, waved bun of hair, piled high and accented with either curls or ringlets, made famous by the Gibson girl sketches. But 21 year old Silver Dollar wanted something more risqué that leaned more towards a common whore, than the daughter of a former Governor.

Posed with her hair loose and seductively wrapped around her head and shoulders, Silver curled up against a taxidermied lion's head, wearing nothing more than a shear gown that bared her shoulders. Her makeup was very pale, with dark red lip stick and an abundance of dark, smoky eye makeup with a finish of black liner.

Silver loved her vamped out new look.

And so did the man who raped her.

Traveling around Denver promoting her book, Silver was invited into the office of a well-respected business man, who falsely filled Silver Dollars head with empty promises while coyly closing and locking his office door.

Later that day Elizabeth received a tearful phone call from her daughter who insisted that she hated Denver and begged her mother to move her back to Leadville, all the while keeping the attack a secret.

She was afraid that the man, with his high connections, would keep his deathly promise to seek revenge if she told anyone about their encounter.

She just wanted to get out of Denver.

But the attack changed her.

With Elizabeth welcomed back to her cabin at the Matchless, Silver moved in with her mother and dove head on into writing, mining and her mother's catholic faith, as she tried to cleanse herself of the sin she felt she caused.

The next few years were a blur for Silver, as she continued her self-imposed exile from the world, leaving the safety of the cabin only to help her mother with supplies. Slowly, Silver began opening up to people but didnt regain her confidence until the end of 1913, when she met the Fitzgerald sisters, May and Josephine.

Nervous for her daughter, but wanting her to break out of her shell and enjoy life, Elizabeth encouraged Silver's new found friendships and watched her daughter move into Leadville's Vendome Hotel and leave her alone in the cabin once again.

With a renewed spirit, Silver Dollar submitted new poems and stories to the Leadville Democrat Newspaper and on January 1st, 1914, her New Year's poem entitled "Here's to you" was published.

"Here's to you-you may be sleeping in an unknown grave tonight. With a wild vineo'er you creeping shyly-in the pale starlight.

Here's to you-a thousand daisies may be scattered 'neath your feet.As your hunted tracks are leading to a vagabonds retreat.

Here's to you-you may welcome in the ranks of fame and wealth where the kings of power and fortune are drinking to your health.

Here's to you- a haunting memory may be calling through the years with a pain that joy can't deaden and a voice that rings with tears.

Here's to you- the sun is sinking O'er your life-if live you do and through all it-are you drinking to the ones who drink to you?"

With her new found sense of worth, Silver Dollar volunteered at a Valentines festival on February 14th, which was held in Leadville's Turner Hall and helped hand out candy and Ice cream to over 250 children who were dressed in wonderful clown and sailor costumes.

Turner Hall, located on East Third Street, was built in 1880 by German immigrants who called themselves Turnvereins. The group, which came to the United States in 1811, originally consisted of 48 political refugee's from Germany who were devote practitioners of Gymnastics.

But only a week after Elizabeth Tabor daughter graced the pages of the local newspaper, in regards to volunteering at the festival, Elizabeth noticed a very short story on February 27th, which made a fleeting mention of her Step-son Maxcy Tabor's only child, Persis Augusta, getting married in Denver.

Persis had met her new husband after befriending his sister Lucy years before, while visiting her longtime friend Mrs. Stanley Walker, who lived in Salida, Colorado. A native of Paris, France, Paul Alain Louis LaForgue had later met Persis while on holiday in Salida with his sister, who introduced them.

The wedding was held at the Tabor families Denver home, which was decorated with Easter Lilies, beautiful assorted flowers and palms and attended by Persis's soon to be mother-in-law, while Lucy stood as a bridesmaid.

As spring began to poke its head out of the Leadville snow, Elisabeth's lessee's William and Lizzie Stephenson filed an extension at the court house, so they could continue working up at The Matchless for another two years. Their original lease was signed on October 28, 1913, but they had discovered enough ore in the ground between shaft #5 and shaft #6 to continue their work and planned to extend their shaft 259 feet.

But despite the best efforts put forth with her new lessee's, it was their new partner that Elizabeth began having problems with. With a one ½ interest in the original lease, Elizabeth quickly discovered that Edward Best had more on his mind than silver ore.

He was smitten with Elizabeth's 24 year old daughter.

Not feeling his intentions were honorable and discovering that he was also a terrible drunkard, Elizabeth made him chose between working at the Matchless mine or courting her daughter Silver.

Edward chose the mine.

Unfortunately, despite the man proving that his love for Silver Dollar wasn't real, Elizabeth couldn't seem to get her heart broken daughter to understand.

STOLEN VIRTUE AND THE TAXIDERMIED LION 211

"Why did you ask him about his intentions regarding marrying me? I told you that in confidence! He has never proposed, I was simply wishing he would and you scared him off by mentioning it!" Silver screamed, as she stomped around her rented room at the Vendome. "He came by today and said goodbye to me!"

Elizabeth tried her best to comfort her youngest daughter, but to no avail. Feeling defeated, Silver Dollar stormed into her room, closed the door, grabbed her writing pad and pen and blamed her mother for ruining her life.

> *"My heart is breaking . . . The end has come with me, life is a barren waste . . . Ed has cut our going together off because he thinks you may make trouble. I love him and would do anything to please him, even living in the cabin as he demanded . . . no, you do not love me. If you did you would not ruin my all, all is over. Ed does not know I love him and I never want him to know, because he is lost!"*
>
> *-The Leaf in the Storm*

Desperate to prove her point, Elizabeth headed down to the area near shaft # 5, confronted her daughter's lover and again asked him his intentions. Seeing in his eyes that he still wished to court her daughter out of lust, Elizabeth told him that if their relationship continued, with no marriage in sight, that she would disinherit her daughter so he wouldn't be able to benefit from his sinful interests.

Feeling that Mrs. Tabor might be trying to force him into a marriage he didn't want, Edward headed over to Silver's room at the Vendome and revealed her mother's threat. But before Silver could beg her lover to stay, he admitted that his love was purely the sinful variety and left the Hotel. Furious, Silver quickly wrote her mother a rage filled letter and dropped it in the mail.

Mrs. Tabor,

Ed told me that you threatened to disinherit me if I had anything more to do with him. And he is not going to have anything more to do with me. I knew that when he said good-bye at the hotel door and no one, not even my mother, is going to break my heart and manage to make the one I love desert me without paying for it, so you are going to pay.

You disinherit me and I will testify with proof so that you will have nothing to keep me out of. And you deed the things away and I shall put my proof in court and when you die, if I am disinherited, I will drag it through the courts and disgrace your name!

And in the future when you wonder where and how I am, just think of me as "The leaf in the storm", suffering, battling for existence, alone and nursing the wounds of love..."

The letter also informed Elizabeth, numerous times, that Silver Dollar was never going to speak to her again, except any letters from her and was planning on moving out of Leadville forever. Knowing her daughter just needed to calm down, Elizabeth began focusing her intentions, once again, on regaining her husband Horace's missing 71,250 shares of stock in the Maid of Erin Mine.

On April 30, 1914 Elizabeth headed up to Denver and filed a claim in the county court against the estate of the late David H. Moffat. She was requesting an account of all the profits from the Maid of Erin mine, since it's reopening and once again wished to have her husband's stolen stock certificates returned to her. The stock represented a $1/9^{th}$ interest in the mine, which she heard had just recently produced almost $1,000,000 in dividends.

Knowing it was a long shot, Elizabeth handing the paperwork over to the clerk, who, with an unsympathetic hand, stamped the document and tossed into the pile.

When Elizabeth returned back to Leadville, she discovered that her brother Peter had bought Silver Dollar a new pony, as his way of getting her out of her slump. Seeming to do the trick, Silver began talking to her mother again and even began a new love interest to erase Edward from her memory.

And his name was Harrison Dewar.

Harrison was an educated man, who had attended college in Madison, Wisconsin after being a linemen for the Newsboys football team in Leadville, as well as playing on the Hockey club. Elizabeth approved of the love affair, which renewed Silver Dollars trust in her mother and helped repair the damage her break up with Edward had caused.

And to boost Silver's self-esteem further, she once again graced the pages of the local Leadville Newspaper, this time as a hero of sorts.

On May 17th Silver and her friend, 17 year old Cora Burnight went to Leadville's Sharver and St. John stables and retrieved their ponies for a day of riding, but poor Cora's pony had other ideas.

Riding down Harrison Ave., the two girls were simply enjoying the weather when Cora's horse became agitated and began bucking wildly, which threw poor Cora to the ground. Stopping her own pony Polly, Silver jumped off her saddle, calmed the animal down and helped Cora to her feet.

Brushing herself off and stating she felt fine, Cora remounted the animal, which quickly bucked the poor girl off again, but this time when she struck the ground, she was knocked unconscious.

With grace and a calm demeanor, Silver pulled her friend and both ponies out of the street and helped bring Cora back to consciousness.

With her confidence at an all-time high, Silver Dollar questioned her current love interest and sent Harrison Dewar a letter that asked his intentions with her, after discovering he had been seeking the company of other women.

"I feel we should have a clearer understanding in order that I may know what to do. I made an agreement with you and I am ready to keep it with pleasure if you keep your part of it. But I do not feel that I should be bound to reject all pleasures, while you go free enjoying yourself apart from me.

You will understand my position as a girl that I cannot afford to reject the company of others if you do not intend to keep your part."

But unfortunately, the man she thought loved her chose his adventurous life style over their relationship, which sent poor Silver into another downward spiral. She spent her days thinking about not only Harrison, but Edward and his drinking problem and wondered if he was possibly the love of her life.

In a desperate attempt to give his niece a change of scenery and maybe a positive outlook, Peter McCourt sent Silver Dollar some extra money, which allowed her to move out of her rented room in Leadville's Vendome Hotel and into a small house at 221 East 10th street. Unfortunately, the house she chose to rent was the same one that she had planned on living in with her now ex-boyfriend Harrison Dewar, which prompted her to seek his approval once again.

As well as the approval of Jimmie Gildea.

Jimmie was a member of the Gentleman's riding and driving club and was known around town for his Horse Prince Hal and his high scores in the trotting and pacing events, so Silver thought he would be quiet the catch.

But as Silver Dollar fought to find favor in numerous men around Leadville, Elizabeth Tabor found herself back in court on May 25th, fighting to regain her husband's mining stock that was in the hands of David H. Moffat's estate.

"All rise, the honorable Judge Rothgerber presiding"

"You may be seated"

"It has been brought to my attention that Mrs. Horace Tabor has filed a claim against the Moffat estate for 71,250 shares of stock in the Maid of Erin Mine, that she believes rightfully belongs to her. Let the record show that the mining shares were given as collateral to David H. Moffat in 1893 for a loan of $40,000. Mrs. Tabor, you have the floor."

"Thank you your honor. It is true that my husband did receive a loan of $40,000 and used the mining shares as collateral, but I feel that since the stock has increased in value, that its worth exceeds the $40,000 that my husband received. I feel that the accrued dividends would liquidate the loan and I am requesting an accounting from The First National Bank, which is the present holder of the stock."

"Mrs. Tabor, I am disallowing your request." The Judge informed her. "Your husband gave this stock as collateral for a loan he was unable to pay back. I understand that the stock has increased in value, but that does not entitle you to have the stock returned to you."

"I'm sorry Mrs. Tabor."

"Dismissed."

Returning to Leadville with her tail between her legs, Elizabeth was pleased to learn that her daughter Silver's spirits were up and that she had been preparing for a pony race, along with her friend Nora, which would be held during the July 4th holiday.

The festival, which began at 10am with a colorful parade, was followed by numerous sporting events ranging from pie eating contests and sack races, to automobile hill climbing , miners cart , harness races and of course the Girls and ladies pony race.

Competing against the best, Silver Dollar and her pony Polly came in second place, while her friend Nora pulled out a first place win.

But Silver found that she was unable to celebrate the festival as a 24 year old young woman should. With no job and a unlimited supply of money being poured into her bank account every week by her Uncle Peter, Silver wanted to enjoy the life of a free spirited young woman, but felt like she was always being watched.

And she was.

Unknown to Silver, her mother's tiny frame was creeping around behind the shadows and peeking into windows, as Silver entertained not only her female friends, but her male friends as well. And on September 3rd, Silver dollar finally discovered who was creeping in the dark.

After moving out of her rented house and into a local boarding house owned by the Walpensky family, Silver decided to throw a party and invite her friends over for some merriment, but seeing so many men enter her daughters rented room threw Elizabeth Tabor over the edge.

With built up anger and disgust, Elizabeth snuck in through the front door of the boarding house and followed the sounds of laughter and music that was flowing down the hall. Finding a room with the door cracked open, Elizabeth peaked inside and watched as her daughter engaged in sin and vile practices, not meant for a decent young, unmarried woman.

Crossing herself for strength, Elizabeth bust through the doorway and confronted her daughter and her sinful ways. In the confusion, the party guests panicked and began escaping the rented room as quickly as possible, jumping out windows and even squeezing past Elizabeth, who was standing in the doorway. Silver, not understanding what was happening, also jumped out the window, which resulted in her shoulder and side slamming against the ground with a violent thud.

With the rented room now empty, Elizabeth began looking around for indications on how her daughter, who didn't work, was affording to pay her weekly rent and throw these shindig's. As she peaked into corners and under the bed for clues, Elizabeth had no idea that her brother Peter had been paying all of Silver Dollars bills and allowing her to live an ungodly life style.

Stealing from his niece the ability to support herself and develop pride in a hard day's work, Peter McCourt allowed the guilt of his sisters situation overwhelm his common sense and in turn, overindulged his yougest niece.

He didn't realize the problems he had created, until Silver called him and poured out a horrific story of shame and embarrassment at the hands of her mother. With a deep feeling of guilt, Peter headed to Leadville to confront his sister and admit the secret he had been keeping from her.

Not only had he bought his niece Silver the expensive pony she had wanted, but had also been depositing $50 a month into her bank account, while his own sister struggled to restore the Tabor name.

He just hoped it wasn't too late to fix what he had done.

A RIVER FULL OF QUICKSAND AND THE LOST RING

Silver Dollar Tabor was gone.

On September 13, 1914, after packing up her pony and all her belonging, she boarded a train for Colorado Springs and whisked herself away from the prying eyes of her mother. Her uncle Peter had already arranged a room for her in a cheap boarding house, until he could attempt to defuse the situation.

Taking a taxi up to his sister Elizabeth's Leadville cabin, Peter immediately admitted what he had done and watched his sister began to break down, out of fear for her youngest daughter.

"Colorado Springs? You sent her to Colorado Springs? She doesn't know anyone there!" Elizabeth explained, as she wiped the tears from her eyes.

"That's the idea." Peter clarified, as he held his sisters trembling hand. "I was wrong for hiding the fact I was supporting Silver and I've explained to her that things are going to change and she needs to find a job. If I would have sent her to Denver, she would just fallen back in with her familiar crowd."

With a new arrangement agreed upon, Silver was informed that her original amount of $50 a month would still be deposited into her bank account, but it wouldn't all be coming from her Uncle Peter. Elizabeth's yougest sister Clotilda McCourt would be contributing $25 of the monthly funds, with Peter depositing the rest. Silver was also informed that in order to receive any of the money, she would have to begin sending her mother letters and end the feud between them.

Silver Dollar, on left, in the movie "The Great Barrier." 1915-Photo by author

And as Peter McCourt had predicted, depositing his niece into an unfamiliar city, prompted her to find a job and in the process, new friends. Using her well-known name to get herself into interviews, Silver was hired by a motion picture company called The Pikes Peak film Company, in the fall of 1914.

Film producer Otis B. Thayer, known as "Obie" started his film company in 1910 while living in Chicago. Originally named the Selig Polyscope Company, he first came to Colorado to film westerns in Canon City, before moving on to Colorado Springs in 1914.

His first western, titled "A Romance of the Rio Grande", was filmed in 1911 and by the time Silver Dollar joined the crew in 1914, he was filming his 39th movie.

As sound was not perfected enough to be used in the movie houses, the films acquired the title "Silent Movies". To compensate for their lack of sound, the actors were trained to over emphasize their body language and facial expressions, in order to convey what was happening in the scene.

When a conversation was spoken, the theatre audience could follow along by reading the words written across the bottom of the screen. To add suspense, surprise, fear or to enforce the feelings of love during a scene, music would also be played by a small band, located inside the theater the movie was being shown in, which also had the added benefit of drowning out the sounds of the noisy projectors.

But by the time Silver Dollar joined the cast of "The Heart of a man", she found her bank account running dry, since she was now employed and no longer receiving her $50 a month allowance. Needing a place to live, she moved into the boarding house provided by the film company and agreed to pay $6 a month for her horse Polly to stay in the barn.

She also found herself not only washing her own clothing, but mending the worn out patches, as she no longer had money for new outfits. Fortunately, she was too busy to focus on her clothing situation, as her roles in the movie varied as the scenes changed, with her being made up as a spinster one day and a beautiful damsel the next.

But it was during a break in filming that Silver learned why the film's producer Otis B. Thayer now chose to shoot his movies in Colorado Springs, when he had previously shot dozens' of movies in Canon City, Colorado.

His leading lady and a camera man had drown.

While filming a western, called "Across the Border", 26 year old actress Grace McHugh was riding in a small boat, down the Arkansas River, when it capsized in the quickly moving water and she was thrown overboard.

Seeing that she had landed in the deep, rushing water and was quickly being washed down stream, cinematographer Owen Carter immediately threw down his equipment and jumped in after her. Reaching her in time, Owen was able to grab Grace and pull them both over to a nearby sandbar, but the film crew watched in horror as the sand began swallowing them both. Unable to reach them in time, due to the rocky terrain, the crew watched the quicksand devour the doomed couple.

Director Otis B. Thayer was later criticized for using the horrific footage in the completed film, when it was released in theater's August 22, 1914 and chose to move his operations to Colorado Springs.

Brushing off the heebie jebbie's, Silver Dollar stayed to film five more movies and as the American public was eager for new, thrilling films, Otis B. Thayer began filming smaller movies called "Short's" and brought them out as quickly as possible.

"The Heart of a man"- a drama released on December 28, 1914

"The Greater Barrier"- a western released on March 12, 1915

"The Cost"-a western released April 10, 1915

"The Parasites"-a western released April 24, 1915

"Told in the Rockies"- a western released May 8, 1915

"The Word"- a drama released June 5, 1915

Using mostly the same actors and actresses for every movie, the lead roles were always held by William Mong, Edmond Cobb and Josephine West, which kept Silver Dollar as more of a background actress whose name never even made it onto the posters.

Annoyed that she wasn't able to move up in the ranks of the movie business, she decided to accept an offer to be a chorus girl in a group called The Minstrel Maid Company, which prompted her to quit the film industry and move into a Denver Hotel, located at 1821 California

St., in August 1915.

But returning to Denver caused a problem that Silver had to find a way to fix and that was how to pay her rent and afford her costumes without any money, which unfortunately she chose to fix on her back. Ollie Underwood, a longtime friend of Elizabeth Tabor's, was living in the same Hotel as Silver when she informed Elizabeth about the exploits of her yougest daughter.

It seemed that the Chamber maid at the Hotel began spreading a bit of gossip about the Showgirl in room #115, who she had seen bring horrible looking fellows up to her room. And when Mrs. Underwood asked if the maid knew the name of the young woman, she peaked over her shoulder before whispering "It's a Tabor."

"She told me that she's leaving town with some company and was making a white costume trimmed in gold to wear on stage", the maid whispered, as she continued telling Mrs. Underwood what she had witnessed. "I'd seen a horrible looking fellow coming up to see her and when I asked, she said it was just an old friend her mother hated, but another maid named Billy said she saw the Tabor girl pick the man up on the street!"

With Silver Dollar trying to make her bills anyway she could, she discovered that her job as a chorus girl was falling apart. The producer was a man named Harry Hart, who couldn't handle his drink and spent his drunken night sharing stories of when he was in a Penitentiary, to anyone who would listen.

After quitting four times, but then coming back to work after Harry sobered up and apologized, Silver was thrilled when she was offered a job at Denver's Lakeside Amusement park, on September 2nd. She knew that Sam Gates, who also worked with the chorus company, worked as a high wire walker for the park and Silver happily accepted an interview with Mr. Phil Fredericks, who was the general manager, for the following morning.

Lakeside Amusement Park was the brain child of Adolph Zang,

Peter Friederich, Godfrey Schirmer, John A. Keefe and Albert Lewin, whose main objective of building the park was to skirt around Denver's "Blue Law's", which prohibited the sale of Liquor on Sunday's.

Their elaborate plan began on March 20, 1907 when the group formed the Lakeside realty and Amusement Company and purchased 0.19 sq. miles of land that encased Denver's Lake Rhonda.

On April 24, 1907 the company then filed a plat with the State of Colorado for a new town, which was accepted and with the paperwork in place, they began to build homes around the lake, with construction beginning on their originally planned Amusement park on September 1, 1907.

On November 12, 1907 the 42 residents voted to incorporate their new little town, which they named Lakeside and now their Amusement Park could not only have liquor on Sunday's, but a Casino.

When Silver Dollar had her interview with the parks manager Mr. Frederick's on the morning of September 3, 1915, she was thrilled with the offer of $100 to slide by her feet on a wire, from the park's 150 ft. high tower and jump into the lake on Labor Day. Her Interview with the park's general manager went so well, that she was introduced to many of the other employee's and discovered that 21 year old Florence Wheeler, who use to dance with Silver at The Minstrel Maid Company, had also been hired, but for the park's theatrical line.

Silver knew Florence, but had found her to be a drunkard, a chronic complainer and a thief. A woman named Blanche had heard from Fanny Borstadt's mother, who lived at a convent, that Florence had been taken in as a charity case once but stole money, clothes and anything that wasn't nailed down.

She had also tried to skip out on her rent at The Page Hotel by lowering her suitcase on a rope out the window, but when the rope snapped it alerted the manager, who had Florence arrested. Harry Hart, the producer at the Minstrel Company had to bail her out of jail, so they could do a show in Sterling. Colorado.

Florence finally got fired after the Minstrel Company discovered she had a warrant in St. Louis for stealing and white slavery charges, which Silver Dollar assumed that Lakeside hadn't yet discovered. Silver was just glad she wouldn't be working with her or sharing a stage again, as Florence was also a terrible dancer.

At twenty five years old, Silver Dollar was so excited about her newly promised job at the Amusement park, that she brought Carl Cameron and J.H. Farran back to her apartment that evening, to get to know her new co-worker's alittle better and to learn about her job. As the men were telling Silver about the new slide that had just been installed at the park, the group heard a loud knock at the door.

Opening the door, Silver discovered Florence Wheeler struggling to stand and reeking of liquor. "Can I use your bathroom?" She asked, as she looked past Silver Dollar at the two men sitting around a small table.

"Florence, we are having a private conversation. Can you go down to the parlor?" Silver asked, as she began closing the door.

"Just let me go to the bathroom!" Florence demanded, as she tried to push her way into the apartment. Knowing that Florence worked with both of the men she was entertaining and not wanting to start problems with her new co-worker's, Silver grudgingly let her in.

Showing her to the bathroom, Silver Dollar sat back down with the men, but as she continued listening to their story regarding the new slide, she heard an agonizing scream. Running over to the bathroom, Silver quickly opened the door and found Florence frantically looking for something.

"Where's my ring?" She wailed, as she began to look around the bathroom. "My ring is missing!"

"Just calm down, I'll help you. What does it look like?" Silver asked as she began looking around on the floor.

"It's a 1/5th carat white sapphire ring! I always wear it on my left hand!" she screamed, before looking back over at Silver. "You stole it!

You stole my ring!"

Shocked by the allegations, Silver looked up just in time to see Florence swing her closed fist towards her face. With a sharp thud, Silver Dollar suddenly felt a stinging sensation engulf her eye, as she lost her footing and fell to the bathroom floor.

"Give me my ring!" Florence screamed, as she pounced onto Silver and attempted to punch her again. Luckily the two men tackled Florence to the floor, which caused her to scream like a banshee. As they picked her up and attempted to throw her out of the apartment, the other tenants at the Hotel over heard the commotion and called the front desk, who in turn called the Police.

Successfully removing Florence from Silver's apartment, the men closed the door and quickly locked it, while the drunk young woman stood screaming about her ring in the hallway. Stumbling towards the elevator, Florence entered the empty car and began angrily pushing buttons, which resulted in her being deposited in the basement, where her screams echoed throughout the building.

When Officer Sam Hughes and Officer Orbach arrived at the Hotel, they discovered Florence crying in the elevator and discovered that the fight was caused by a missing ring. Calming her down with promises to find it, the Officers took her to the front desk and learned that Silver Dollar Tabor was the resident of the room in question.

Knocking on Silver's door, the Officer's explained the problem and asked if they could bring Florence in to look for her ring. Seeing Silver's swollen eye, the men began questioning her about her injury as Florence started screaming about her missing ring again. Not sure who was at fault, the Officers chose to arrest Florence, Silver, Carl and J.H, piled them all into the police car and headed down to the station.

At 8am the next morning, after a terrible night behind bars, Silver was removed from the cell so the Detectives could return her to the Hotel and watch her search for the ring, while Florence continued to sleep off her bender. Satisfied that the ring was not in the room, Silver was returned to the station and back into her cell, where her accuser was starting to wake up.

Standing tall and giving a stretch, Florence began straightening up her skirts when she felt something pinch her finger. Taking a peak under her layers of fabric, she happily discovered a safety pin, which was holding her missing ring, fastened to the underlining of her skirt.

"Look Silver, I found my ring!" Florence proudly announced, as she held it up to the light." Now I remember that when I was in your bathroom, I pinned it under my skirt with a safety pin."

"You need to tell the Officer's, so we can get out of here." Silver explained with an irritated tone, as she gently touched her swollen eye. "I need to get a beef steak, so the swelling will go down."

With a nervous expression, Florence returned the ring to the safety pin and flattened her skirts back down. "No! I'll have the case dropped, but I don't want the police to know that I found it, for it will make me look foolish."

Shocked, Silver rose to her feet and started to rattle the cell door, over the insistent hushing of her frantic cellmate. "Excuse me! Excuse me! Florence Wheeler has found her ring and I wish to be let out!" Silver Dollar yelled, as the attending officer agreed to call back the Detective.

Removing the combative accuser from the cell, Silver instructed the Officer on where to find the ring, which allowed Silver Dollar and her two male companions to be set free, but resulted in a violent threat from Florence.

"If I don't get released when you do, I will hunt you down Silver Dollar Tabor! And I will kill you when I get out! I swear I'll do it!" She screamed as she struggled against the officers.

Slightly startled and seeing the psychotic look in Florence's eyes, Silver Dollar knew she was telling the truth and she kept thinking about the threat as she headed back to her apartment at The California Hotel. But when she walked into the lobby she was greeted with smiles and stares, as a woman approached Silver and handed her the Newspaper.

"SILVER DOLLAR TABOR 24 DENVER IS NURSING
A DEEPLY DISCOLORED EYE"

The Herald Democrat September 4, 1915

"I'm 25, not 24" Silver explained as she handed the paper back to the woman." And I'm going to bed."

With her record clean and no charges brought against her, Silver Dollar kept her Labor Day job and earned her promised $100 by hanging by her feet at the lakeside Amusement Park, but she found herself looking over her shoulder for any signs of Florence Wheeler.

She needed to get out of Denver.

Packing up her trunks, Silver Dollar explained her situation to both the Minstrel Company and Mr. Phil Frederick's from the park and how she feared for her life. Bringing Silver into his office, Phil handed her not only the $100 she had earned, but an additional $100 for a train ticket. "Head to Chicago, you won't have any trouble finding a job there", he told her with an understanding smile.

Writing to her mother, Silver explained to her what had happened and that she was struggling finding a job as a chorus girl in Chicago, as she discovered she wasn't as talented as The Minstrel Maid Company had led her to believe. So far ,she had only been able to find random jobs that paid $5 to dance at social functions, which she earned by performing an Egyptian dance she had learned years before. It seemed that her time touring with the Lambert Minstrel Company and performing in small Colorado farming towns had come in handy after all.

Still fearful of Florence finding her, Silver began going by the fictitious name Ruth Knight.

But as Silver Dollar struggled to find work, her mother had problems of her own, as she suddenly found herself homeless and her beloved mine at risk.

At 9am on October 10, 1915, Mrs. Tabor's lessee's James Gildea and Louis Springhetti were deep down inside shaft #7, doing some Sunday repairs, when Springhetti came up to the surface to fetch some supplies that were located in the engine house, near shaft #5. But as he got closer to the building, he began hearing a hiss, which caused him to run towards the building at top speed.

Both Springhetti and his partner had just invested a pretty penny in the new equipment that the building housed and when he reached for the door, he saw smoke start to billow out. Ripping the door open he saw that flames had already engulfed the inside of the engine house and was spreading so quickly, that he instantly jumped back.

Seeing the fire equipment off to the side, Louis Springhetti went to reach for it when something caught his eye…Mrs. Tabor's cabin. In his moment of fear, he had almost forgotten that 61 year old Elizabeth was still inside her cabin, less than 500 feet from the ever raging fire.

Abandoning the equipment, he screamed for Mrs. Tabor as he ran towards her cabin, which attracted the attention of George C. Miller and Tom McClure who were working the nearby Robert E. Lee Mine. Seeing that Louis was going after Mrs. Tabor, the men from the Robert E. Lee grabbed all available hands and headed over to the fire equipment next to shaft #5 and attempted to extinguish the inferno that was threatening to burn down The Matchless.

With no time for a polite entrance, Louis kicked open the front door of the cabin and despite being out of breath, was able to point and explain the danger she was in. Looking back at all the men from The Robert E. Lee fighting to save The Matchless, Louis felt confident in helping Mrs. Tabor remove her beloved belongings and get them and her far away from the raging fire.

Settling Mrs. Tabor and her personal possessions on a hill, a safe distance away from her now ignited cabin, Louis returned to help assist the men in the battle.

When the fire was finally extinguished, all the surface buildings at shaft #5 were gone, including Elizabeth's cabin. Over $4,000 worth of new equipment that included a compressor, a hoist and a steam boiler were damaged beyond repair, which caused Louis to take of his hat and say a farewell to the vein of good ore they had just started hoisting to the surface.

Looking back over at the hill he had left Mrs. Tabor on, he saw the tiny woman silently standing with her salvaged belongings and holding a blanket. Seeing that she was staring at the smoldering ruins of her cabin, he couldn't help but wipe his eyes, before looking away.

Which is when he heard it.

"What did I miss?"

Turning towards the familiar voice, Louis Springhetti looked into the confused face of his mining partner James Gildea, who had been deep inside shaft #7 while the fire had raged. But as they filled him in, he asked a question that hadn't crossed anyone's mind.

"Hey guys? Why didn't the gasoline tank explode?" he inquired, as he pointed to the nearby container, damaged by the heat.

Curious, the men carefully approached the tank, and discovered that it was in fact empty, despite just recently being filled. It now appeared that The Matchless had been the latest casualty in a string of intentionally set mining fires, which had plagued Leadville in recent months, with the Morning Star Mines shaft #5 suspiciously burning just the day before.

With the fire out and the gossip and assumptions discussed, the men from the surrounding mines returned to their work with a bit of a story to share with their co-workers come Monday morning. Helping Mrs. Tabor into his wagon, Springhetti then packed her surviving belongings into the back and took her into town, so she could get a room at the Vendome Hotel.

As they made the short trip, Elizabeth thanked him for saving her life and then praised God for the guidance that led her to store her most valued possessions inside Denver's Bekins moving and storage company, instead of up at the cabin.

With a smile, she looked up to the heavens and knew that the precious memories of her beloved husband and the childhood keepsakes from her precious daughters, were safety tucked inside locked trunks, ready for her eyes to gaze on them once again.

The Frozen Boa Constrictor, The Blue Bird and Another Bout of Appendicitis

With her little mountain cabin gone, Elizabeth Tabor found herself, once again, living in Denver's Windsor Hotel. She didn't mind the memories it provided of her sweet husband or of her children when they were little, but she did miss watching the deer graze up near her mine in Leadville, as chipmunks scurried around under her feet.

Finishing her breakfast, Elizabeth Tabor walked out of the Windsor Hotel and began her familiar walk downtown to visit her memories. With October's weather being quite pleasant, she happily walked the one block over to Lawrence Street and then headed down the 5 blocks to Bekins moving and Storage Company, located at 1411 Arapahoe street.

"Good morning Mrs. Tabor", the uniformed gentleman announced, as he tipped his hat, "Would you like to look through one of your trunks today?"

After a smile and some pleasant conversation, Elizabeth was led over to a small room, where she sat and waited for the man to wheel in one of her trunks. With her beloved Horace gone and both of her living children off on their own adventures, her memories brought her peace.

Hearing the familiar sound of the carts wheels squeaking as it approached her, Elizabeth stood up, straightened her skirt and peaked down the hallway. Seeing the large wooden trunk, with the rounded metal corners, being wheeled towards her made Elizabeth smile.

Pulling the cart into the room and parking it at her feet, the storage company's employee locked the carts wheels and excused himself from the room, as Elizabeth began lovingly wiping away all the dust and grime from the old trunk.

And with the twist of her key and the lift of the lid, she was instantly transported back to a time when money was no object and diamonds rained down from the sky.

With her eyes gently closed, she let the smell of the wonderful perfumes rise up out of the tightly packed trunk and engulf her senses. The combined aroma of lavender and roses brought back memories of her beloved Horace, that were so strong ,she could almost feel him standing next to her.

Slowly opening her eyes, she laid her hands on the cloth that encased her beloved Ermine fur opera cloak and removed it from the trunk. Sitting on a nearby bench, she carefully unwrapped the cloak and allowed it to cover her tiny body. Its weight and the softness of its fur reminded her of all the cold winters that beckoned her to wear it, along with the matching fur muff, in order to keep from freezing on those long winter carriage rides to the Opera house.

The cloak was constructed from the pelts of a small white weasel called a stoat, which is simply German for weasel. The animal's body is white, with a black tail, which is where the word Ermine fur comes from. The fuzzy black tails allow the creation of a pattern that consists of a white back ground with a pattern of black shapes, which creates

Little Lily Tabor in big dress-Oshkosh Public Museum-P2001.47.11

its unusual look.

Laying the cloak carefully off to the side, Elizabeth lifted up a small velvet photo album and slid open the golden latch. With a smile she was greeted by her beautiful Lily, her precious first born daughter, covered in a large wreath of flowers and ribbons and wearing a dress that was just alittle too big for her.

As she flipped through the photos, she laughed at the memory of how hard both her and Horace had worked to get Lily to look at the camera, as she kept trying to wiggle out of her oversized dress and push away the numerous flowers that kept tickling her little nose.

Gently closing the album and latching it shut, Elizabeth continued removing items from the trunk until she stumbled upon a small velvet bag. Lifting it out, she set it into the palm of her hand and gently bounced it to feel the weight, which caused its contents to give off a slight rattle.

Laying a scarf on the nearby table, Elizabeth carefully poured out the bags contents and glanced upon her children's baby teeth. Moving them around with her fingers, she was brought back to a time when she left gold coins and gifts under her daughter's hand embroidered satin pillows, in exchange for these tiny little gems.

After spending most of the afternoon reminiscing, Elizabeth lovingly packed up her memories and locked her trunk backup tight. Leaving the room, she alerted the gentleman that she was done for the day and with a friendly wave of her gloved hand, headed back to the Windsor Hotel.

With no cabin in Leadville to return too, as of yet, Elizabeth spent her days visiting with old friends and reading the newspaper for any tidbit of information on her or her family, which she would happily squirrel away.

As 1915 came to an end and the world welcomed in 1916, Elizabeth came across a newspaper article on January 24, which made her thank her luck stars she lived in Denver and not in Montana.

Starting out at a mild 44 degrees, the town of Browning, Montana was hit by a violent artic freeze that plummeted the temperature down to a frigid -56 degrees in just one day. Announced as the largest 24 hour temperature change in United States history, the town's thermometer's steadily dropped 100 degrees and the town slid into a record nobody in Montana ever wanted to achieve.

One resident told the press "Upon retiring for the night, I tried to blow out the candle, but the flame was frozen, so I had to break it off."

As February began peaking its head into the New Year, Elizabeth received a letter from Silver Dollar on the 14th, which bashed her for failing to respond to any of her previous letters and left a guilt trip

Elizabeth Tabor in a fur cloak-89.451.4639 History Colorado

inside its ink filled pages.

But with Silver's constant traveling and all the various names she went by, her mother found it increasingly difficult to know where her daughter was or who some of the letters were actually from.

> *"I was in such a serious condition that the dance company sent me to the Harrisburg City Hospital where I laid in agony for three weeks. I wrote you a card from there and signed it R. Knight."*

Elizabeth re-read the sentence and thought back to the unknown card she had received weeks back that simply asked her to contact a woman named Maria Holzen about her niece, but Elizabeth had no idea that her own daughter had sent that card to her.

And who was this Maria Holzen?

Looking back to the letter in hand, Elizabeth learned that Silver Dollar had had a nasty abscess that needed to be lanced and that the pain had been so bad, it had caused her to fall into a faint. And the reason she had entered the hospital, for her 3 week stay, was because she had contracted blood poisoning after the abscess had become infected.

Needing her job as a chorus girl, Silver also talked about working through the pain by drinking Whiskey, then contracting food poisoning from a Lobster salad, which racked her body with a terrible fever and violent pains throughout her body.

The letter ended with Silver Dollar

Older Silver Dollar in a stylish hat-Legends of America

whining that her mother was allowing her little girl to die and suffer alone in a Hotel room she couldn't afford, but luckily for Elizabeth the letter head, above the tear drenched correspondence, listed her daughters address as The Hotel Hannah at 1122 Superior Ave. N.E , Cleveland, Ohio.

Quickly leaving for the bank to withdraw some money, Elizabeth just hoped it would reach her daughter before she moved again.

As winter passed and spring was in the air, Elizabeth received another letter from Silver on April 5, 1916 that was again full of sorrow and pain. Her daughter talked about how she had gotten into a quarrel with the manager of a traveling show and quit, then found herself sick again and fighting to stay in a hotel room she couldn't afford.

Silver's letter also mentioned that she was again suffering from blood poisoning, but this time it had infected her glands and prompted a Doctor to remove one of her ovary's, which made Elisabeth's heart drop, as the letter described the horrific results of a botched abortion, rather than a simple physical aliment.

This time the return address on the envelope was listed as Hotel Savoy in Omaha, Nebraska.

In Elizabeth's return letter, she begged her daughter to come home to Colorado or move in with her sister Lily, but she knew she was just wasting ink and the price of a stamp.

Still reeling from the heartbreak inflicted by her youngest daughter, Elizabeth was shocked to see the name Tabor splashed across the headlines in an unexpected fashion, which threatened to change the way the people of Colorado thought of her family.

On April 25, 1916 the Daily Journal ran a story about a pair of children who had been abandoned by their father and were being taken to the Home League Orphanage in Denver. The story of children being abandoned normally wouldn't have batted an eye to any ordinary Newspaper editor, but these children had been graced with the last name of Tabor, which meant it warranted front page exposure.

Abandoned by their nameless father and with no mention of their mother, the story read that Sherriff Edgar Kracaw of Telluride had boarded the Ridgeway passenger train with eleven year old Zelmar Tabor and thirteen year old Vernia Tabor in tow, after Judge M.L. Brown had failed to find any family to take them in.

Elizabeth knew who their nameless father was.

But he was only a father to Vernia.

Horace Tabors family, like most families in that time, was quite large. His father Cornelius Dunham Tabor, who was born on July 23, 1799, was one of 16 children, where Horace was one of 10.

This large amount of children had, in turn, left Horace with numerous aunts, uncles and cousins scattered around, which is where Zelmar and Vernia came in.

Vernia's parents were Milton B. Tabor and Lela Tabor who had moved to Colorado to work the mines years back and had birthed 8 children, but according to the newspaper story, the father had only given up Vernia to the state.

The second child the newspaper story mentioned, Zelmar Tabor, was actually one of Vernia's cousins and not a sibling as the story had incorrectly reported. But sending the two children to Denver's Ward #15 actually was quite fitting, as this was the same orphanage they had both spent time in back in 1910, along with their cousin Noah Tabor.

As Elizabeth read the heart breaking story of the Tabor children, she lowered her head in silent understanding. She and Horace had struggled so much themselves to support their own children on a miner's salary, after they lost their fortune and they only had two children to feed.

Needing a distraction from all the heartbreak and worry she had been experiencing, Elizabeth was happily caught off guard by a story, spreading around Colorado, about a Boa Constrictor that had been found frozen inside a bunch of bananas, up in Victor, Colorado.

The bananas had been delivered to the local Victor Grocery from

South America and to the store owner's surprise, a large, frozen snake was found coiled amongst the fruit. Afraid the animal was dead, and not wanting his customers to find out about this frozen castaway, the shop owner carefully removed the snake and laid it outside the back of his shop, where the sun unexpectedly began waking it up.

Drawing a crowd, the snake was soon identified as a three foot long Anaconda Boa Constrictor. Seeing that the exotic animal was accepted, the store owner laid the bunch of bananas next to it and allowed people

The Boa in the bananas, Victor, Colorado -Photo by author

to take pictures, while the snake slithered around its former home.

Unfortunately, despite numerous attempts to feed it, the snake died 18 days later.

Ironically, an almost similar snake had been found wrapped around a delivery of bananas in Greeley, Colorado back on December 7, 1914, but this one survived and became quite a showcase.

S.E. Davenport, an employee of the local Grocery store, had been separating bananas from the bunch hanging in their back room, when he saw a beautiful, red snake frozen around the stalk. After carefully removing the animal, he laid it inside a box and called the State Teachers College to retrieve it.

The College later reported that the almost three foot long Anaconda Boa Constrictor had not only woken up, but was eatting very well.

As the year continued, the name Tabor once again graced the local Newspapers, but this time it was to announce a miracle of sorts.

Seventeen year old Madge Tabor, the oldest child of Charles M. Tabor, had survived surgery to treat her appendicitis on October 12th, to the great relief of her mother Mariah.

Charles, Horace Tabor's youngest half-sibling, was born when his mother was 46 and his father was 73. Unfortunately, after having six children of his own, Charles died at the age of 40 when his oldest child Madge was only 13 years old.

Little Madge improved very slowly following the surgery and wasn't able to sit up in bed until November 23rd, but thankfully she went on to make a full recovery.

And it was just around 11 days later, on December 4th, that Elizabeth found out that her lessees up at her Matchless mine were asking her to edit their lease agreement with her, in order to prevent a former lessee turned thief, from ever working at her mine again. And to sweeten the pot, Elizabeth discovered that her lessee James Ryan had built her a brand new cabin up at the Matchless, which was waiting for her when she arrived in Leadville to sign the papers.

Built near shaft #6, the cabin was 15' X 20' with a 6'x5' enclosed porch on the front, which would give Elizabeth some protection from the bitter cold drafts, caused by Leadville's frigid winters. The walls and ceiling were insulated with thick padding, covered in brown construction paper, which gave the cabin a finished look and it was furnished with a cast iron bed, a small table, a few chairs and a heavy duty rocking chair, set up next to the wood stove.

It was perfect.

The court hearing in regards to the lease agreement, was held on

December 3, 1916 and was simply a revision to Elizabeth Tabor's earlier agreement with her current lessees, which was originally signed back on November 18, 1915.

The changes were made to assure that Silver Dollars former love interest, Edward Best, was not only barred from leasing the mine, but that he was also not allowed to step foot on the property. Edward had been causing problems again with the current lessees and it was this rift that prompted James and Michael Ryan to call for the revision, as they also felt that Edward was stealing ore

The current lease would now run for three years and end on November 18, 1919, but with an added change regarding the royalties paid for the ore. For ore valued at $10 or less, the lessees would pay Mrs. Tabor 10%, but on ore worth between $75-$100 or more, they would pay her 30%.

And to keep her lessee's honest, 62 year old Elizabeth Tabor left Denver's Windsor Hotel and moved into her new , little cabin up at the Matchless, with every intention of working one of the shafts herself for a little extra pocket money.

Elizabeth soon found that life back up in Leadville was just what she needed and happily settled into her new daily routine. As 1916 came to an end and she turned her wall calendar over to 1917, she finally got news of a large body of silver ore down in shaft #7, but Elizabeth almost lost two of her lessee's in the process.

In February, Elizabeth Tabor was sitting outside and enjoying the bright day, when James Ryan's wife and two year old son James Jr. came up for a visit. Being a nice day, Bridget had walked the mile up to the Matchless with her little son in tow, in order to bring her husband and his brother Michael a hot lunch.

As the two women began making small talk, the hoist cable, attached to the head frame, suddenly tightened and gave a quick jerk. Jumping up from her seat, Elizabeth ran over to the hoist house and discovered that a cave-in was feared. As the dust began to settle, from around the entrance to the shaft, the frantic group finally saw Michael Ryan slowly immerging… but he was alone.

"James is trapped, we need help!" Michael announced in his deep Irish brogue. "The shaft collapsed and it's quite a fucking, brutal mess down there. One of those gammy looking timbers fell on us!"

Grabbing a group of nearby miners and a few necessary tools, the men quickly headed back down into the shaft and after what seemed like an eternity, managed to free James and hoist him up to the surface.

"Mrs. Tabor, we found a vein of Silver ore! A bloody ton of it!" James happily announced, as he was helped out of the shaft. Hearing the squeal of his little boy, he carefully stood up and began dusting himself off, before picking up the child.

"Don't worry Bridgie, me leg isn't banjaxed." Jim announced to his worried wife, with a quick slap to his pant leg, "The timbers fell when the ceiling collapsed and one of them pinned me legs, but thanks to the Holy Mother, it kept me from falling down the bloody shaft."

"Papa, blue bird! Blue bird!" little James announced to his sore and dusty father, as James Sr. found a nearby place to sit down. Looking over at his relieved wife, he smiled up at her and learned that a little blue bird might have predicted the discovery of the silver ore pocket, inside the Matchless.

The day before the collapse, Bridget had walked to the Matchless with her little boy, to bring up the hot lunches, when she saw an unusual site at the front gate of the Matchless.

A blue bird.

Being February, it was extremely early for blue birds, so she pointed the bird out to her son, who squealed with delight as the little bird began following them back home.

Flying ahead of them and landing in snow drifts, the little blue bird continued following the pair until they reached the front gate of their home on East 7th street, over a mile away.

According to folklore, the blue bird is considered a good omen and as a symbol of change and passage, as it predicts that those who previously attempted to block your progress, will now find themselves blocked and hindered themselves.

Elizabeth Tabor was pleased that the little blue bird's prediction had come true, in the form of an unblocked vein of rich silver ore, but she secretly wished that she could send a thousand blue birds to her daughter Silver Dollar, whose latest letter reeked of bad choices and lies that were threatening to destroy any future she might have.

The angry Circus midget and a dead German fighter pilot

Lies.

All her youngest daughter does is lie.

Silver Dollar fills her tear filled letters with one lie to her mother and then changes the story when she writes to another, without any realization that the people she writes might compare her stories.

On July 14, 1917 Elizabeth Tabor received yet another letter from 26 year old Silver Dollar asking for a favor, but this time, she was asking her mother for more than money.

This time she was asking her mother to lie about her life of poverty up at the Matchless, but she wasn't just asking her to lie, she was trying to guilt her mother into lying for her, so Silver could win the heart of her latest suitor.

The man of the hour was Clair E. Sloninger, from Lincoln, Nebraska and he was very rich, which was one of the traits Silver Dollar looked for in a man. He came from old money and his elaborate lifestyle had reminded Silver of how her life used to be and how it could be again.

So she lied.

Silver had met Clair while she was working as a chorus girl for The Beach review dance company and never thought that he would stick around more than one night, so she cozied up to him, let him buy her a expensive dinner and told him her family was just as rich as his.

And he liked it.

He liked it so much that he spent every free minute with her and even began talking about marriage, but luckily for Silver Dollar, his National Guard unit shipped out before he could head over to Denver to meet her family. His Unit was heading out to join The Punitive Expedition, in order to protect the town of Columbus, New Mexico and Silver Dollar couldn't have been happier.

From March 16, 1916 to February 14, 1917 a force of over 14,000 United States soldiers, under the command of Brig. General John J. "Black Jack" Pershing, entered northern Mexico in pursuit of Mexican bandit Francisco "Pancho" Villa.

An additional 140,000 members of the National Guard were also sent to protect the Mexico/United States border and the small town of Columbus, New Mexico from further attacks, after Pancho Villa's men burned down part of the town and killed some of its residents.

But Silver Dollar didn't care, she was simply hoping her current love interest Clair Sloninger wouldn't come back

Confident that she had seen the last of him and his insistent wish to meet her "Rich" family, Silver Dollar relaxed and continued life without him, until Clair returned from the war in February 1917, with a shiny Mexican Border service metal pinned to his jacket.

Which is when the real problem started.

Where Silver normally gave men a false name, such as Ruth Reed or Ruth La Vode, she had accidently told her rich suitor her real name, which he had no problem finding when he make a quick stopover in Denver, Colorado.

And Clair learned a lot more about his lady love than he bargained for.

When he arrived in Denver and began throwing the name Tabor around, he heard rumors that Silver was actually married to a man named Jack La Vode, that she had spent a night in jail under suspicion of theft and that her family had lost their fortune when the Silver market crashed.

Ashamed of her collections of lies and to stubborn to tell Clair the truth, Silver begged her mother to write to her suitor and hide the truth from him.

> *"Mamma, you are my only friend and I ask a favor of you. I told Clair that you were very religious and was so modest in your living that no one would know you were wealthy. If you see him or hear from him, for my sake, Please tell him you are wealthy."*
>
> *"And if you write to him, tell him that it is a lie about Jack La Vode, but please use fair stationary with no return address."*

Silver's letter ended with her decision to leave Lincoln, Nebraska and go into hiding until her mother could smooth things over with Clair.

But with Silver Dollar in hiding, Elizabeth had nowhere to send her daughter an answer to her demands and despite having Clair Sloninger's name and address within the pages of her daughter's latest letter, Elizabeth Tabor had no desire to clean up another one of her daughters messes.

Instead of dwelling on her daughter Silver Dollar's newest drama, Elizabeth tried to focus her energy on her daily trips into the deep, dusty shafts of her Matchless mine in search of the next silver vein and the chance for a bit of pocket money.

But surprisingly, as summer began to fade into fall and the Aspen leaves began their festival of colors, Elizabeth received an unexpected invitation from an old friend she hadn't heard from in years, which she quickly accepted.

Eva Luise James and her husband Even had been friends of the Tabors since the old mining days and Horace Tabor had even gifted the family a house on Denver's Clayton Avenue, before the Silver strike stripped Tabor's bank account bare.

The letter read that Eva's husband Even had died the previous August and with the house feeling a bit empty, Eva was offering Elizabeth to spend the winter with her and the children, once the weather turned and began showing its frosty face in Leadville.

And with the first signs of an early winter appearing in early-August, Elizabeth Tabor packed up her bags, locked her cabin up tight and headed to Denver.

"Mom, Mrs. Tabor is here." Numa announced, as he removed the over flowing grocery sacks from Elizabeth's tiny gloved hands, before helping her with her coat.

"Mrs. Tabor, you shouldn't have spent your money on this food for us, you don't have money to spare." Eva explained, as she continued wiping her damp hands on her apron.

"Now pet, you know I never need money for food when I come to Denver." Elizabeth explained with a smile, as she handed her coat to fourteen year old Numa. "I just picked this up at John Thompson's Grocery. Why, years ago Mr. Tabor and I spent thousands of dollars with them and sometimes I used to think they over charged me, so I'm just taking it back now when I need it."

Sitting down at the kitchen table and accepting a fresh cup of hot tea, Eva and Numa began unpacking the wonderful meats and fruit their guest had brought, while Elizabeth began idol chit chat with her old friend.

"I'm very sorry to hear that your Even had passed, may I ask what did he died of?" Elizabeth inquired, as she continued to let her tea seep.

"Even got sick with consumption last summer. "Eva explained, with a mournful tone to her voice. "He started getting fevers, chills and he was always feeling tired, but he still continued working hard to support us. We hoped it was just the flu, but when he started coughing up blood, we finally had to admit what he had."

"Please don't tell anyone, Mrs. Tabor." Numa begged, as he turned towards his mother's solemn gaze and then back over at Elizabeth "We don't want anyone to judge our family due to the dirty disease my father contracted, so we have told people he died choking on grape seeds and not the dreaded consumption disease of tuberculosis. He was already known as a gambler and a man who loved his drink, so we don't want him to also be judged in death."

Hearing the front door open, Elizabeth turned towards the sounds of children's laughter, as Numa's younger siblings walked into the house and removed their coats. But as the children walked into the kitchen to greet their guest, Elizabeth noticed some of them were missing.

"Eva, I hope you don't think me harsh, but I thought you and Even had five children and I only count three." Elizabeth asked, as she peered down the hallway looking for the missing children.

"Yes Mrs. Tabor, we did, but we lost little Jessie back in 1910 to the flu." Eva explained, as she set out cookies for the children over at the table. "Poor little dear was only three years old when he passed away."

"And were would Byron be?" Elizabeth asked, as she watched the children happily bite into freshly baked goodies.

"Now that's a long story, for another time." Eva, responded with a slight laugh. "After Even died of the consumption, the boys had to drop out of school and get jobs selling newspapers, but my Byron just kept getting in trouble. Finally I had no choice but to ship him off to an orphanage in Lancaster, Nebraska. I signed him off last year, right after he turned eleven."

"But Mama made us keep Mud!" Both Numa and Even Jr. laughed, as they teased their eight year old little sister. "My name is Maudella! Not Mud!" the little girl insisted, as she tried to finish her cookie in peace. "Stop calling me Mud, I don't like it!"

THE ANGRY CIRCUS MIDGET AND A DEAD GERMAN FIGHTER PILOT 249

As Elizabeth settled into her new winter home, she decided to take a quick trip to see her lawyer and as it turned out, another man who owned Horace Tabor money had recently died.

John Francis Campion, a wealthy Leadville mine owner who invested his gold profits in sugar beets and cement, had died on July 17, 1916, at the age of 67 with an unpaid debt due to H.A.W Tabor.

In 1889 Campion had approached Horace Tabor about purchasing stock in one of Tabor's many mines in the Leadville area and had agreed to purchase $50,000 worth, but didn't yet have the funds. Being kind hearted, Horace had agreed to place the unpaid stock in a Leadville bank, on hold, until Campion could come up with the funds.

Unfortunately, behind Horace Tabors back, John Campion made a back room deal with one of the bankers and had the unpaid stock turned into useable shares, which they split them between themselves.

In turn, Campion used the money to improve on his Little Jonny Mine, up in Leadville, which allowed him sinking a 120 foot shaft and hit a gold vein so wide and so pure that it was heralded as the world's richest Gold strike. And by October 29, 1893 the Little Jonny was shipping out 135 tons of gold a day.

And now the famous millionaire was dead.

On August 12, 1917 Elizabeth Tabor's lawyer Charles E. Friend filed a claim in the Denver court house, against the estate of John F. Campion for $50,000, which she stated was due her husband's estate. Given a September 16th court date, Elizabeth and her lawyer thanked the clerk, before walking down the now familiar court house steps.

Returning to her winter home, Elizabeth went into her friend Eva's kitchen to pour herself a cup of tea, to help relax her mind and grabbed a nearby newspaper as she headed outside to the porch. But Elizabeth's solemn expression quickly turned into a smile, as she stumbled upon a comical story in the Herald Democrat newspaper about a very angry circus midget.

CIRCUS MIDGET WHIPS WILD MAN AND GIANT

"Have care when you are working with the Midget Men in the side show of the Circus, when they pass through your town, as they are vicious. Very vicious.

Carl Morris, a midget in the show with W.M. & F.M. recently became enraged and beat up the wild man and the Giant. When interviewed by Police, they said they had only been kidding. Morris is not sorry and says they have no business picking on someone smaller than them."

- Tabor, Oklahoma August 24, 1917

"All rise. Court is now in session. The honorable Judge Ira. C. Rothgerber presiding"

"You may be seated"

As Elizabeth sat in a Denver court room, on September 16th, next to her lawyer, she prayed that maybe, just for once, someone who had stolen money from her precious Horace would be brought to justice, but today wouldn't be that day.

"Mrs. Tabor, I am aware that on August 12th you filed a claim against the estate of Mr. John Francis Campion, for the sum of $50,000, but I'm sorry Mrs. Tabor, despite what you have presented in court today, I will be denying your claim." Judge Rothgerber announced with the strike of his gavel.

"Dismissed!"

With her tail between her legs once again, Elizabeth Tabor thanked her lawyer and boarded the trolley. The ride seemed longer than usual, as she thought about how hard she had tried to regain her beloved Horace's stolen fortune and reset history into thinking highly of the

Tabor's once more.

But when she arrived back at Eva James home, in a bit of a funk, she discovered a phone message asking her to call Mr. Edward Ruter, the manager at The Matchless. Praying it was good news, she quickly called the number and was relieved to hear that they had finally located the silver vein from Shaft #7, which had collapsed back in February.

After almost a year of digging out the collapsed shaft and resetting the timbers, Shaft #7 was back up and running. Elizabeth's lessees James and Michael Ryan, along with their manager Edward Ruter had spent countless hours repairing the engine room, black smith shop and the housing over the shaft, as well as installing modern electricity to work the hoisting machinery.

Continuing the shaft an extra 246 feet, they dug out the old workings on the second and third levels until they found the silver vein, as well as iron and low grade carbonate.

The mines manager also informed Elizabeth they had begun sinking the shaft even lower, through a layer of quartzite, around four feet of porphyry and a thin sheet of lime, which revealed another layer of quartz. His was predicting that another layer of lime was expected at any time, as they had already dug the shaft an additional five feet.

After thanking her Mine manager and reassuring him that she would be returning to Leadville in the spring, she sat back in her chair and smiled. Maybe soon she could restore the Tabor name to its rightful place in history.

Within a few months, Colorado was graced with the New Year and welcomed in 1918. Eager to return to her Leadville cabin, Elizabeth Tabor waited until the first hummingbird of Spring buzzed passed the windows before she packed up her suitcases, gave Eva and the children hugs and kisses and boarded the train back to her Matchless mine.

Elizabeth was thrilled to find, upon her return to her cabin, that progress was still being made down shaft #7 and with stories of the World war, also known as the war to end all wars, filling the front pages of every newspaper she read, she had found herself becoming slightly numb to the daily headlines.

That is, until the Red Baron was finally shot down on April 21, 1918.

Manfred Albrecht Freiherr Von Richthfen was a 25 year old German fighter pilot who confirmed his 80th kill just the day before he was shot down by a combination of ground fire and Canadian fighter pilot Captain Arthur "Roy" Brown's expert aerial maneuvers.

Manfred's title as a Freiherr, which meant "Free Lord", was a title of nobility that all male members of his family were given and was commonly translated as "Baron". And when the young pilot began his career in May 1915, his choice to paint his plane bright red, combined with his nobility status as a Baron, quickly earned him the title of "The Red Baron."

His first confirmed aerial victory was on September 17, 1916, which he celebrated by ordering a silver cup to be engraved with the date and type of aircraft he had shot down. He continued this new tradition until his 60th confirmed kill, when the dwindling supply of silver in Germany forced him to have his cups crafted from a basic base metal instead.

As Manfred Richthofen was promoted to squadron commander, his new crew chose to also paint their planes red, in order to make their commander less conspicuous and prevent him from being singled out. The squadron soon earned the name "The flying circus", due to the colors of their planes and the unit's choice to use tents, trains and caravans when they traveled.

But his deadly career almost came to an abrupt end on July 6, 1917, when he suffered a serious head wound while airborne, that instantly caused him to experience temporary blindness and disorientation. Spinning out of control, but determined not to crash, he was able to regain enough eye sight to land his plane in a nearby field before he collapsed.

THE ANGRY CIRCUS MIDGET AND A DEAD GERMAN FIGHTER PILOT   253

Surviving his injuries, Manfred endured multiple operations to remove the bone fragments from his head, before being placed in an unfulfilling desk job. But with the German military keeping his status under wraps, they chose to boost moral by spreading false rumors that the British had offered a large award and an automatic Victoria Cross metal, for any allied pilot who shot down the Red Baron.

When Manfred Richthofen learned of the false propaganda being spread on his behalf, he quickly decided that he had no desire to finish his military career behind a desk. Climbing back into his infamous red aircraft, he continued flying until he encountered gunfire, which left him with a fatal chest wound, at 11am April 21, 1918.

Aware of his impending death, Manfred regained enough composure to save his beloved plane and land it safely in a nearby field. Following the path of the doomed pilot, two gunners, along with Sargent Ted Smout of the Australian Medical Corps arrived to find a badly wounded Manfred, who turned to the men and said "Alles Kaputt", as he took his last breath.

With the War raging in Europe and enveloping every country in its path, the local newspapers continued to cover the senseless bloodshed that poured out as a result. But on July 18th a news story blared out of the Matchless mines radio that was so heinous and so heart wrenching, that it made every mother, within ear shot, grab their own children just alittle bit tighter.

· The reported stabbing death of five children, the youngest being only 13, after attempts to butcher them in a rain of gunfire had failed.

Nikolay Aleksandrovich Romanov, known worldwide as Russia's Emperor Nicholas the 2nd, had just been slaughtered along with his wife, five children, three servants and their son's Doctor, inside the basement of a safe house. The emperor's wife Alix, being of German decent, was thought to have deliberately sabotaged Russia and aided Germany in the war.

Nicholas Romanov was bestowed the title of the Emperor of Russia at the age of 26, after watching his father Alexander 3rd die of nephritis, an ailment of the kidneys, at the age of only 49. In order to secure an heir to the throne, Nicholas married Alix of Hesse-Darmstadt, who went by the name Alexandra and their first child, a daughter named Olga, was born the following year, in 1895.

Unfortunately, the royal couple made a terrible first impression the following year, when thousands of people were stampeded to death during Nicholas's official crowning as the Tsar of Russia. Unaware of the deaths, which occurred during a public celebration near Moscow, the newly crowned Tsar and his wife were shunned as they happily enjoyed themselves during the coronation ball, held in their honor.

The couple then went on to have three more daughters, before giving birth to a son they named Alexei, who sadly was diagnosed with hemophilia.

When Russia entered into the World war, in August 1914, their soldiers performed so poorly that Nicholas the 2nd took control of the military and chose his wife Alexandra to aide him, which caused extreme tension with their subjects, as extreme poverty and hunger began ravaging the country.

On March 15, 1917 a newly elected legislature called Duma forced Nicholas the 2nd to step down from the throne and his family, joined willingly by their three devout servants and their son's Doctor, were placed under house arrest. In the void left by Russia's Tsar, The Bolshevilk's, later named the Russian Communist party, overthrew Duma and by order of their newly appointed leader Vladimir Lenin ordered the former Tsar and his family assassinated.

"Revolutions are meaningless without firing squads."
Vladimir Lenin- October 1917

At 2am, the morning of July 17, 1918 the Royal family and their four loyal subjects, were led into the basement of their safe house, where they were met by a firing squad, composed of seven Communist Soldiers from Central Europe and three members of the Bolshevilk's party.

The former Tsar was shot several times in the chest, as he pleaded for the lives of his children, while the rest of the group was barraged by a hail of rapid gunfire, which left his four daughters miraculously still alive.

Full of anger, the gunmen searched the surviving children and discovered that they had lined their clothing with diamonds and precious stones, which had given them some protection from the gunfire. Desperate to finish the job assigned to them, the armed men began stabbing the girls with their bayonets, before shooting them all in the head at close range.

The location of the bodies was unknown.

A FRESHLY BAKED PIE AND THE DIAMOND NECKLACE

Despite being sickened by the murder of Russia's Tsar and his family, people continued to swarm the movie houses in hopes of catching all the latest information from the front lines, in the form of News Reels.

News Reels had been the brain child of the Lumiere brothers, Auguste and Louis, who improved Thomas Edison's cinematograph and created a style that allowed simultaneous viewing, instead of Edison's peep show styled kinetoscope.

The Lumiere's first public viewing of their News Reels was exhibited on December 28, 1895 and showed a bull fight in Madrid Spain, while their second News Reel showed the coronation of Tzar Nicholas the 2nd in Moscow in May 1896. Each film was 17 meters long, which, when hand cranked through a projector, ran for approximately 50 seconds.

When the United States entered into the World War on April 6, 1917, President Thomas Woodrow Wilson saw the possibility of using film to promote the war and with the assistance of Hollywood film Companies, he was able to make it happen.

President Wilson began an aggressive pro-war, film driven public relations campaign in the fall of 1917, when he signed a contract with Universal Pictures, to produce Official State films. Along with the News Reels, the film companies were also asked to make war propaganda films such as "100% American" staring Mary Pickford and "Sic 'em Sam" with Douglas Fairbanks.

But too much war propaganda can really wear on you.

Between the movie houses, daily Newspapers and radio News briefs reporting on the war, Elizabeth Tabor welcomed the distraction that her little mining town of Leadville provided for her. As summer turned into fall and the aspen leaves began to glow with their gilded brilliance, she politely refused Eva James return invitation to spend the winter in Denver and decided to stay put.

But winters can be very lonely.

November 4, 1918 gifted Elizabeth with not only her normally scheduled grocery delivery, but her mail as well. At 64 years old, Elizabeth was quite content inside her cozy cabin, but welcomed any company, no matter how short.

After paying the delivery boy and giving him her list for the following week, Elizabeth walked over to her small table to unpack her box. Sifting through her mail, she noticed a letter from her yougest daughter Silver Dollar. Holding the letter in her hand for a moment, Elizabeth took a deep breath and sat down on a nearby chair, before she opened what she already knew would be pages filled with misery and desperation.

Sent from Chicago's Marion Hotel and using the name Ruth La Vode, Silver's letter told the now familiar story of being homeless and immediately needing money in order to survive. She claimed to of lost her job due to her clothes being thread bare, which had resulted in her losing her room and being cast out onto the street, with only 47 cents to her name.

The short letter ended with a request of $45 to pay her old hotel bill, as they were holding her personal possessions for ransom, as well as money to purchase new clothes so she could get a job.

Elizabeth laid the letter in her lap before looking out her cabin window, which gave her a clear view of the snow covered head frame of shaft #7. With the winter winds howling and the snow drifts around her cabin getting deeper, she prayed that her child would stop being so bull headed and move back in with her family, until she could straighten out her chaotic live style.

As 1918 came to its blustery end and welcomed 1919 with the sparkle of freshly fallen snow, Elizabeth Tabor added more coal to her stove, pulled her rocking chair closer to the warmth of the fire and prayed for her daughter.

As the months passed and March drew near, Elizabeth received a letter from her daughter Silver on February 28, 1919 that made her heart drop. Within its pages, Silver Dollar wrote that she wasn't only recovering from yet another bought of pneumonia, but that one of her teeth had become so infected that the doctor had to cut a hole in her jaw to drain the pus.

But surprisingly, Silver didn't ask for any money.

As a nice distraction, Elizabeth Tabor's neighbor John Mahoney stopped by the next day to drop off his weekly supply of Denver Post newspaper's for her, with an added surprise of fresh pie from his wife. But it was always his usual silly greeting that made Elizabeth smile.

"Hello the house!" Mr. Mahoney announced, as he walked towards the front door of the cabin, with his gifts in hand.

Popping her head out the window, Elizabeth replied "I am the maid and if you like I will relay any message to the lady of the house."

"Yes, can you please tell her that Mr. Mahoney just came by to drop off her newspapers and a fresh pie?" He laughed, as he held the pie up for her to see. "It's her favorite."

Elizabeth quickly closed the window and drew the curtain, only to quickly pull it back and reopen the window." I am Mrs. Tabor and you are?"

"I am Mr. John Mahoney and I am here to drop off this wonderful pie my wife has just baked." He announced again, as he held out the pie.

With a girlish giggle, Elizabeth pulled her head inside, closed the window and came out the front door to retrieve her treat. Her neighbors were wonderful friends and in the warmer months she would walk over the hill to have tea with his wife Mary while she tended to the children, 15 year old Margaret, 11 year old Rose and 7 year old Richard.

"You will be missing today's paper I'm afraid, as we had a slight accident this morning with one of the pies." Mr. Mahoney explained, as he set the pie down on Elizabeth's kitchen table, so he could retrieve the papers from under his arm.

"Since we don't have one of those fancy Frigidaire's, Mary cools her pies in the snow bank outside the kitchen window." He began, as he set down the newspapers. "So, I was reading todays paper, minding my own business, when she leaned out the window to retrieve the pies while doing a ballet pirouette. Well, the filling in the pie shifted when she spun back into the kitchen and all the filling spilled over the top of my head!" he added, as he pointed to his sticky hair.

"Did you get burned?" Elizabeth asked, as she began noticing tattle tale signs of the pie filling on his shirt.

"No, but I told Mary, thanks be to God that you had a pie and not a cast iron skillet!" John Mahoney added with a laugh.

After some idle chit chat, Mr. Mahoney headed out the door, leaving Elizabeth alone with over a weeks' worth of newspapers to keep her busy. As she cut a piece of pie and poured herself some tea, she happily grabbed the top paper, which surprisingly was an older paper dated Jan 15th, 1919 and it talked about a flood of molasses covering the streets of Boston.

Located at a Boston rail yard, where workers were loading freight cars, was a 58 foot high tank filled with 2.5 million gallons of crude molasses. But without warning, the bolts holding the bottom of the tank suddenly broke loose and shot out like bullets, as hot molasses began rushing out.

As the bottom of the tank finally gave way, an eight foot wave of molasses poured out and began sweeping away freight cars and caved in doors and windows of nearby buildings. Men working in the building's basement stood no chance, as the basements quickly filled with molasses, drowning the men.

Passing the freight cars, the deadly wave continued its carnage by knocking over a firehouse and pushing over the support beams for an elevated train line, before it ran out of steam.

In all, 21 people and dozens of horses drowned or were scalded to death and the city feared that it could take months to clean up the sticky mess.

It sounded horrible.

In Leadville, with March leading into spring, Elizabeth was soon able to spend more time outside her cabin and watch the blue birds perch themselves on the Matchless Mines many head frames and to tweet about the arrival of warmer weather.

As 1919 continued, the newspapers began talking about a possible peace treaty between Germany and the nations of the world, now that the World War had ended the previous November.

The Paris Peace Conference had begun on January 18, 1919, with 21 nations in attendance, minus Germany and Russia who were not allowed to attend. The conference was dominated by the "Big four",

President Wilson of the United States, Prime Minister Lloyd George of Great Britain, Prime Minister George Clemenceau of France and Prime Minister Vittorio Orlando of Italy and at one point President Wilson had to step in between Lloyd George and Clemenceau to prevent a fist fight.

The split between France and Great Britain was caused by France's desire to dismember Germany to make it impossible for them to start any future wars with France, where Britain, the United States and Italy were fearful that if Germany was dissolved, it would renew the War.

The treaty, known as the Treaty of Versailles due to it being signed inside France's Palace of Versailles, was finally signed on June 28, 1919 by two German representatives, who stood in for Germany's leader Kaiser Wilhelm the 2nd.

The final draft of the treaty focused mainly on Germany's roll in the war and further stipulated that Germany would be forced to pay for the devastation they caused. Germany was also stripped of 13% of its pre-war territory, all its overseas possessions and its remaining territory would be occupied by allied troops.

Another condition of the treaty was for Germany's leader Kaiser Wilhelm the 2nd to be formally tried, which was not a possibility, do to him being held captive by the Dutch Government, who refused to surrender him.

But the treaty was a start.

Unfortunately, the stress almost killed the President of the United States.

While Woodrow Wilson helped to draft out the Treaty, a suggestion was brought up for all the countries involved to form what would be called "The League of Nations". This concept was thought to maintain World peace and prevent future World Wars, by settling International disputes through negotiations and the idea was supported by many of the world leaders involved, including President Woodrow Wilson.

To promote the idea to the American People, President Wilson was sent on a 22 day, 8,000 mile tour of the United States, which set out on September 2, 1919, as Republican's opposed the formation of the idea and Democrats wanted the President to rally up support.

But the trip proved too much for the 62 year old President, who suffered from constant headaches and loss of appetite during his tour, finally collapsing of exhaustion in Pueblo, Colorado on September 25th. Returning to Washington for a much needed rest, the President suffered a massive stroke on October 2, 1919 that caused his entire left side to become paralyzed.

But unknown to the American public, this was not President Woodrow Wilson's first stroke.

Before Woodrow Wilson was President, he had been an instructor at Princeton University and in 1896, he suffered his first stroke at the age of 39, which left him with profound weakness and loss of dexterity in his right hand. Six years later, in 1902, he suffered from his second stroke, which added to his limited inability to use his right hand.

As Wilson shooed off his ailment's, by using the excuse that he had simply been writing too much, he suffered his third stroke in 1906 which almost blinded him in his left eye. Desperate to hide his condition and continue his political career, he pushed forward and was elected Governor of New Jersey in 1910 and then President of the United States in 1912.

Unfortunately, President Wilson suffered his fourth stroke in 1913, which caused his left arm to become partially paralyzed, but as was his way, he denied anything was wrong. But his stress level was really pushed to its limit on August 6, 1914 when his wife Ellen died of kidney disease at the age of 54 and her sudden death put the White House doctors on alert.

Marrying his second wife Edith Galt on December 18, 1915 seemed to put the President in a better mental state, but his doctors discovered that he was still suffering from a combination of hypertension and hardening of the arteries, but he again shooed off their claims.

But with the President's fifth stroke plastered across the front page of every newspaper in October 1919, Woodrow Wilson was no longer able to hide his secret from the world. But people have a tendency to forget about headlines and turn to the next page, which happily began containing more community events, than talk about the War.

Which was perfectly fine for Elizabeth Tabor.

While the world was focusing on peace treaties, kidnapped German dictators and unhealthy Presidents, Elizabeth had been spending her days climbing up and down the ladders of the Matchless Mines shaft #7. And always welcoming company, Elizabeth was alerted to the sound of a truck coming up her driveway, which always brought a smile to her face.

"Hello house!' John Mahoney announced, as both he and his wife Mary got out of their truck and approached Elizabeth, who had been throwing bread crumbs to the chipmunks. "Would you be able to alert the lady of the house that we would like to visit?"

Not able to play her usual game with her friends, as she wasn't inside her cabin, Elizabeth Tabor quickly covered her eyes with her hands for a second, before responding to the request. "Hello, I am the maid and I will tell the lady of the house that you wish to see her." She said with a giggle.

"Please tell her that we have brought over our new brownie camera." Mary announced, as she held out the small, black, leatherette covered box. "It cost us $2.00."

Covering her eyes again, Elizabeth waited a few seconds before exposing her face back to her friends. "Well Hello John and Mary, so nice of you to drop by!" Elizabeth announced, in a silly tone. "And what is that little black box in your hand?"

"It's our new brownie camera and I was hoping to take some pictures of you and Mary next to shaft #7" John announced, as he wound the camera to the next frame.

"Well, let me go freshen up first. "Elizabeth announced, as she began dusting bread crumbs off her blue and white plaid skirt. Going into her cabin, she quickly found a white scarf to tie around her hair and a clean, wool sweater to cover up her grease stained blouse.

With a smile, Elizabeth and her friends snapped a few poses near the head frame of shaft #7, with one photo showing Elizabeth and Mary holding on to a ladder, that had been leaning against the frame. Mary found that she had a hard time smiling, the closer she stood to the open mine shaft, but Elizabeth spent her waking hours climbing up and down those ladders, so she had no problem putting alittle spin on her poses.

With Leadville's mild October weather turning to snow, Elizabeth finished gathering up the coal and firewood on her enclosed porch and made sure her cabin was buttoned up tight, for the harsh winter storms she was expecting to endure once again.

But as the months flew by and Christmas came near, Elizabeth was shocked to see gifts from her daughter Silver Dollar delivered to her cabin, along with her groceries. Opening the packages, she discovered a beautiful, soft bathrobe and a bouquet of white lilies, which came with a simple card that said "Merry Christmas, Love Silver."

As Elizabeth cuddled the soft present, she prayed that this was a sign of a new start, for your youngest daughter and that all her problems

Elizabeth Tabor, on the left, next to the mine shaft's ladder-Legends of America

were past her.

As Elizabeth flipped her calendar from 1919 to 1920, she tried to keep herself busy until spring showed the beautiful tips of the daffodils poking through the snow. Her neighbors were unable to drop off their previously read newspapers until the snow melted, as the road up to her cabin wasn't easy to navigate and could get quite muddy.

But when the blue birds finally arrived and the Chipmunks came out of their burrows to have a much needed stretch and yawn, John Mahoney arrived at her front door with a mountain of old newspapers and a smile.

"I kept this paper on the top of the stack for you Mrs. Tabor", John announced, as he placed the twine wrapped stacks of papers on the table. "It seems your Isabella diamond has been stolen from the people who bought it at the auction."

Taking the paper off the stack, he folded the paper so the article was evident, before pointing to the headline. Taking the paper from John, Elizabeth was surprised to see that her former wedding present had again switched hands, before being stolen from its newest owner.

TABOR DIAMOND IS STOLEN

> "The famous Isabella diamond, formally the property of the late Senator Tabor and purchased by Mrs. Joseph Danz of Seattle, Washington last May for $15,000 was among the jewelry valued at $20,000 stolen by armed robbers, as she was about to enter the private garage of her Seattle home."

-Oak Creek Times-February 21, 1920

It did sadden Elizabeth that her precious diamond necklace was now in the hands of thieves, instead of lovingly being cared for by a woman who would treasure it like she had, but she had been apart from the diamond covered bauble for so long now, that it felt like a distance memory.

Thanking John for her new reading material, she poured herself a cup of tea and started to catch up the stories she had missed.

But the story she really wanted to read would be anything from your daughter Silver Dollar and finally on September 16, 1920, Elizabeth got her wish.

Elizabeth had been sending letters to her daughter, but rarely received one back, so her newest letter was quite a relief.

In the letter Silver asks her mother to please live at the Hotel for the winter, instead of up at the mine, but with money tight, Elizabeth didn't want her daughter to know she would rather not empty her purse for a different bed, if she didn't need to.

Silver also surprised her mother with the news that she doesn't have just one, but two suitors eager for her attention, but feels that neither man would make her happy. She mentions that both men are simply ordinary, working men that are clean and refined, but doesn't see a future with either of them, simply a home and a living.

She did talk about possibly marrying one of them, just so she doesn't have to worry about struggling again and that she would be better off. But she recently had her fortune told by a Medium, who told her that if she married, she would be terribly dissatisfied.

Silver's letter then quickly took a sinister turn, saying that the Medium also informed her that 1921 would bring a change for her, but was then very empathetic that she saw Silver Dollar dead.

Shocked, Elizabeth reread the last line, before grabbing her crucifix.

God, please don't take my precious Silver Dollar!

THE BURIED STEAMER TRUNK AND A BOX FULL OF POMEGRANATES

Still fearful for the life of her youngest daughter, following a mediums prediction of an early death, Elizabeth couldn't help but notice the similarities between Silver and her late father, whose own death was predicted by a palm reader so many years before.

Desperate for answers, Elizabeth decided to take up tea leaf readings to answer the questions her faith could not, despite the fact that predicting the future was considered a sin.

> *(Leviticus 20:27),"A man or a woman who acts as a medium or fortune teller shall be put to death by stoning: They have no one but themselves to blame for their death."*
> *(Deuteronomy 18:10-12) "Let there not be found among you anyone who immolates his son or daughter in the fire, nor a fortune teller, soothsayer, charmer, diviner or caster of spells, nor one who consults ghosts or spirits or seeks oracles from the dead. Anyone who does such things is an abomination to the Lord."*

Finding directions on reading tea leaves in the newspaper, Elizabeth Tabor began educating herself and found it a fascinating way to keep herself entertained on lonely winter nights.

1. Drink the contents of your tea, leaving about a teaspoon of liquid in the cup.
2. Take the cup by the handle, with your left hand and silently ask your question.
3. Swirl your cup three times in a counter-clockwise direction.
4. Carefully invert your cup over the saucer and leave it untouched for one minute.
5. Carefully turn your cup up the right way and read your fortune.

To keep track of her predictions, Elizabeth began recording her findings on scrap pieces of paper she would stack inside an empty box, so she could refer back to them later.

As winter began to take hold of Leadville, Elizabeth was pleasantly surprised by not only a letter from her daughter Silver Dollar, on November 10, 1920, but the promise of another Christmas gift.

In the very short letter, Silver informed her mother that she was sending her a box of a new, exotic fruit called a pomegranate, as they were quite popular in Chicago.

"You peel them somewhat like an orange, by peeling the thin skin off, but be careful of the insides. Then you pull the sections apart and eat the coverings off the seeds, but spit the seeds out after you have sucked off the juice"

With the bitter wind blowing out 1920 and a snow storm dumping 1921 onto Elizabeth Tabor's door step, she made sure to keep her wood stove stacked with coal, while happily sitting back in her rocking chair and sucking the juice off the seeds of her bright red pomegranates.

The New Year also brought Elizabeth another letter from her

THE BURIED STEAMER TRUNK AND A BOX FULL OF POMEGRANATES

daughter Silver, written from Chicago's Groveland Hotel, which hinted that the end could be near for her precious daughter.

In the short letter, dated January 15, 1921 and signed Mrs. Ruth Reid, Silver tells her worried mother that she is once again very sick. She also adds that she will explain her decision, to once again use a fake name, after she recovers, which causes Elizabeth to hang her head low in defeat.

Laying down the disappointing letter, Elizabeth Tabor sat back in her chair and gazed out at the whirling snow, which was doing a ballet of twirls around the wooden frame of shaft #7. Elizabeth had been desperately trying to raise the name Tabor back up to its original high standing around the country, yet she feared that despite all her hard work, Silver Dollar was doing her best to destroy it.

As the months continued and spring began to poke its sleepy head out from between the patches of ice and snow left behind by old man winter, Elizabeth made her way over to her neighbor Mary Mahoney's house for a cup of hot tea and some much needed idle chit chat.

After a few hours of catching up, Mary excused herself from her guest to work on the laundry, which gave Elizabeth some personal time to catch up on the large stack of old newspapers her neighbors had saved for her to read. But as she flipped though the headlines, she noticed a newspaper story that threatened to send the name Tabor into yet another downward spiral.

The discovery of a dead Tabor locked inside of a steamer trunk.

```
"Lying in a bed, in the very room
formally used by her daughter Mrs. Maude
Tabor, Mother Sarah Tabor solved the much
discussed Lawton, Michigan Trunk Murder
Mystery and declared her daughter's death
a suicide."

Eagle Valley Enterprise -February 11, 1921
```

But as more information came to light… the young woman's death was far from a suicide.

The unfortunate Emma Maude Tabor was the daughter of Luther Tabor, whose Grandfather Church Tabor was Horace Tabor's Great Uncle, which made them distance cousins, but still blood.

Luther Tabor had married Sarah L. Johnson and together they had three children: Florence: born in 1869, Emma Maude: born in 1873 and Walter O.: born in 1878. Sadly, Luther, a very successful attorney, died in 1911.

Emma Maude took a while to find love and didn't marry until she was 41, becoming the third wife of an embalmer named Joseph C. Virgo. Unfortunately, according to the numerous police reports surrounding her death, she died on May 1, 1916, but nobody could agree on the cause of her demise.

The original report was that the trunk, which held her body, was discovered inside the bedroom she originally occupied at her mother's house, but it was later revealed that it was found in the basement underneath a pile of old shingles.

Emma Maude's older sister Florence had moved back into her mother's home, after separating from her husband and was instructed by her mother not to touch the shingles in the basement, as they were being saved for kindling.

But on November 20, 1919 Florence noticed something sticking out from underneath the shingles and quickly noticed it was a trunk. Grabbing it by the handle, she began pulling it into the center of the basement, only to have the side of the truck rip away, exposing a human foot.

Frantic, Florence immediately ran out of the basement and over to a neighbor's house, where she called the police.

Florence and Maude's 80 year old mother Sarah Tabor explained to the police that the body belonged to her daughter Maude and that her daughter had died, in her arms, from an overdose of chloroform that

THE BURIED STEAMER TRUNK AND A BOX FULL OF POMEGRANATES 271

she used to treat her asthma. But once she discovered Maude had died, she had chosen not to contact the police and instead laid her daughter on a nearby couch and packed it with salt to preserve it.

And if the story wasn't already strange enough, the 80 year old frail woman then reported that by herself, she folded her daughter's body in half and placed it inside a steamer trunk full of coarse salt and locked the lid. The trunk, originally referred to as her daughter's "Hope chest", was then reportedly lowered into the basement by her elderly mother, by herself, with no help from anybody.

"I slid the steamer trunk down the cellar stairs by means of a rope snubbed about the door knob and then hid the trunk under a pile of shingles", Sarah Tabor explained to investigators, with a nonchalant twitch of her shoulders

"Why didn't you report her death?" the Coroner asked her, with a quizzical look, as he turned his gaze back to Dr. A.S. Warthin, the University of Michigan pathologist who had conducted the laboratory analysis on the body.

"Because we had made a pact that we would be buried together, so I kept her in the house." Mrs. Tabor replied, with a shrug.

"Ma'am, you originally stated that your daughter died from an accidental overdose of chloroform, following an asthma attack, but her autopsy showed that your daughter died of hemorrhages incident to the inducement of an abortion" Dr. Warthin informed her, as he flipped though his notes. "And I do find it quite disturbing that no infant, dead or otherwise has been located."

"She had an asthma attack and died." Sarah Tabor stated once again, with a face lacking any expression, "There was no child."

Pending a trial, set for March 27, 1922, Mrs. Sarah Tabor was sent to the Van Buren county Infirmary.

As the horrific story of "The Van Buren Trunk Murder" spread across the county, Elizabeth Tabor tried to keep her mind focused on her lessees and any silver ore she could hoist up from the dark depths of her beloved Matchless Mine. More than ever, Elizabeth needed to do whatever she could to restore the Tabor name.

As the year flew by and the aspen leaves changed from the bright, emerald green of spring, to the fall festival of golden light, Elizabeth's heart continued to ache, as she hadn't heard from her youngest daughter since January.

What if the fortune teller's prediction was true?

What has happened to my Silver Dollar?

But thankfully Elizabeth received a letter on November 5, 1921 that eased her mind at first, but then caused her to pray for daughter's immortal soul.

Written from Chicago's Groveland Park Hotel, but once again using her given name, Silver apologized to her mother for not keeping her updated on her condition, which was only now beginning to improve.

Writing from her sick bed, with no real explanation about the cause of her illness, Silver Dollar informed her mother that the Doctor had instructed her to rest and to forgo any excitement, coffee, tea or alcoholic beverages if she wanted to recover.

Silver did respond to her mother's repeated requests for her to move in with family, with the explanation that she just couldn't travel until she got stronger, but Elizabeth knew it was just another one of her daughter's stubborn excuses not to improve her lot in life.

With a disheartened spirit, Elizabeth Tabor responded to her daughter's letter and included a newspaper clipping about Father Dominic Pantanella, who held an inspiring sermon at Denver's Sacred Heart church, in hopes it would encourage Silver with whatever private demons she was facing.

As the year came to an unfulfilling end and 1922 exposed its promising face, Elizabeth was delighted to receive another letter from Silver Dollar on February 18, 1922, that held a tiny bit of promise for her troubled little girl.

Silver began her letter with another mention of a new illness, as well as a re-sprained ankle, but then mentioned that her Aunt Tilly and Cousin Andrew had visited her while they were Chicago and had promised to help her open up a flower shop.

Seventy seven year old Tilly was Elizabeth Tabors oldest sister and had been christened Matilda, but people had been calling her Tilly for as long as she could remember. Her husband Andrew had passed away in 1908, so their youngest son, Andrew Jr. put his life on hold to care for his mother.

Silver Dollar also mentioned that she was planning on sending her mother her old black, satin dolman jacket, so she could wear it around Leadville and cover her warn out clothes. Elizabeth's original reaction was of instant delight, until she read the remainder of the paragraph, which threatened to tear her own soul from her body.

"The jacket is a long one and you can get a lot of good out of it this summer around Leadville. It will cover up all your other clothes and I used to go out lots of times with only an apron under it."

Feeling a sudden shock run through her, Elizabeth sank into her rocking chair and held the letter to her heart. She had hoped that her precious daughter had not been selling her body to survive up in Chicago, but her description of what she wore underneath a shear jacket, confirmed Elizabeth's long standing fears that Silver's illnesses were caused by venereal infections.

With Mercury being the main cure used in the attempt to cure syphilis , some of the side effects, such as tooth loss and mouth ulcers would help explain Silver Dollar' letter from February 28, 1919. Inside its pages, Silver had informed her mother that a Doctor had found it necessary to cut into her jaw to drain a terrible ulceration.

Other symptoms such as fever, headaches and extreme fatigue also filled so many of the letters Silver had sent to her mother, that Elizabeth finally had to admit the unspoken truth…that her daughter was a common whore.

Fearful of what she might write in response to her daughter's letter, Elizabeth Tabor instead obtained a prayer card of Saint Anthony and mailed it back to Silver, until Elizabeth could pray on the information at hand.

Saint Anthony's life patterned Silver's, as they had both been born into wealthy families, only to be sent on a path of poverty at a young age and separated from life's luxuries.

Known as the Patron Saint of lost things, Saint Anthony's personal book of psalms and notes on the Lords teaching was stolen by a fellow Friar, only to be returned after Anthony preached a sermon to a school of fish.

But while Elizabeth hoped that the prayer card would help her daughter get right with God, a distant relative of her beloved Horace was facing trial in the murder of her own daughter, who was found salted and folded in half, inside a steamer trunk.

On March 27, 1922 Sarah Tabor, now 83, sat in a Van Buren County, Michigan court room, to face charges of killing her daughter Maude and hiding her body inside her basement.

Still sticking to her original story, for the time being, Sarah insisted that her daughter had indeed been suffering from a terrible asthma attack, but died after she accidently gave her too much chloroform, in an attempt to calm her down.

But as the questioning continued and the evidence was presented that proved that Maude had suffered a botched abortion, Sarah Tabor's story quickly changed.

"My daughter had left her husband, over his ill treatment of her and she came back to live with me. She was quite despondent and I found her dead with chloroform spilled on the bed. So, I put her in the trunk so nobody would find out." Sarah Tabor told the court, as she wrung her hands.

The officer then called Sarah Tabor's son Walter to the stand, where he gave a different account of his sister's death.

"Mother first told me about my sister's death on August 15, 1916, when she said that Maude had died of Asthma in a Colorado Springs Sanitarium, but when I came to see Mother around April 19, 1917, she took me into the basement and showed me my sister's body inside the trunk. It was hard to look at, as rats had eaten her nose off, but I could still tell it was my sister." Walter explained, with his head held down.

"Did your mother tell you how she died?" the officer asked, with his notebook at the ready.

"Yes, she said that Maude was pregnant, but had left her husband and Mother didn't want the child to get part of the families inheritance, so she over dosed Maude with Chloroform. She said she was sorry for what she did and said she wouldn't do it again, if given the chance." Walter explained, his head still held down.

"Joe Virgo did it!" Sarah Tabor announced, as she stood up from her chair and pointed at her ex-son–in-law, "He knew she was pregnant and forced her to have an abortion, then brought her to my house to die! I had to give her Chloroform to ease her suffering!"

"Order in the Court! Order in the Court!" the judge commanded, as he pounded his gavel. "By any chance are we able to interview Florence Tabor, the sister who originally found the body of Maude Tabor in the basement?' The Judge asked, as gazed over the officer, who was trying to calm down the accused.

"No, your Honor, we are not." The officer responded, "Mr. Florence Tabor poisoned herself last night, after she was released from police custody. We had detained and questioned her yesterday, in regards to her refusal to testify against her mother at today's hearing and we found her dead this morning."

With the trial continuing, the jury heard testimony from Sarah Tabor, Walter Tabor and the victim's former husband Joseph Virgo, who had quickly married his 4th wife only 9 months after Maude's death, but eventually the evidence all pointed towards Mrs. Sarah Tabor.

Her first trial resulted in a hung jury, after 36 hours of deliberation, while her second trial was dismissed due to lack of evidence.

After draining her life savings defending herself, she was a free woman.

With the verdict of the now infamous "Lawton, Michigan Trunk Murder" plastered on front pages across the nation, Elizabeth Tabor watched in silent shame, as the name Tabor was dragged through the mud, yet again.

And to add to her sorrow, her daughter Silver Dollar just sent her another tear filled letter and a request for more money.

On April 22, 1922 Elizabeth received a letter from her troubled daughter, which now contained the return address of Chicago's Hotel Carleon, but she was pleased to see she was back to using her given name again.

In the letter, Silver talked about how she had been laid up in bed for two months due to a sprained ankle, which was quickly followed by a bought of the flu, which had manifested itself into pneumonia. Due to her ailments, she was unable to work, so she was asking for $70, since the Groveland Hotel was holding her belonging hostage again.

She also mentioned how her stay at the Hotel Carleon would be short, as a friend of hers was getting a ten room flat and was going to be allowing Silver to room with her. She also apologized for not mailing her black, satin dolman jacket out yet, as it was unfortunately still locked inside one of the trunks being held hostage.

With a heavy sigh, Elizabeth Tabor grabbed her coat and bundled up tight for the now familiar one mile walk into town, to withdraw more money for her daughter. With newspapers packed inside her miners boots, to help keep out the cold breeze and her patched scarf tied tight around her ears, she spent her brisk walk saying the rosary for her beloved Silver Dollar.

A TINY MESH CAGE AND THE FRIENDLY PHARMACIST

"**Thank you for** the ride, young man", Elizabeth said with a smile, as 41 year old Charles Koch opened up the passenger door of his delivery truck, took Mrs. Tabor's dainty hand and helped her step down onto her snow packed driveway.

Elizabeth had been visiting the German run grocery of Koch and Pfannenschmid at 204 Harrison Ave. for a few years now, as they allowed her to pay what she could without question and always had a smile for her. As Charlie Koch retrieved her box from the back of his delivery truck, he looked over at Mrs. Tabor's cabin and was happy to see a small bit of smoke coming from her chimney pipe.

Unknown to Elizabeth, her brother Peter McCourt had made arrangements with the store's owner Fred Pfannschmid year's back, to send his sisters grocery bill to him, but with the understanding that he wanted Elizabeth to keep her pride and never know the truth.

As Mr. Koch carried the groceries into Elizabeth's cabin, he made mental notes on the size of her firewood stack and the warmth of the cabin, as he had also been asked to keep Peter updated on his sisters living conditions.

"Will there be anything else Fraulein?" Charlie asked, as he took a quick glance around the tidy little cabin.

"Thank you Charles's, but a ride back up to the cabin was all I needed." She said with a smile, as she began to take off her oversized jacket.

"Guten Abend", Charles Koch replied, with a polite tip of his hat.

"And good evening to you too, Sir", Elizabeth responded, with a laugh, as she gave him a quick curtsey.

Luckily for 67 year old Elizabeth's dwindling savings account, her daughter Silver hadn't asked for any more money as the year continued, but Elizabeth still watched every dime just in case. She really wished she could spent the bitter winter's at Leadville's Vendome hotel , but she feared that the next letter she received from Silver Dollar might be another request for a large amount of money, so she needed to keep her purse tight.

On October 19th Silver sent her mother a letter containing yet another address change, as well as informing her that she was once again going by the name Ruth Reid, which disappointed her mother, but Elizabeth was just thankful her daughter didn't ask for any money.

Elizabeth's youngest daughter would be turning 32 that coming December 17th and Elizabeth Tabor prayed that one day her precious Silver would decide to grow up and finally take control of her life.

Locked up tight in her cozy cabin, as the chilly November snow began creating a blanket of white crystals to welcome in the end of fall, Elizabeth received a letter from Silver that sounded a tiny bit optimistic and gave her mother just a glimmer of hope for her daughter's future.

In her November 9th letter, Silver Dollar mentioned how all her friends felt Elizabeth was a wonderful mother, which normally would be followed by a request for money, but this time it wasn't. Instead, her letter talked about how a friend of hers was planning on opening up a flower shop and that despite Silver's disappointment on not being able to start a dress shop with her cousin Andrew, as he had promised, she felt that a flower shop would be wonderful replacement.

Silver completed her letter by talking about her lifelong love of Ferns, how Chicago's Hotel Huntington, where she was currently renting a room, was full of stray cats and kittens she could pet and by telling her mother how she was finally optimistic about her future.

And despite feeling that this might be the last letter she would receive from Silver Dollar, before the calendar changed over to January 1, 1923, Elizabeth recieved a letter on Christmas that described the loneliness Silver felt, being away from her family for the holiday.

> "Dear Mamma,
>
> This is a lonely Christmas for me. It always is, for I think of home and the snows of Colorado.
>
> It is very warm today. Few people are wearing their heavy coats and that seems strange to me.
>
> Next Christmas I hope and pray that we are together. Maybe you can come here to live with me and I am going to make an effort to go to Colorado for a visit this coming spring.
>
> Mamma dear, always remember that you are the nearest and dearest thing in my life and that if God will help me, we will be together this coming 1923."

The letter itself was signed Silver, but the envelope held a return address with the name Ruth Reid, which caused Elizabeth to let out a disappointing sigh of discouragement. How was her daughter ever going to find herself if she kept hiding behind fake names and lies?

Needing a mental distraction, Elizabeth got up out of her chair and made her way over to her dry wood bin in the corner of the kitchen. She always made sure to bring enough wood and coal inside her cabin to carry her through the first few months of winter, while the rest of her wood stood stacked on her enclosed front porch, but she really missed the luxury of the steam heat that the Vendome Hotel offered its winter guests.

After grabbing a few small logs, she laid them next to the woodstove before opening the small metal door. Poking at the embers with her fire iron, she continued thinking about the hospitality she enjoyed during her past visits to the Vendome and the long hours spent swapping old mining stories, inside the Hotel's dining room.

But as she glanced over to her youngest daughter's latest letter, she instantly felt a wave a of guilt flow through her body. Adding an extra log to the fire, Elizabeth slowly closed the door to her woodstove before standing up to add water to her tea kettle.

Any money selfishly spent on herself, for even for the slightest creature comfort, would take money away from her child.

As the water in the kettle began to simmer, Elizabeth went over to her book shelf and pulled down a box of old newspaper clippings that she had been saving. Full of wonderful old stories, about the mines around Leadville and all the great things her beloved Horace had done for the city ,Elizabeth decided that reading them out loud to herself would just have to do for now.

Flipping through the pile, she stumbled upon a few stories on the construction of Leadville's Tabor Opera house, which always made her smile. Pouring herself a cup of hot water, she placed some loose tea leaves inside her tea ball and watched as the tiny mesh cage quickly sank to the bottom of her cup, before she made herself comfortable.

In August 1879, the location chosen for the Leadville Opera house was originally occupied by Horace Tabor's wood framed home, that he shared with his first wife and young son, but with Harrison Ave. becoming a mecca for new businesses, Tabor decided to move the house.

The family's home was carefully jacked up and logs were placed underneath of the structure, while a team of horses slowly pulled the house towards its new home, soon to be located at 116 East 5th street.

A TINY MESH CAGE AND THE FRIENDLY PHARMACIST   281

It was a slow, carefully done procedure, as the team would be constantly stopped to allow the back logs to be placed in the front of the home, to allow a seamless flow.

Horace Tabors friend William Bush had the original vision for Leadville's Opera house, which he had named The Bush Opera house, but unfortunately he ran out of money. Horace was quite willing to become an investor, to help his friend out with the funding, but once the amount of money Tabor invested became more than his friend Billy Bush, the name of the Opera was changed to the Tabor Opera house.

Which did not hold well with his friend.

To prevent hard feeling, Horace Tabor bought his friend out of his share of the Opera house, so he would be free to build something else, but the hard feelings still persisted.

The buildings original contractor J.T Roberts had broken ground on August 1, 1879, before selling the contract to L.E Roberts, but despite a rocky start, the Opera house still only took 102 days to construct. The handsome three story brick building, with its decorative trim work constructed of Portland cement, had a foot print of 60'x 100' and placed one spacious store front on either side of the buildings grand front entrance.

But it was the store on the North side that held history for Elizabeth.

This store was rented by Elizabeth's former lover Jake Sands, who placed his clothing store Sands, Pelton and Company within its walls, to give him and Elizabeth a fresh start, after leaving Black Hawk and her husband behind on October 1, 1879.

In regards to the materials used for the buildings construction, since most of it didn't exist in Leadville, Horace Tabor had to have his supplies brought in by wagons over Mosquito Pass. The large 6'x11'panes of glass, used on the store fronts windows, were tightly packed in straw to survive the bumpy journey and as soon as they arrived in Leadville, they were installed in mere 30 minutes.

With the Opera houses opening night scheduled for November 2,

1879, Horace Tabor gave one last inspection, by sitting in each seat, to assure that each theatergoer had a clear view of the stage. Unfortunately, Horace soon discovered that the entire second row of seats, in the balcony area, couldn't see the stage.

With only 12 hours before the doors opened, Horace had work crews come in and carefully remove the iron columns supporting the front of the balcony. Cutting them down 8", the workmen then placed them back with such expertise, that not a single crack formed in the plaster.

Not to be left out of opening night, Tabors friend Billy Bush, who owned the Clarendon Hotel next door, was allowed to build a connecting covered walk way on the third floor, so his Hotel guests wouldn't have to leave the warmth of the Hotel to see the shows.

Small price to pay when your friend's former Opera house now has the name Tabor plastered across the front of it.

But as Elizabeth Tabor spent her lonely winter nights reading old

Leadville Opera house- The Denver Public Library, Western History Collection-X-172

newspaper clippings, adding wood to her stove and watching her wall calendar change to 1923, her youngest daughter Silver Dollar was contemplating the true meaning of life and wondering if the rules could be broken.

It was almost May before Elizabeth heard from her daughter again and her letter was quite worrisome, as it appeared she was once again homeless and living with another friend. Her letter gave no mention of the flower shop she was supposto to help manage and listed her return address as Ruth Reid, Grant

Park Hotel, all the while complaining that colored people had moved into her former apartment building, which is why she left.

"Perhaps things might be different, if I were different. I'm so afraid to wander away from the legitimate path. I'm afraid of danger and the price that people pay for breaking the law.

I guess it is your prayers that give me the fear, to keep me back. Sometime we may all be rewarded for our struggles."

But all the worrying and praying for her dear Silver, couldn't have possibly prepared Elizabeth Tabor for what was written inside the pages of her daughter's May 15th letter, as Elizabeth discovered that her own sisters son had made sexual advances towards his own cousin.

Elizabeth's oldest sister Matilda, called Tilly by her family, had visited with Silver the previous February along with her son Andrew, who had made promises to Silver in regards to a dress shop. But now it seems he wanted sexual favors in exchange for his help.

In Andrews's defense, he may have thought that perhaps since Silver's sister Lily had married one of her first cousins that perhaps Silver Dollar might follow in her footsteps in regards to Andrew, but Silver was having no part of it.

It appeared that Aunt Tilly was also offering for Silver to live with them, since she was still homeless and simply living with friends, but when Andrew tried to sweeten the deal in private, by turning it sexual, Silver turned tail and ran.

Heartbroken, Elizabeth laid the letter in her lap and started to cry. She had prayed so hard for her daughter to move in with family, any of her family, so she could get help for her self-destructive life style, but just when she was finally ready to take that first step, the rug was pulled out from under her.

But Elizabeth's fears were happily set aside, for a while at least, when a package arrived from Silver Dollar, to celebrate her mother's 69th birthday on September 25th, 1923.

Opening up the parcel, Elizabeth discovered a beautiful bathrobe and a box of candy, which she quickly began to eat. Not wanting to dirty the robe, she carefully placed it back inside its box and sat it on her bed.

But it was her daughter's next letter, which Elizabeth received on October 11th that shook her to her core.

When Elizabeth Tabor first discovered that her youngest daughter was a lush and wasn't able to control her drinking, she hoped and prayed that something would happen to turn her away from her liquid poison. And when Prohibition went into effect on January 16, 1920, which banned the production, importation, transportation, sale, possession and consumption of alcoholic beverages, Elizabeth felt her prayers had been answered.

But every law has its loop holes.

The legal exemptions allowed Pharmacists to prescribe liquor for any type of ailment, ranging from anxiety to the flu, while churches were able to purchase wine for religious purposes. This resulted in the number of registered Pharmacists to triple, while churches and synagogues saw record increases in church enrollment, as the men of the cloth were legally allowed to obtain wine for the members of their congregations.

And it was one of these loopholes that her precious daughter was

A TINY MESH CAGE AND THE FRIENDLY PHARMACIST 285

bragging about in her current October 11th letter.

Talking about her latest illness, Silver informed her mother that she once again had contracted pneumonia, but thankfully her new boyfriend was a Doctor and could write her prescriptions for her beloved whiskey.

> *"I have friend here who is a Doctor. I go out with him very often and if it had not been for him, I might not have pulled through. He has a drug store and he gave me all my medications and whiskey and was a great help to me."*

Silver continued her letter by saying that she had moved into The Drexel Hotel, but was looking for a new place to live, as the hotel's manager locks all the exterior doors at 1am and if you are not inside by then, you can't get into your room until morning.

She also apologized for not visiting her mother during the summer, like she had originally promised, claimed that travel is just too expensive and how "Money doesn't just grow on trees."

The letter ended with her talking about a marriage proposal from a man in California, that she really didn't like and how she regretted running from her former lover Clair Sloniger, who now no man can match.

But according to her last letter of 1923, Silver Dollar must have changed her mind.

> *"My Dear Mamma,*
> *Did you receive my last letter, in which I told you about getting married this past August?"*

Shocked, Elizabeth found herself frozen for a second, before laying the letter to her heart.

My baby girl got married!

She finally settled down.

Giving a silent prayer that the marriage was a good match, Elizabeth continued holding the letter, as she made her way over to her rocking chair. Sitting down, she closed her eyes and took a deep breathe before opening the letter once more. As her eyes began filling with tears of joy, she read that her new Son-in-law William James Ryan was a good man, who thought the world of Silver Dollar and promised that she would never want for anything.

But as the letter continued singing her new husbands praises, Silver's words suddenly began to turn dark, as she started complaining of her new husband's lack of wealth and the feeling that she had simply settled.

> *"I have only a few more years before my looks are gone. I planned all along on getting a rich man and paying up all your mortgages and all our old bills in Colorado and all that, but I couldn't make the grade. God may help us sometime unexpectedly."*

Upon reading the last part of her daughter's letter, Elizabeth's heart began to sink. All she wanted was for her daughter to be happy and be with a man who would treat her right, but now it sounded like Silver was getting ready to chase the rabbit, once again.

And the next letter Silver sent her mother, described her doing just that.

Waiting until the calendar flipped over to 1924, Silver's first letter of the New Year proved that all of her mother's hopes and prayers for her future had been for not.

Despite using the name Mrs. W.J. Ryan on the outside of her envelope, Silver confessed to her mother that she had quickly divorced her husband for a new man, who wished to marry her in the Spring. She gave no reason for the divorce, except the quick line "I guess you

A TINY MESH CAGE AND THE FRIENDLY PHARMACIST   287

never know a person until you live with them."

Silver mentioned that she was once again rooming with a friend, this time with a woman named Mrs. Norman, who had a large apartment on Michigan Ave. But it was the comment. "This large apartment is extremely comfy, so I think this address will be permanent", that confused Elizabeth.

If Silver Dollar was planning on marrying a new man in the coming spring, who had a sweet little daughter, then why would she be talking about staying permanently with her friend Mrs. Norman?

Elizabeth wouldn't get that answer, or even hear back from Silver, for another year.

Desperate for answers, Elizabeth spend her free time attempting to discover what was happening with her youngest daughter, through the shapes the tea leaves made as they settled along the inside rim of her tea cups.

Known as Tasseography, the diviner looks for familiar patterns in the leaves, with each shape holding different meanings, in regards to the questions asked. A shape that resembles a snake can be interrupted as meaning a falsehood, a spade could mean good fortune through industry, a mountain could mean a journey of hindrance and a house could mean change or success.

Each leaf pattern that Elizabeth saw, she sketched out on small pieces of paper with the name of the object she felt it resembled and the date, in hopes of seeing a pattern form.

But Elizabeth's frantic plea every night was to simply hear back from her daughter.

Turning her wall calendar over once again, this time to 1925, Elizabeth finally received her next letter from Silver Dollar on January 18th.

Seeing that the return address on the envelope was listed as R. Tabor, it was quiet obvious to Elizabeth that her youngest daughter never married the previous spring, but it was nice to see she was not using another of her many aliases.

Silver started out her letter by apologizing for not writing sooner or sending her mother a Christmas gift, followed by the confession that she was still recovering from numerous burns, caused by being scalded. She explained that the burns covered her face, chest, one shoulder, both arms, as well as both hands and had caused her to be bed ridden for months.

Without explaining how she burned herself, be it from a tea pot or possibly from working as a laundress, she went on to praise her friends who helped care for. Without the money for a hospital stay, a lady friend and her husband tended to her wounds, which had healed up wonderfully, with no signs of lasting scars.

She went on to mention that her chest received the majority of the steam, which was still covered in red blotches where the skin hasn't yet healed, but at least her face looks normal again.

A second letter sent on April 18th was quite optimistic, in regards to the possibility of starting a dress shop with a lady friend, but it appeared that another injury had sidelined any progress in the job department.

As Elizabeth read about Silver Dollar recovering from a fractured knee and how she is now just relearning how to walk, she gently laid the letter in her lap and started to cry.

Since Horace died, Elizabeth had tried her hardest to give her daughters the best life she could, considering the circumstance her husband's death had left them in, yet both girls went in directions she couldn't have ever possibly imagined.

Originally when her oldest daughter Lily married her first cousin, Elizabeth felt that was the worst sin that could have ever been cast onto the Tabor name, but her youngest daughter Silver Dollar, her sweet Honey Maid, seemed desperate to burn the name Tabor to the ground.

I am so sorry Horace! I'm so sorry! Please tell me what you want me to do!

As Elizabeth dove deep into her religion and prayed for a miracle,

A TINY MESH CAGE AND THE FRIENDLY PHARMACIST

a sliver of hope arrived in the form of a short, but desperate letter from Silver on August 4th, which hinted at her desire to be near her family again.

> "My Dear Mama,
> Please write me, as I worry so about you. I have dreamed of you and Papa so often lately. Please let me know how you are.
> Your loving child Silver"

But all the prayer's and desperate plea's to God, to save the soul of her precious baby girl, fell on deaf ears. On September 18, 1925, Silver Dollar Echo Honeymoon Tabor succeeded on giving the Tabor name its final push over the edge.

Silver Dollar was dead.

The Stench of Embalming Fluid and the Heart Wrenching Lie

"**Ma'am, there is** an urgent call for you at the store and I've been asked to bring you into town." Charlie Koch informed Elizabeth Tabor, with a solemn tone, as he held his hat in his hands.

Wiping the silver ore dust from her apron, Elizabeth turned to see the face of a man who normally greeted her with a smile, but now appeared to be struggling with a terrible secret.

"Charlie, what happened? Whats wrong?" Elizabeth asked, as the grocery store owner silently began to walk her towards his delivery truck. Opening the passenger side door, he couldn't' even meet the eyes of the woman who he drove home from his store twice a month ,as he knew he needed to keep his demeanor for the drive back into town.

Their truck rides had been filled with so many of Elizabeth's stories about her life and that of her children over the years, that Charles knew the struggles his elderly customer had gone through and now he wanted to be there for her as she faced the inevitable.

Closing the trucks door, he gazed through the passenger side window for a second and saw the frightened face of a woman who was

THE STENCH OF EMBALMING FLUID AND THE HEART WRENCHING LIE   291

only seven days shy of her 71st birthday. With his hands still on the door, he quickly looked off to the side, before pushing himself away from the truck.

Walking around to the driver's door, he quickly jumped in, closed his door and shoved the truck into gear. Feeling Elizabeth's fear, he wiped a tear from his eye as he headed the truck back into town.

"I'm sorry, my dear Fraulein…but its' not my place."

As the silent truck approached its destination, Charlie noticed that reporters were already starting to swarm Harrison Ave., desperate to get that first comment from Mrs. Horace Tabor. "Fraulein, I need you to keep your head down for a minute my dear, while I make this corner." He instructed, as he placed his right hand over her shoulders.

Taking a side road towards Harrison Ave., Charlie Koch pulled down the alley that led to the delivery entrance of his store. Pulling up to his building, he saw his partner Fred Pfannenschmid pop his head out of the back door and quickly look around, before walking over to the truck and opening the passenger door.

As the two men led Elizabeth Tabor into their store, they made sure to lock the door behind them, before taking her over to the phone. As she walked, Elizabeth noticed that the store was free of customers and that newspaper reporters were looking through the stores large glass windows and demanding entry, as they frantically shook the locked front door.

Guiding Mrs. Tabor over to a large wooden desk and pulling out the chair so she could sit down, Elizabeth could hear her name being screamed at her through the glass. Looking over towards the sound, she could see men frantically waving their arms, in a desperate attempt to gain her attention.

"Lily's number is right here Mrs. Tabor Ma'am, she is waiting for your call", Mr. Pfannenschmid informed her, as he slowly backed away.

Within 5 minutes, Elizabeth was screaming.

Horace and Elizabeth Tabor's youngest child's life had ended in severe agony, surrounded by fellow apartment dwellers on Chicago's Ellis Ave., who couldn't do anything but watch her die. Hearing the screams, they had run into her apartment, where they found her body severely scalded, the floor pooled with water and a large kettle laying nearby.

As Silver Dollar fell onto the floor and began going into shock, her neighbors did what they could to cool her wounds, while others called for a doctor, but she died before help arrived.

Removing her body from the building, the police began interviewing witnesses who gave very similar stories. Words like vamp, drunkard, party girl and boozy were used to describe the dead woman, as well as stories of false names, strange men and that she had severely scalded herself only a year previously, which might help explain why she went into shock and died so quickly.

Following a search of her room, the officers found proof of many different names the woman had used, but the name Silver Tabor was discovered on the many letters that littered her room, as well as on a letter from a family member in Chicago. A framed photo of a colored man was also found, with a disturbing note taped to the back of the frame, which led the officers to believe the Tabor woman might have been murdered.

The photo was of a saloon owner, with a note that read "Jack Reid would be responsible or know all about it, if I am ever killed." Luckily, with help of the buildings tenants, the man was quickly apprehended.

As Silver Dollars body cooled in the city's morgue, Reid was questioned by officers and explained that the woman had frequented his saloon, but he hadn't seen her for almost a year. And with no evidence to hold him on and the fact that none of the witnesses to the woman's death mentioned him anywhere near the apartment when she was scalded, Jack Reid was free to go.

Happy to be walking out of the Police station a free man, Jack had a smile on his face and a little skip to his step…but back in Colorado,

THE STENCH OF EMBALMING FLUID AND THE HEART WRENCHING LIE   293

Elizabeth Tabor was just getting started on her journey.

With the Koch and Pfannenschmid Grocery store surrounded by reporters, the owners knew they had to get Mrs. Tabor out of Leadville while things calmed down. Composing herself for a few minutes, Elizabeth was able to call her friend Eva James in Denver and ask if she could come stay with her, which is the only thing that brought even a little smile to Elizabeth's face.

The next trick was getting Mrs. Tabor onto a train to Denver, without being seen, but luckily Colorado reporters are easily distracted. But the ones back in Chicago were keeping a very close eye out for anyone who might be attempting to identify the body of the scalded woman, who was lying in their local morgue.

Dodging reporters, Clotilda McCabe, Elizabeth Tabor's 58 year old sister and Lily Last, Silver Dollars 41 year old sister, traveled to Chicago to see who was really underneath the sheet.

The cities morgue was located inside Chicago's Bethany Hospital, but with Silver's body not yet identified, she was listed under the name she had used to rent her last apartment, which was Ruth Norman.

Wheeling the sheet draped body into the room, the mortician explained to both Clotilda and Lily that an autopsy had already been performed and that the body was covered in large incisions, as well as the burns. But nothing could have prepared them for what they saw.

Upon removing the sheet, the women were immediately faced with 35 year old Silver Dollar's nude body and the overwhelming stench of embalming fluid and Listerine. Quickly covering up their noses with their gloved hands, the women glanced down at Silver's horrific burns and the large, crudely stitched up incisions, which began at her neck and ended at her groin.

Her scalded skin appeared to have peeled off in sheets, leaving behind deeply grooved areas of muscle, which exposed the bone beneath. The parts of her skin that were still partially intact where covered in blisters, ranging from pea size to the size of a tea cup and had already turned the bluish, purple shade of death.

"The deceased was also found to be suffering from sclerosis of the liver. We discovered old scars on her upper body, arms, hands and face from previous burns, which may have weakened her body when she suffered the current burns and might help explain why she died so quickly." The mortician explained, as he used his pencil to point out the scarred areas

"Sorry, but this woman is not my sister." Lily told the mortician, as she looked away from the body on the gurney. "This woman is too tall. My little sister was only 5'2"."

But as the mortician began recovering the body, Silver's Aunt Clotilda took one last look and felt certain this was the remains of her niece. "Sir, unlike my niece Lily here, I do believe this is my sister's youngest child and I would like to claim the body."

After agreeing to make the arrangements, Ruth Normans chart was changed to the name Silver Dollar Tabor and with no desire to remain in the hospitals morgue any longer than needed, the two women quickly headed outside for some fresh air.

"Were you here to claim the body of the scalded woman?" a reporter yelled, as a swarm of men wearing grey suits pounced on the two women. "Is this really Senator Tabor's daughter?" another man asked, as the women held their heads down and tried their best to dodge the men.

"Is it true that your sister was a whore?" a man in the back yelled, while he held his pencil at the ready.

Stopping dead in her tracks, Lily turned towards the voice, held her head high and decided she needed to set the record straight, once and for all.

"My sister Mary Echo Tabor, who was nicknamed Silver Dollar by our father, is not the dead woman in Chicago. My sister entered a convent against the wishes of her family. Our family will respect her wishes to lose her identity from the entire world and I am not at

THE STENCH OF EMBALMING FLUID AND THE HEART WRENCHING LIE 295

liberty to tell you were that convent is." Lily answered, as the reporters continued to ask questions.

"Can you explain why people say she looks like your sister?" another reporter barked out, above the voice of the rest.

"The description of the woman in Chicago is not of my sister. This Chicago woman was of medium large stature where my sister is five feet two inches tall, with reddish brown hair. This woman is not my sister!" Lily explained, as she grabbed her Aunt Clotilda by the arm and began leading her through the sea of reporters.

"If your sister is in a convent, then why did you travel to Chicago to view the burned woman's body?" a reporter yelled, as the swarm of men continued to follow the women.

Realizing that the reporters had just caught on to Lily's lie, the two women quickened their pace, entered their waiting car and slammed the door fast.

Returning to the safety of their Hotel, Clotilda called her brother Peter back in Colorado, to give him the bad news and asked if he would pay to keep Silver from a pauper's grave. After contacting the mortuary, Peter McCourt wired $300 to Chicago and requested no head stone be placed on the grave, in an attempt to discourage souvenir hunters.

Lacking the public viewings and elaborate parade that led her father Horace Austin Warner Tabor to his final resting place, the child whose voice had the ring of a Silver Dollar was laid to rest surrounded only by her friends. The only clue that the scalded woman, who laid inside the box, was ever loved by her family, was her mother's request for a burial in Chicago's Holy Sepulchre Catholic cemetery.

A lost, poisoned child lying beneath consecrated ground, without the gift of final rights to save her soul.

But unfortunately, the newspaper reporters still wanted to hear from Elizabeth Tabor and grab that last interview for their front pages, but nobody could locate her. Luckily, a few reporters had discovered the area's she would frequent in Denver and she was finally located while shopping at Johnson groceries.

"Mrs. Tabor! Mrs. Tabor! Can you tell us about your daughter Silver's death?" the eager suit clad men asked, as they gathered around the tiny woman.

"I have no idea what you are talking about. My daughter is serving our Lord in a Convent." Elizabeth replied, as she calmly answered the man's question. "Now if you will excuse me…"

"Mrs. Tabor! Is it true your daughter died in the black belt of Chicago?" another reporter barked at Elizabeth, as he blocked her path.

Taking a deep breathe, Elizabeth looked at the men holding notebooks, with their pencils at the ready and let out a sigh of total disgust. Their overly excited expressions and eager eyes showed her that these snakes lacked even a drop of sympathy, over a mother's loss of her child.

They just wanted a story.

"My daughter is not dead." Elizabeth announced, with her head held high. "The woman they buried in Chicago is nothing but an imposter. Like I said before and so has my older daughter Lily, Silver is in a convent serving our Lord and savior. Now if you will excuse me, I have shopping to do."

Studying her face for any signs of sorrow, the reporters finally shrugged their shoulders and printed that the family denied that the scalded woman was Silver Dollar.

And the story was dropped.

With the local newspapers focusing on new stories and no longer filling their headlines with shameful stories about her daughter, Elizabeth was finally able to focus on her grief. Her precious baby girl was dead and buried in an unmarked grave, over a thousand miles away, while her own mother lied to the world to protect the Tabor name.

Elizabeth Tabor's penance would now come due.

Like a deadly virus eating at her soul, the many sins of Elizabeth

Elizabeth Tabor and Eva James walking-Legends of America

Tabor could potentially be damning and unforgivable, if she doesn't chose to throw herself onto the feet of God and beg for forgiveness. She believed that her sin of adultery caused the death of her first child, before he could even take a breath and now her youngest daughter lies in consecrated ground, due only to the guilt of her mother, not because the right was earned through her devotion to God.

Silver Dollar was buried within the walls of a Catholic Cemetery, with a soul full of unrepented sin and now it was on her mother's shoulders to save her soul from purgatory.

Which meant Elizabeth Tabor needed to start attending daily mass.

And with Elizabeth now living with her friend Eva James in Denver, inside the James family's new house, Elizabeth's temporary address put her closer than ever to her beloved Sacred Heart Catholic church.

After becoming a widow in 1916, Eva James had struggled to make ends meet. She had pulled her son's out of school to work and sent yet another son to a Nebraska Orphanage, but she still found it necessary to sell their family home on Clayton Ave. But luckily, with the money from the sale, she was able to purchase a small framed house at 1812 Logan Street.

Which suited Elizabeth Tabor just fine.

Originally, when the James family lived on Clayton Ave., Elizabeth found that the sacred Heart Church was an un-walkable three miles away and she had to rely on her friend Eva to drive her. But now that the family lived on Logan Street, Elizabeth discovered that she simply needed to walk one block down to 17th street and catch the trolley, which dropped her almost onto the door steps of her cherished church.

Located at 2760 Larimer Street, the brick, Gothic styled house of God greeted Elizabeth like an old friend. As she stood on the sidewalk and faced the church's raised front entrance, she glanced to her left and smiled at the sight of the white, wrought iron fence that still surrounded the church's rectory.

Also known as a Clergy house, the Rectory was a simple styled, two story tall brick building that housed the church's devoted Priests and Nun's within its walls. But it was the fence that encompassed the almost 4,000 sq. ft. building that brought back wonderful memories for Elizabeth.

Back when the Tabor's money flowed like fine wine and gold coins were passed out in celebration of the birth of their first daughter, Horace and Elizabeth had donated the beautiful iron fence to the church, so it could border the rectory's lush green lawn, which in itself was a show of status.

But today, as Elizabeth ran her dainty hands slowly across the top of the fence, she thought back to the sermons her husband Horace had attended at this church, simply to appease her, then to except the Lord in his final moments of life and die in his glory.

It was the sound of the churches heavy, wooden doors opening themselves up to the outside world that snapped Elizabeth back to her task at hand. With one last loving pat on the wrought iron fence, she turned towards the steps of the churches raised entry and began her assent into righteousness.

As the terrible year of Silver Dollars passing came to a close and the years began to pass, Elizabeth found she was quite content living with her friend Eva and playing Grandmother to her three children. Eva's son Numa, who just turned 24, had been sleeping on the family's sofa so Mrs. Tabor could have his bed, as the little frame house didn't have room for another.

It was tight, but they managed.

In the spring of 1927, Elizabeth received a letter from her Granddaughter Caroline, which announced her graduation from Washington high school, in Milwaukee, Wisconsin. Elizabeth's oldest grandchild was the prettier of the two girls, as she was fortunate enough not to of inherited her Grandfather Horace's tall forehead.

Listing her graduation as May 24th, Caroline filled her Grandmother in on what she had been doing during her senior year of high school and it was quite impressive. She belonged to the Girl's club and the math club, which they called Philomathea. This title was taken from the word Philomath, which meant "A lover of mathematics".

Caroline also was quite involved with the year book, as she was not only the panel editor, but the art editor as well. In her letter she continued telling her Grandmother about her senior year, by explaining that her nickname was "Kelly" and that her year book quote was going to be "Her name belies her fame", but gave no explanation for either.

As the year continued and ended in a glorious snowfall, 1928 soon peaked its head into the New Year and informed Elizabeth Tabor of the next high school graduation to grace her family, this time for her Grandson John Last the 4th.

Looking a lot like his Grandfather Horace, John was a handsome young man with a long, thin face and the tall Tabor forehead. Where the extended forehead was a curse for his little sister Jane, John's long face allowed his prominent forehead to balance along with his other features.

Caroline Last Graduation picture- Year book photo-The Oshkosh Public Museum.png

Ready to receive his diploma and don his cap and gown, John wrote to his Grandmother about his senior year in school and it appeared he had kept himself quite busy.

John explained that the kids in school called him Jack, instead of John and he was known to be quite an athlete. He was involved in Track, Football, the Tennis Club, as well as the Chemistry Club, the Harvard Club and was even the sports editor and reporter for the year book. And if he wasn't busy enough, he

THE STENCH OF EMBALMING FLUID AND THE HEART WRENCHING LIE 301

also belonged to the athletics association and National Honors Society.

His year book quote, next to his picture, would read "At whose sight all the stars hide their diminished heads', which was a line from the 1674 poem called Paradise lost, by John Milton.

But where May 24, 1928 was full of wonderful stories of yet another graduation Elizabeth Tabor couldn't afford to attend, it also brought about a terrible letter that showed her that the rug can be pulled out from under your feet at a moment's notice.

On July 7th the Matchless mine was once again headed to the auction block.

Since 1920, the mine had only been worked during the warmer months, while quarreling lessees and creditors fought over the profit from each cart load of manganese silver ore that came out of its great depths. Elizabeth had made a small percentage from each load, but unfortunately it wasn't enough to pay the taxes or make her creditors happy.

Without a dime to offer towards the mine, that put the name Horace Austin Warner Tabor on the map, Elizabeth spent auction day inside the walls of the Sacred Heart church, praying that the Lord would help her, as now it looked like 73 year old Elizabeth Tabor would have nothing.

But the Lord works in mysterious ways.

John Kernan Mullen had just turned 81, 26 days earlier, when he purchased the rights to Horace Tabor's famous Matchless mine, with the sole purpose of gifting it back to Mrs. Tabor. Mullen had, like most Coloradoans, watched the rise and fall of the Tabor's and witnessed Horace's second

John Last Graduation picture-Year book photo-The Oshkosh Public Museum

wife's extreme devotion to his memory, after he left this earth.

Where Tabor had made his millions in mining endeavors and investments, J.K. Mullen had made his millions from wheat, flour mills and Grain elevators.

Born in Ireland on June 11, 1847, Mullen was a devote Catholic who contributed to the church as his wealth multiplied, as well as starting a pension fund for his numerous employee's. On October 23, 1921, J.K. Mullen watched Denver's Immaculate Conception Cathedral, at Colfax and Logan, be consecrated after he donated the money needed for its completion.

Due to his service regarding the Cathedrals construction, the Vatican accepted him into the Order of Saint Gregory, which was an award that honored members for their service to the church.

And now he could continue serving the Lord by purchasing the Matchless Mine and gifting it back to Mrs. Elizabeth Tabor.

A TUB OF LARD AND THE DANCING SQUIRRELS

"**Mrs. Tabor, my** name is John Mullen and this is my Attorney." Mr. Mullen explained with a friendly smile, as he stood on the front steps of Eva James Denver home and motioned towards the man standing next to him. "We would like to discuss my companies' purchase of your Matchless mine yesterday. May we come in?"

After some confused smiles and a few cordial handshakes, Eva and Elizabeth invited the two men to sit down at the homes small kitchen table, as Mr. Mullen's attorney laid a contract in front of Mrs. Tabor.

"Mam', we are here today because my client wishes to inform you that he has no intention of leaving you destitute and without a home to call your own." The overly dressed attorney explained with a smile, as he removed a fountain pen from his jacket pocket. "Mr. Mullen wishes to offer you some options in regards to you continuing to live in the cabin, up at the Matchless mine."

"As I'm sure you are already aware, your mine went up for auction on July 7th, due to a unpaid mortgage of \$15,000 and \$25.65 in delinquent taxes", the Attorney reminded Mrs. Tabor, as he pointed to the amount listed on the contract. "We would like to offer you the ability to live on the property, free of charge, until the time of your death. You may also work the mine or sell off any of the old machinery if you wish without question, but if you would like to purchase the Matchless mine property, to say… leave to a family member or friend, my client would be asking $16,711.00."

"I can live in my cabin again?" Elizabeth asked, as a smile began crossing her face.

"Mrs. Tabor", Mr. Mullen responded with a smile of his own. "That was my sole reason for buying your mine in the first place."

Blessed with a fresh, clean, creditor free contract in her hands, Elizabeth took the next train out of Denver and headed back up to The Matchless mine. She had kept her distance the last few years, due to what seemed to be constant bickering and lawsuits between her numerous lessees, creditors and people who just wanted to stick their nose where it didn't belong, but now she could return to her cabin with a clean slate and a fresh start.

With July's weather full of warm sunshine and promise, Elizabeth stopped by Koch and Pfannenschmid grocery, once she arrived in Leadville, since she was sure her cupboards were bare up at her cabin. After some pleasant chit chat, Charles Koch packed her boxes of groceries into the back of his truck and gave her a ride up to the Matchless.

As the summer continued, Elizabeth spent her days visiting friends and enjoying the peace and quiet Denver's city life could never offer her. But as winter approached, she found herself spending more time alone in her cabin and began longing for the excitement of Denver's city life once again. Using the telephone at the grocery store, during her next trip into town, she called her friend Eva and was pleased to find that she was welcomed back for a winter visit.

But this visit was more than Eva James ever bargained for.

"Mrs. Tabor? Mrs. Tabor is that you?" Eva asked, as she opened her front door to find what appeared to be a heavy set woman covered in snow, standing on her front porch.

As the curious visitor looked up, Eva could see Mrs. Tabor's sparkling blue eyes looking back at her. "Oh, Mrs. Tabor! It is you! Oh, dear, oh dear, please get inside! You will catch your death!" Eva announced, as she took the large, knit grocery bags from Mrs. Tabor's gloved hands.

Setting the bags down, Eva quickly began helping her friend remove her worn out linen coat, scarf, gloves and finally her old veiled auto cap, before leading her over to a kitchen chair. Sitting down, Elizabeth began untying the strings that held the layers of burlap fabric over her shoes, as Eva hung up her guest's damp clothing near the wood stove.

"Mrs. Tabor, you shouldn't be out in weather like this! It's bitter cold outside!" Eva scolded her friend, as she took more of her wet things over to the heat of the stove.

"I know just how bad it is, but it's not as cold as Leadville!" Elizabeth laughed, as she continued to untie the strings. "I came down last night and stayed at the hotel. I will admit I walked here from down town, because I didn't have a nickel for car fare and they won't let me ride the trolley anymore without paying my way. But I did stop by John Thompsons' Grocery store and brought you some excellent things for a lamb stew, which is just right for a night like this."

Seeing that the snow had soaked Mrs. Tabor to the bone, Eva led Elizabeth into one of her children's old bedrooms and handed her a starched, gingham dress, as well as a pair of warm slippers to wear.

"Thank you pet, this dress fits wonderfully." Elizabeth announced, as she walked out of the bedroom and revealed her true, slim figure. She had hung her long woolen dress and underthings above the bedrooms radiator so they could dry, as well as laying out the newspapers she had used to stuff her clothing, for added warmth from the cold. Using a towel, she then began drying her reddish blonde hair, which was deeply streaked with layers of gray and white.

"Now, I'm not here to impose like I did before." Elizabeth informed her friend, as she sat down next a wonderful hot cup of tea. "I have a rented room up at the Windsor for the winter, I just wanted to come see you for a few days, but this blizzard really snuck up on me!"

But after a few hours of catching up and a couple games of cards, Elizabeth discovered that she wasn't feeling well. "Pet, I think I'm going to turn in." she announced, as she slowly stood up and began to shuffle over to her bedroom door. "I'm not feeling like myself."

And by morning, Eva knew what was wrong with Mrs. Tabor

She had the flu.

With Elizabeth normally being an early riser, Eva was surprised to find that her friend wasn't up when she awoke. Putting on her robe, she quietly knocked on Elizabeth's door, but the only response she received was more of an intelligible mumble, then a clear answer.

Slowly opening the door, Eva discovered that Elizabeth was drenched in sweat and slightly thrashing her body, as she mumbled that someone was trying to steal the Matchless. Running over to her friend's side, Eva placed her hand on Elizabeth's forehead and discovered she had a raging fever.

Quickly heading into the kitchen, Eva pulled out a tea kettle, filled it with water and set it on the stove to boil. As the liquid began to heat, she took out a tub of lard, bottles of turpentine and Coal Oil, as well as a large number of old flannel rags she stored under her sink and laid them all on the counter.

Pouring the turpentine and coal oil into a sauce pan, she placed it on a burner to heat, before she headed back to lift up Elizabeth's head and placed a dry towel over her sweat soaked pillow case. Returning to the kitchen, Eva filled the hot water bottle, closed the cap and continued to stir the turpentine and coal oil, which she was pleased to notice was beginning to bubble. Adding a couple spoonful's of lard, she continued to stir the mixture together, until she had a hot, gooey paste.

Taking a wooden spoon, Eva submerged two rags into the sauce pan and coated them thoroughly, before placing the goo soaked rags onto a nearby plate, which she carried to Elizabeth's room along with the hot water bottle.

Pulling back the covers, Eva unbuttoned Elizabeth's night shirt and carefully placed one hot rag on her chest and the other around her neck, before placing the hot water bottle under her feet, to draw out the fever. As the day passed and the treatments repeated, Elizabeth's rambling began to slow and she was becoming more coherent.

"Pet, you are one of God's precious angels. Only you and him and Father Paul, could have saved my life… I owe it to you. Someday the Matchless will again make a fortune for me and when it does, you are going to have a wonderful home for your children and fine clothes and plenty of food. The children will go to the best schools and never have to do hard work. But will always have plenty…you wait… and see…"

Within a few days, Elizabeth Tabor was able to sit up in bed to take her cough medicine, which consisted of a teaspoon of coal oil mixed with molasses, to disguise the taste.

Coal oil, also known as kerosene, was a common cure-all for many ailments, such as the flu, coughs and wounds of any type. Taken internally, it was mixed with sugar cubes, honey or molasses, while externally it was applied to wrappings or poured directly onto the affected area. The use of coal oil was thought to of prevented infections and heal the body of anything that ailed it.

As Elizabeth Tabor grew stronger, her friend brought in a collection of old newspapers for her to read and Elizabeth was pleased to see that the Tabor name, was once again, being mentioned in a positive light.

Sitting in a place of honor, inside Denver's State Historical Museum, was an old iron prospector's pan, believed to of been owned by none other than H.A.W Tabor. Found under a gravel pile, near a tumbledown shack in Pecks Gulch, the old, battered pan was thought to of been left behind in the 1850's, while Tabor began his hard climb to fortune and fame.

But wishful thinking doesn't make something true.

While it was well known that Horace Tabor prospected in the vicinity of Peck's Gulch, which was around the Black Hawk and Central City area, historian's seemed to of forgotten that Tabor and his first wife Augusta didn't arrive in Colorado until June 20, 1859.

But Elizabeth wasn't about to correct any positive stories involving her family.

As the week continued and Elizabeth grew stronger, she packed up her small travel bag and happily accepted a ride, from Eva James, back to Denver's Windsor Hotel.

As the year 1928 left the countries wall calendars and was ripped off to reveal 1929, Elizabeth counted the days until the first buds of spring appeared on the tree's, so she could return to her mountain cabin.

Finally, as April began showing its face and the squirrels started dancing around the newly exposed leaves, Elizabeth knew it was just a matter of weeks before she could pack up her bags and head to Denver's Union station.

But 1929 would not be a good year for Mrs. Tabor, in more ways than one.

After a year of ill health, Elizabeth's younger brother Peter McCourt Jr. died in his Denver home, on April 5th, at the age of 72. His first wife Emma had died in 1912, at the age of 50 years, but when Peter married his second wife Jessie years later, she brought her son Sherman into their marriage, which became Peter's only child.

Joining her family at both her brother's funeral and burial, into the McCourt family Mausoleum located inside Denver's Fairmount Cemetery, nobody was aware of the secret Peter took to his grave. Unknown to even his wife Jessie, Peter had been paying his older sister's grocery bill's at both John Thompson's Denver grocery store and Koch and Pfannenschmid grocery in Leadville.

And with Peter gone, Elizabeth's days of carefree grocery shopping would be coming to a sudden and abrupt end.

With Elizabeth's family finally dispersing after Peter's funeral, Elizabeth headed over to Denver's Union Station and traveled back to Leadville. Unaware of Peter's death or that the grocery bill would no longer be paid, Koch and Pfannenschmid Grocery happily allowed Elizabeth Tabor to choose any supplies she wished and Charlie drove her back up to the Matchless.

The Matchless Mine looking run down- The Denver Public Library, Western History Collection-X-22029

Upon learning that Mrs. Tabor was back in town, her neighbor John Mahoney came right over for a quick visit and to drop off his winter collection of Denver Posts for her to read. But when he arrived, he soon discovered that Elizabeth had invited someone to live on the property, as a type of watchman, but Mr. Mahoney wasn't too sure about the man's intentions.

"Hello, the house!" Mr. Mahoney happily announced, as he stepped out of his truck and headed towards Mrs. Tabor's front door. Playing along, Elizabeth quickly opened the window of her cabin, and stuck her head out to respond. "I am the maid, but I will relay any message you have to the lady of the house." She giggled.

"Please tell Mrs. Tabor that I wish to check to see if the ladder in the shack is secure and if the cables are ok. And I also brought her newspapers." he responded, as he held up the box.

Closing the window quickly, she counted to three before opening it back up. "Oh John, nice to see you. I'll be right out." Elizabeth replied, as she once again closed the window and latched it shut.

"Mrs. Tabor, I would like to check the ladder in the shack and make sure the cables are secure, as I have a feeling you will soon be climbing back down into the mine again." John teased, as he held onto the box of newspapers. Heading into the cabin, John placed the box on the floor, near the table, before he tapped the top of the pile with his knuckles.

"All the papers that have stories about the Tabor's I placed on the top of the stack for you, so they wouldn't get wrinkled." He explained to her, as he turned to head back out the front door. "Now let's check out your mine, shall we?"

Like he had done for a dozen or so years, John began inspecting the numerous buildings on the property, checked the tightness of the cables and made sure everything up top was secure. But when he walked toward a small cabin, located on the side of the property, he was caught off guard by an older man sitting on a tree stump, smoking a cigarette.

"Names George Schmidt and you must be John." The old miner stated, as he held out his dry, cracked hand in introduction. "Yeah, I worked for H.A.W back when this mine produced $10,000 a day and now I figured I can at least help Mrs. Tabor pull up enough scraps of ore, out of that hole over yonder, to buy groceries and such."

"Now, don't you worry, I will be checking on them there cables, measure the water levels inside the shaft, stuff like that. But to be perfectly honest, being back here at the Matchless, all I keep thinking about is getting back down there and hitting that silver vein!." He added with a hardy laugh, which was followed by abought of uncontrollable coughing.

Making his excuses, Mr. Mahoney tipped his hat towards Mrs. Tabor and reminded himself to check up on her alittle more often.

As evening arrived, Elizabeth poured herself a cup of tea and happily sat down to read the newspaper stories that mentioned the Tabors, but quickly found herself quite embarrassed by the article in front of her. She had tried so hard to restore the Tabor name to his rightful place in history, even at the expense of her daughter Silver's untimely death, but now it appeared that Elizabeth herself was now the subject of ridicule.

> "The widow of the mining magnate, once the darling of fortune, clings tenaciously to the property that produced its millions. She stalls off the mortgage as it becomes due and manages to hold on in some way. Considering what Tabor did for the up building of Denver, the citizens of that town could well afford to pay off the mortgage and give it to this old woman, who lives in the past, yet clings with pathetic regard to the property that was the foundation of the Tabor fortune."

As the years passed, Elizabeth Tabor continued with her newly set routine, of spending the warm months at her cabin, while spending the winters at the Windsor Hotel. She also continued to allow Mr. Schmidt to live in the old foreman's cabin, up at the Matchless and felt just a tad bit safer knowing that he was keeping an eye on the place, while she was out of town.

But during the spring of 1930, she was shocked to discover his cabin empty, when she arrived back in Leadville and many of his belonging tossed out into a nearby snow drift. Looking through the discarded items, Elizabeth picked up Mr. Schmidt's wire bird cage and found that it contained the remains of his pet.

"I'm sorry Mrs. Tabor, but George Schmidt was found dead on April 4th. I thought you knew." John Mahoney explained to her, when he arrived at the mine to greet his elderly neighbor. "I had come up to check on the Matchless, as I expected you would be returning soon and I just found him."

"What happened to his little bird?" Elizabeth inquired, as she pointed to the skeletal pile of feathers stuck to the bottom of the cage.

"It appeared that the poor, little creature either starved or froze to death after Mr. Schmidt died." John informed her, with a shrug of uncertainty.

George M. Schmidt was only 65 years old, when he was found dead of a suspected heart attack. His body was discovered reclining in his favorite chair, next to a cold wood stove, but nobody could pinpoint when he passed. It was well known that Leadville's cold winter temperatures tended to keep bodies of the deceased in a state of hibernation, until late spring.

But as Mrs. Tabor continued listening to the details surrounding her late watchman's death, 76 year old Elizabeth felt a cold shiver pass through her soul. Her beloved Horace's slow, agonizing death had graced the headlines, as people eagerly grabbed each day's newest addition to check on his condition and her daughter's Silver's violent, untimely death had done the same.

Elizabeth just hoped that when it was her time to leave this world, that her own death wouldn't take center stage and would instead simply become a small side note in Colorado's history.

Luckily, Elizabeth was soon able to focus on something pleasant, when she received a letter regarding her youngest grandchild's high school graduation on May 24th. Jane Last was Elizabeth Tabor's only grandchild that resembled both her Grandmother and Grandfather, which was both a curse and a blessing for the young girl. Where her face was sweet and dainty, her tall Tabor forehead caused the poor child to become creative in regards to hairstyles.

Jane explained to her grandmother that her senior year had been very busy, as she belonged to The National Honor society, was the yearbooks Editor in chief, the Vice president of The Washington Players group, Vice president of a math club that the school called Philomathea and Vice president of the Tennis club.

She also told her grandmother that her nickname in school had been Widdibus, without any explanation and that the motto, next to her picture in the year book was "Always energetic and busy, it is true. But never too busy to say hello to you."

How Elizabeth wished she could visit with her grandchildren again.

In July, Elizabeth was thrilled to receive a visit at the Matchless, from her 71 year old younger brother Phillip McCourt, who lived down in Denver. Phillip's wife Blanche had died back in 1926 and with a lot of free time on his hands, he decided to help his big sister try to get the Matchless mine back up and running.

Bringing in a crew, the property was cleared of broken mining debris and garbage and after an inspection of each of the shafts, it was decided that they would focus all their efforts on shaft #6. A functioning boiler was discovered on the property, moved over to the shaft house and the real work began.

The work men spent the next few months shoring up the timbers, deep within the shaft and removing buck load after bucket load of ore, until the workmen were told to stop digging. Philip McCourt had been keeping close taps on the amount of profitable metals each bucket of ore had been containing and by October he saw that he was losing more and more money every day.

With a heavy heart, Phillip convinced his sister to sell off all the remaining machinery to Guilda Swift, on October 4th and he returned to Denver.

And with no Forman to keep an eye on The Matchless, Elizabeth

Jane Last Graduation picture-Year book photo- The Oshkosh Public Museum

decided to spend the upcoming winter in her cabin.

As the month's passed and the snow began to fall, 76 year old Elizabeth Tabor checked the wood inside her stove, poured herself a nice, hot cup of tea and pulled down another box of old newspaper clipping to keep herself entertained with.

At the bottom of one box Elizabeth found stories from when Leadville was just beginning to stretch its legs and in turn, disgust any prim and proper New York City reporters that chose to write about.

One article was written by a reporter named Helen Hunt Jackson, back when she visited Leadville and Oro City for a story back in 1878. Working for "The Atlantic Monthly", Helen had traveled by stage coach to see the new mining camps first hand and was so repulsed, that she painted quite a picture for her readers back home.

> "The residential districts were covered in freshly hacked stumps, litter, plain log cabins, unpainted board shanties, tents and various combinations of the three- not very inspiring home architecture.
>
> The business district was something else, here the town pulsated. Business and residential sections alike poured smoke from reduction works, contaminating the air with a lurid column of almost rainbow tints. I quickly boarded a stage coach and went home."

Another East coast reporter named Mary Hallock Foote, was warned by her friend Helen Hunt Jackson not to visit Leadville as "The place was too unnatural. Grass would not grow there and cats could not live."

But she just had to see for herself.

> "The road over Mosquito pass to Leadville began to look like the route of a demoralized army. There was no road-there were wheel ploughed tracks, upon tracks and sloughs of mud, dead horses and cattle by the hundreds scattered along wherever they dropped. And human wreckage in proportion."

With a slight chuckle, Elizabeth Tabor placed the articles back into the box and continued sipping her tea. She remembered the stories, her beloved Horace had told her and the children, where he had hired men to dig through the ice and snow, just to lay the water pipes down Harrison Ave. The men, chilled to the bone, had to build bon fires all over town, in order to thaw the frozen ground.

But as Elizabeth listened to the wind howl outside her cabin, she peeked over at the empty water buckets near her front door. It sure would be nice if the city would set fires and lay water pipes up to her cabin, instead of forcing her to fetch water from across the street.

But she wouldn't have been able to pay the water bill anyway.

Due to all the standing water, inside the Matchless mines numerous shafts, the water on her property was contaminated and undrinkable. And with no extra money left to spend on the water boy, Elizabeth had been sneaking down the street every night to use her former neighbor's pitcher head pump.

The house in question had been torn down a few years back, but their water pump was still functional and thankfully hidden from the site of nosey neighbors. But due to Elizabeth Tabor's desire to avoid running into any passersby's, she tried to keep her visits to the late evening hours.

Looking over at her clock, Elizabeth could see that it was getting close to midnight, which was her preferred time to fetch her water. Families where normally asleep and the earth was quiet, minus the sounds of her gunny sack covered boots crunching though the newly fallen snow. Wrapping up her feet and layering her clothes, she reached for her warmest winter coat, which she got for a song, despite its extremely decorated appearance.

Her wonderful wool winter jacket was an old high school marching band jacket, which was decorated with numerous, shiny gold buttons in rows down the front, gold braids on the shoulders and a nice high neck to keep out the cold. Wrapping a scarf tightly over her hat and then snuggly around her neck, Elizabeth slipped on her gloves, grabbed her buckets and headed out the door.

"Mrs. Tabor? Mrs. Tabor? Please come inside dear." Mrs. Robert's pleaded, as she spoke to the shadowed figure slowly walking past her house. "You will catch your death, please come inside."

Bertha and her husband John had been living across the street from the Matchless mine for over ten years and had watched Mrs. Tabor struggle with basic necessities, while attempting to hold onto her pride.

"Thank you pet, it would be nice to get out of the cold." Elizabeth admitted, as she knocked the snow off her sack covered boots. Bertha smiled down at the elderly woman, as she took the buckets from her tiny hands.

"Mrs. Tabor, you know you are always welcome to come fill your water buckets whenever you like. I'm home all day with the children." The young woman reminded her stubborn neighbor, as the buckets began to fill, "You don't need to fight with that old frozen pump next door."

But she knew, that despite her offers, she would still see Mrs. Tabor sneaking past her home the following night.

When John and Bertha Roberts first moved across the street from the Matchless, they had heard the stories of Mrs. Tabor and her pride. But they weren't aware of Mrs. Tabor's nightly visits to the old water pump, until John started working the night shift.

Bertha was up around 11pm, with their youngest child Murrill, when she saw something moving outside in the darkness. Afraid it could be a bear, she turned on the outside lights and instead saw a tiny, hunched figure holding something in its hands. Letting her curiosity get the best of her, she laid the baby down in the crib, grabbed her gun and headed outside.

And she had been watching Mrs. Tabor repeat her nightly track ever since.

Just that past spring, when Bertha and her husband were shopping with their children, at Zaitz Mercantile at 717 Harrison, they had overheard the grocery clerk and the shoe maker discussing Mrs. Tabor. As the young couple listened in, they felt a sense of pride in their little town, knowing that so many people were trying so hard to help the stubborn old woman.

"I remember the time Mrs. Tabor came in with a terribly worn out pair of shoes and asked if I could fix them." George explained, as he continued his shopping." Those old shoes were worn away to nuthin, but she wanted me to fix them anyways. Well, when she leaves, this man standing at the door says to me, Hey George, give me them shoes and I'll find a new pair that matches them and you can just tell Mrs. Tabor you fixed'em up good."

"Did the old woman accept them?" the clerk asked, as he began boxes up the groceries. "Hell, no she didn't' except them!" George laughed, as he slapped the counter. "She took one look at those shiny new shoes, handed them back to me and said if you don't think you can fix my shoes, I'll take them to a shoe maker who can."

"You know, it's the welfare that pays for her groceries." The clerk added, as he continued boxing up the shoemaker's purchases, "But we can't tell her, because we know she won't take it. So we have to tell her that the money was put into her account by some old miner who owed her husband Horace money!"

"Hey, did you tell him about how I caught Mrs. Tabor digging through our trash awhile back?" Elmer Kutzlub chimed in, as he came out from the back of the store, wiping his hands with a towel. "Poor old woman."

"Ok, I've got to hear this one!" George insisted, as he sat down at one of the stores counter stools.

"So, I drive Mrs. Tabor home twice a month and put her groceries in the back of my truck, but I would sometimes notice a few extra things in that old knitted bag she carries around. Didn't really think much about it. "Elmer began, as he continued to dry his hands. "But one day, I headed out to the alley to throw out some old vegetables and I see the old lady digging around in our bins!"

"What did you do?" George asked, with an eager expression.

"Well, I know how tight things are, with the mines closing down and all. Hell, I have a wife and two young'uns myself to feed." He explained, as he set the towel on the counter. "So, since the old woman comes around about the same time every month, I've been setting aside some of our discarded merchandise in a box, until she comes into the store and then I quickly set it outside, on top of our bins, for her to go through."

"Hell, a few times I've even shown up at her cabin with a basket of peaches or something… but never tell her anything is for her! She will refuse it on the spot! Might even get out that shotgun of hers. " Elmer, explained, with a serious tone, as he slammed his fist down hard onto the counter. "No, sir! Never just give her something! I have learned to ask her if she could please give the peaches to families in need. That's the trick!"

"Have you ever seen the inside of that cabin of hers?" George questioned, as he leaned forward a bit to hear the answer.

"Neat as a pin." Elmer replied, with a smile. "Neat as a pin."

A FALSE NAME AND THE UNDIAGNOSED BRAIN TUMOR

"Mrs. Tabor? Mrs. Tabor? May I please speak to you?" Mr. Karsner asked, as he rapped his knuckles on the front door of Elizabeth Tabor's cabin. The author had traveled over 2,000 miles just for a chance to meet her, as the book he was writing about the Tabor family was almost complete.

"Mrs. Tabor, my name is David Karsner and I've traveled all the way from Manhattan just to meet you Mam'." He called out, as he thought he had heard rustling behind the bolted cabin door. Within few seconds, he listened as the bolt slide out of its lock and watched the cabin door slowly crack open.

Through the small gap in the opened door, Mr. Karsner peered down to see a tiny, elderly woman with blue eyes. As he continued his attempts to convince her that his visit was a friendly one, the heat from the cabin began warming his body, as it found its way past the woman and into the frigid April morning.

As usual, Leadville was proving it's self a late starter in regards to the arrival of spring and 1931 would prove to be no different.

After giving the stranger the once over, Elizabeth felt he was harmless enough and allowed him to come in, but kept her shotgun at her hip as he entered her cabin. "I don't normally have visitors, as I prefer to be alone." She announced as she offered him a seat.

Feeling an uncomfortable tension in the room, David quickly glanced around Mrs. Tabor's tiny cabin and sat down on a small, wooden kitchen chair close to the wood stove. Pulling over a nearby chair for herself, Elizabeth never took her eyes off the overly dressed man as she sat down, spread her knees apart just a tad and made a comfortable resting spot for her rifle to lay across her lap. As the man glanced around her cabin, Elizabeth continued to intimidate him by stroking her weapon, as though it was a loving pussy cat.

With an author's mind, David began filing away a mental picture of the inside of the tiny cabin, as he didn't feel it wise to remove his note pad and pen. He spotted an old iron bed frame, with a mattress covered in both blankets and clothing along one wall, as well as a nearby rocking chair, with the rockers tied with twine. Nearby, he noticed yet another chair, this one with a tin basin and a lid, which he felt might be used as a makeshift toliet, as well as a tall shelf stacked with what appeared to be newspapers and garbage.

Turning his head towards yet another corner, he noticed a two-burner oil stove, thick with grease, before turning his attention back to the small, round wood stove, which was supporting a metal dishpan full of snow.

"I normally fetch my drinking water in a pail, but I do it at night." Elizabeth chimed in, after noticing the stranger looking at the small pile of snow, for just alittle to long. The sound of her voice quickly snapped the writer out his trance, but as he looked back over at Mrs. Tabor, he discovered that the gun in her lap was pointed directly at him.

Letting out an unprofessional sounding shriek, David Karsner quickly moved his chair back, in an attempt to get away from the receiving end of the menacing weapon.

But 76 year old Elizabeth Tabor just laughed at him.

"Don't be alarmed dear, I won't shoot you", she explained, with a sinister expression, while turning the barrel towards him once again and never breaking eye contact. "Since Schmidt died, I always keep my trusty at hand when strangers come up here and I make no exceptions. You know, I am the sole guardian of this wonderful mine."

"Yes, Mrs. Tabor, That's why I came to talk with you." David explained with a nervous tone to his voice, as he watched the elderly woman continue to lovingly stroke her rifle. "Could you tell me why you chose to live up at this mine?"

"We Tabor's are proud. We have never taken a cent in charity from anyone and that will not begin now." Elizabeth began, as she kept her eyes set on the stranger. "Anything that can be done to save the mine, will be on a strictly business basis. This mine is dearer to me than my life and I guess God gave me a strong back to carry the burden."

As Elizabeth spoke lovingly about the Matchless, the man couldn't help but stare at her thread bare blouse, which exposed layers of newspapers through its numerous tears. It was funny to think that this tiny, elderly woman, who was once married to one of the richest men in the state, now lined her disintegrating clothing with discarded garbage.

And yet, despite having the subject of his soon to be completed book sitting right in front of him and traveling across almost the entire country just to meet her, the author shooed away any desire he had to even ask her one question about her past.

Not even one.

Bringing the uncomfortable visit to an end, the author quickly stood, which prompted Mrs. Tabor to display her cat like reflex's and within seconds David Karsner was faced ,yet again, with the barrel end of the shot gun.

"You have a fine day Mrs. Tabor." The author announced, as he held his hand out in a friendly manner, all the while trying to avoid looking at her weapon. Seeing the man's fear, Elizabeth relaxed for a second and set her rifle at parade rest, before shaking his hand.

"It must be fine to live away up here in the Rockies, with the gilded sky almost within reach of your hand and this mine of silver beneath your feet." He added, as he opened the cabins front door and walked outside towards his waiting car.

"Yes, it is. But you have forgotten something," Elizabeth added, as the author began looking over himself to see what he might of left inside the small cabin.

"What is that?" the author asked, still unsure of what he may have left behind.

"God is in my heart." Elizabeth replied, as she touched the cross dangling from her torn blouse. "Think of it, Mr. Karsner. Spring is nearly here again."

Returning to his Hotel, David Karsner retrieved the notepad from his satchel and added his meeting with Mrs. Tabor to the final chapter of his book, which he had already named "Silver Dollar". All of his research was comprised of newspaper clippings, magazine stories and interviews with people who personally knew the Tabors, yet not a single sentence in his book was passed by Elizabeth Tabor herself.

Hell, he never even told her he was writing it.

When the author was originally compiling his research on the Tabors, he had come across a newspaper story written for The Republican, on March 1, 1883, the day divorcee Elizabeth Bonduel Doe married divorcee Horace Tabor, which poked fun at the young, tiny, new bride.

```
"On Thursday night, at Willard Hotel,
Washington, Senator Tabor and "Baby" Doe
were married."
```

And as author David Karsner finished writing about his visit with Elizabeth Tabor, he happily closed his notebook and smiled at the lie that he had created for the elderly widow.

The lie of a false name.

Which would follow her for eternity.

Welcome to the world Mrs. Baby Doe Tabor.

Welcome to the world.

With the author long gone, Elizabeth headed back inside the warmth of her cabin, with no idea that the stranger who just visited her would be the one to bring the story of her beloved Horace to life, while causing her so much heart ache.

As the year passed and 1931 came to its usual blustery end, Elizabeth could of never imaging the fire storm she would be facing in the New Year.

Walking into town, as the spring of 1932 began arriving in Leadville, Elizabeth was surprised to hear talk of a new book out about the Tabors. Heading over to the library to investigate the claim, the librarian handed her a small, hardback book entitled "Silver Dollar."

"Mrs. Tabor, I never realized that your husband Horace called you Baby Doe." The librarian, commented with a smile, as she watched Elizabeth flip through the book.

"He didn't." she replied, with a confused look. "Nobody has ever called me that."

Checking out the book, Elizabeth was shocked to discover that not only had a false name been given to her and listed as truth, but that the details of her youngest daughter's death were shamefully smeared all over its pages.

With a hand on her rosary, Elizabeth prayed that the interest in the book would wane and be quickly forgotten.

As the year continued and it appeared that the hype about the book was slowly ebbing away, Elizabeth was shocked to hear that her old friend Margaret Brown had died on October 26, 1932, at the age of 65.

After suffering from terrible migraine headaches for years, Margaret was found dead in her Barbizon Hotel room in New York City, by the Hotels manager. The woman who was known worldwide as "The unsinkable Molly Brown", was discovered at 10:55pm, but despite the original assumption that she had simply died in her sleep, an autopsy later revealed a large brain tumor.

Margaret Brown had risen to fame as a survivor of the luxury cruise liner the Titanic, after it struck an ice burg and sunk to the bottom of the Atlantic, in the early morning hours of April 15, 1912. It was reported that not only did she help people into the life boats, but stayed with them on the rescue ship the Carpathia, until all the survivors were either claimed by family in New York or sent to area hospitals for care.

Margaret and her daughter Helen had been vacationing with John Jacob Astor and his family in Cairo, Egypt, when she learned that her first Grandchild, Lawrence Brown Jr., was sick. Deciding to return to the states together, the group bought tickets aboard a new ship called The Titanic, but when they arrived in London to board, Margaret's daughter Helen decided not join them.

John Jacob Astor died in the sinking of the Titanic, along with his servant Victor Robbins and the Astor's dog "Kitty", an Airedale, but his pregnant 18 year old wife Madeleine, her maid Rosalie and private nurse Caroline Louise Endres survived.

Yet despite all the hype surrounding Margaret Brown's heroics aboard the Titanic, Elizabeth Tabor simply remembered her friend as an activist.

In August 1893, Horace Tabor had given his wife Elizabeth his blessing to offer up two rooms inside Denver's Tabor opera house, for the Women's suffrage movement. One of the rooms was used as an office for the group's secretary, while the larger room was to be used as a meeting place, as it could hold hundreds of people.

And it was during their first meeting that Elizabeth Tabor and Margaret Brown became friends.

Both being wives of wealthy mine owners, the women rallied that the vote was intended to prove to men that women were intellectually capable and deserved the vote.

> "Woman pay taxes! Women clean homes! Let them clean the city! Your vote will give the women a square deal. It will give your girl the same chance as your boy."

At 8pm, on November 8, 1893, the Tabor Opera house was a place of ecstatic celebration, as Colorado became only the second state to allow women the right to vote, with Wyoming being the first, having granted that right on September 30, 1889.

Unfortunately for Elizabeth, she wouldn't' have much time to reminisce about her old friend, as her own life was about to turn upside down and her quiet, private live permanently disrupted.

"Mrs. Tabor? Mrs. Tabor? Could I please have a minute of your time?" Robert Nelson asked with a shiver to his voice, as he knocked on the front door of Elizabeth's cabin.

Not used to visitors, especially on an icy, late November morning, Elizabeth quickly put on a jacket and grabbed her rifle. "Who may I ask is calling?"

"Mam, my name is Robert Nelson and I'm the Manager of the Denver Theater. I'm here about the movie Silver Dollar, we are showing about you and your husband." The man stammered, as he tried to keep himself warm." Mrs. Tabor…It's really cold out here."

Cracking open the door, Elizabeth looked up to see a half frozen man, who didn't look like much of a threat. Opening the door all the way, the theater manager practically ran Mrs. Tabor over to get to the warmth of the wood stove.

With a giggle, Elizabeth closed the cabin door and watched the man frantically rub his hands next to the flames. "A little nippy outside?"

With a shiver, the man turned around and saw Mr. Horace Tabor's tiny, 78 year old widow smiling back at him. "Yes, Mam'. It's rather cold outside."

Molly Brown -Legends of America

Turning around, but keeping his backside near the wood stove, he opened up his jacket and quickly handed Elizabeth a flyer, before placing his hands once again towards the stove.

The picture showed a clean shaven, round faced man, with dark brown hair on one side of the poster, while a beautiful blonde haired woman, with a scandalous dress and veil, graced the other. The title "Silver Dollar", which was splattered across the bottom of the flyer, made Elizabeth's heart sink as she realized that the book she despised, had now been made into a moving picture.

"Is this man in the corner supposto be my Horace?" Elizabeth asked, as she held up the paper and pointed to the drawing of the man. "He looks nothing like my husband."

"Yes, Mam'", the manager replied, finally warmed up enough that he could tell her about the movie. "The man's name is Edward G. Robinson, he has been in six movies, before staring as your husband. But be aware that your husband's name was changed to Yates Martin, for the movie."

"I already don't like him. "Elizabeth replied, with a sour expression. "How tall is he?"

"He is about 5'7"." The manager replied," And I think he is a Jew from Romania."

"Hummm and I guess this half naked woman with the blonde hair is supposto be me then?" Elizabeth asked, with an undecided tone.

"Yes, that's Bebe Daniel's, but your name was changed to Lily Owen's for the movie." The manager added, as he pointed to the picture." And I believe she is around 5'2" tall. She was a child actress and she is very popular."

"Her I like." Elizabeth responded with a sincere tone, as she studied the flyer again.

"Mrs. Tabor, the reason I'm here is to invite you to introduce yourself and walk onto the stage of my theater on December 1st, for the premier of the movie in Denver." He explained with a sincere smile,

"All expenses paid, of course and we are also willing to pay you very handsomely for your troubles as well."

Looking back at the movie flyer, Elizabeth thought a minute before handing it back to him. "I'm sorry, but my husband was a tall, handsome man and I just can't support the studio's choice to cast a shrimp like Edward G. Robinson to play him."

Robert Nelson took back the flyer, as Mrs. Tabor walked over to a pile of split logs in the corner of her cabin, before heading over to the wood stove. As she opened the stoves door and began stirring the coals, the theater manager finally had a chance to take a quick look around her cabin. It was quite obvious that this elderly woman, the original queen of Silver, was quite destitute, but her love for her husband was commendable.

"Besides, young man, I really don't like to be gone very long from the Matchless." Elizabeth explained, as she added another log to the fire. "I prefer my little mountain cabin over the glitter of 16th street."

Taking a seat, Robert continued to listen to the adorable, elderly woman talk lovingly about her husband's former mine, as well as her interest in writing her own biography about her family.

"Mrs. Tabor, do you think you could allow me to take something of yours to Denver for the premier?" the manager asked, as he glanced around her cabin.

With an ornery twinkle in her blue eyes, Elizabeth walked the man over to the back window of her cabin and pointed towards the head frame of shaft #6. "Underneath that snowbank, you will find all the silver ore samples you could ever want and I'll even give you a box to put them in."

Within the hour, a very happy, but rather frozen theater manager waved goodbye to Mrs. Tabor and headed back towards Leadville. Elizabeth had also given him the idea of asking the Elks lodge if perhaps they would allow him to borrow some items from the Tabor Opera house, on Harrison Ave, which thankfully, they did.

Despite not being able to convince Mrs. Tabor to join him for the movies premier on December 1st, the theater's Manager was not only able to show off an original stage drop and wonderful velvet curtains from the Leadville Opera house, but hand out small Matchless mine ore samples, to each movie patron, on opening night.

But as Elizabeth Tabor sat quietly alone in her cozy cabin and watched Christmas snow fall gently over the mine dumps, that surrounded her little home, she could never have imagined that another woman was traveling 58 miles, up from Salida, in a desperate attempt to live with her.

The woman's name was Susanna Bonnie.

Sue was a southern girl who was raised in New Orleans, Louisiana and had the southern twang to prove it. Surprisingly, the young man Sue found to marry was originally from the Railroad town of Salida, Colorado and he thought that they should start their new married life, living in Salida with his mother.

Who instantly hated her.

Sue had been educated in a Louisiana Convent and when she graduated, she celebrated her freedom from the Catholic order, by getting a tattoo. But Sue didn't just get any tattoo…she got a full chest tattoo of a burro!

Extremely proud of her decorated chest, the young woman would unbutton her blouse and lower the sleeves to expose the animal, then rotate her right shoulder to make its head move and then rotate her left shoulder to make the tail move.

This parlor trick might have impressed the boys, but it not only got her kicked out of her new mother-in-law's house, but she was also handed a freshly printed divorce decree as she was shown the door.

With nowhere to go, she was able to find employment at Salida's Starbucks dairy farm for a bit, but when she lost her job, she was again left homeless. Desperate for idea's, a former co-worker jokingly suggested she go up to Leadville and ask old Mrs. Baby Doe Tabor if she could live with her, inside her little shack.

Taking the suggestion seriously and with no other options, Sue Bonnie hitchhiked to Leadville, on December 30th and began the frigid walk up to the Matchless Mine.

"Excuse me! Excuse me! Miss? Miss? Are you lost dear?" John Mahoney screamed to the figure he saw in the blowing snow. Not receiving a response, he tightened up his coat and trudged through December's deep snow drifts, only to find a young woman wearing nothing but an evening dress and open toed shoes. Quickly taking off his coat, he covered up the woman and brought her back to his house to warm up.

"What were you thinking? You could have frozen to death!" John announced, as his wife grabbed a nearby blanket and tried to warm up the young woman.

"I came to stay with Mrs. Tabor. "Sue replied, through the chattering of her teeth. "I want to live with her."

John looked over at his wife, who quickly exchanged the same confused expression. "Young lady, Mrs. Tabor doesn't take in boarders. Why don't I just drive you into town?"

But as the young woman warmed up and the feeling returned to her toes, she continued her insistence that she was going to live with Mrs. Tabor. "Fine Miss, I'll drive you over to the cabin, but after Mrs. Tabor tells you to go away, then can I drive you into town?"

Giving Sue an old jacket, John started up his truck, drove to the base of the driveway, which led up to the Matchless and parked. "My truck won't make it any farther Miss, but just follow the driveway up to the cabin and I'll wait for you right here. Just look for the smoke."

John watched as the stubborn young woman trudged through the snow, until she disappeared from sight. Pulling out a newspaper, he kept himself occupied until she returned, with a defeated tone to her voice. "I could hear her inside, but all she kept saying was that she was the night watchman and I don't want to be disturbed."

As the young woman pouted, John couldn't help but laugh, as he shoved his truck into gear and started towards town.

Piles of beautiful gifts and the burning Newspaper

Despite below zero temperatures and snow drifts taller than the average man, the frosty start of 1933 didn't stop the managers of the nation's movie houses from knocking, at all hours, on Elizabeth Tabor's front door.

She was really starting to regret giving Denver's Theater Manager that box of ore samples.

The Manager from Denver had turned each sample of ore into a thing of beauty for his theater guests, by wrapping them in a piece of cellophane and then attaching a miniature flag to each one. On one side, the flag read "This ore donated by Mrs. H.A.W. Tabor for the world premiere of Silver Dollar. Was taken from the Matchless Mine, from which Mr. Tabor took millions of dollars during the days of the silver boom", while the other side was a picture of Leadville, Colorado and showed the mining district, as well as the mountains.

The Warner's Theater in Los Angles had requested a shipment of ore, for their opening night, but scoffed at the shipping price of $10 a ton, in order to deliver it by train to California.

Ironic how Warner Brother's movie studio had no problem changing the names of Mrs. Tabor and her husband in their motion picture, to avoid paying out any royalties, yet showed disappointment over Mrs. Tabor's refusal to foot the bill for the delivery of ore, in order to promote a film she would never receive a penny from.

But despite Elizabeth's hatred of the book, as well as the actor chosen to play her husband in the movie, she did enjoy the press the Tabor's were receiving, even though some of it wasn't exactly favorable.

> "For all his crudity and love of pomp, there wasn't anything niggardly and crooked about this man, who shared as long as he had something to share."- Grand Junction Sentinel

> "It is certain that H.A.W Tabor would be very proud to see this magnificent reproduction of his career, as he enjoyed so such glamour and desired always to be the center of attention."- Steamboat Pilot

But as the showing of the movie "Silver Dollar", spread across the United States, so did the realization that the real Mrs. H.A.W Tabor was still alive, up at Leadville's Matchless Mine. Elizabeth was stunned by the number of vehicles that arrived daily at her tiny cabin to take pictures or to beg for her to autograph the book that she despised.

In an attempt to discourage the constant intrusion, Elizabeth eventually put a note on the front door of her cabin, which read that she was away on important business, but the smoke from her chimney would always give her away. But surprisingly, despite her adamant refusal to speak to any of her well-wishers, she would be greeted, every night, by piles of gifts left sitting outside her door.

Wonderful gifts.

Clothes, shoes, warm coats, blankets, cook ware and beautiful

Silver Dollar movie premiere- The Denver Public Library, Western History Collection-X22003

dishes…but she couldn't accept any of it. With her head held high and the cold wind blowing through her disintegrating clothing, she reminded herself that she owed the Lord a great penance and her gift of poverty was her vow of eternal remorse.

Under the darkness of night, Elizabeth would collect the gifts and stack them either on her enclosed front porch or in corners of her tiny cabin, cover them over with old rugs and blankets and pray the visitors would stop coming.

Elizabeth Tabor just wished people would allow her to finish her penance, before she left this earth, so she could one day be reunited with Horace.

Charity, disguised as either an old unpaid debt, found money from a fictitious Tabor property or from well-wishers, no matter how sincere the intentions, was still charity, which Elizabeth's immortal soul would still have to suffer for.

Please Lord, speak to their hearts and continue to give me the strength to refuse charity, no matter how much my body aches from hunger or want of material possessions.

Lord give me strength.

As the warm weather began to pass and the aspen trees began to allow their autumn leaves to gently cover the Rocky Mountains, Elizabeth Tabor was relieved to finally be freed from her forced confinement and once again was able to walk around her beautiful mine, without the fear of Tourists trespassing on her property.

She rejoiced in the fact that she had successfully battled the demons that taunted her to use the beautiful items, left by the numerous well-wishers and once again Elizabeth felt enlightened.

"Mrs. Tabor, its Loretta. Can I come in?" Loretta Walsh inquired,

Elizabeth Tabor talking to girls outside her cabin-The National Mining Hall of fame and Museum archives

as she stood in the deep snow, brought the night before, by the towns' first winter blizzard. Mrs. Walsh was the secretary of the Leadville Community Center Association and was bringing a food box, that Elizabeth Tabor had been misled into believing was paid for by a man who owed the Tabors an unpaid dept.

"Just a minute, Loretta." Elizabeth answered with a cheerful tone, as she put on her moccasins and went to unbolt the front door.

"Oh, I'm so glad to see you!" Elizabeth announced, as the woman leaned down to give the tiny Mrs. Tabor a hug. "And who is your friend?"

"My name is Alice Young, Mam', so nice to finally meet you." The young woman announced as she held out her hand in introduction. With a smile, Elizabeth responded by placing both of her hands, around the young woman's out stretched hand and incasing it with hers.

Inviting both women into her cabin, Loretta placed the food box on the nearby table, while Mrs. Tabor motioned for Alice to sit in a padded rocking chair, that the young lady was sure was Mrs. Tabor's coveted seat. With Loretta unpacking the box, Alice glanced down at the filthy rocking chair and saw it was a high backed wicker rocker, covered in a heap of soiled blankets, with a faded cushion for the seat.

Not wanting to insult her host, she carefully sat down and thanked her lucky stars that the rickety looking rocker held her weight. As she looked back over at Mrs. Tabor, Alice watched the dainty woman light a small, kerosene lamp with a twisted piece of newspaper, which she ignited from the constant flame inside her wood stove. Seeing that Alice was watching her, Elizabeth smiled and announced with a comical, sour expression. "Don't worry, it's just the Denver Post."

As the kerosene lamp brightened up the room, Alice glanced down and noticed that Mrs. Tabor's was wearing moccasins that appeared to be constructed out of a heavy, ribbed hose, bits of woolen fabric and strips of an old blanket, which demonstrated her resourcefulness.

Above the shoes, she was wearing a heavy, full, brownish skirt with rough, frayed, saw tooth edges that just touched the top of her moccasins and a long sleeved, high necked, navy blue jacket, which hung loosely on her tiny frame.

Her throat was also covered in what appeared to be a kind of chinchilla collar, fastened around the front with a safety pin and dangling over the front of the blue jacket was a piece of thin wire, which held a brown, two inch crucifix, which she noticed Mrs. Tabor grasping every few minutes.

The feature that stood out about Mrs. Tabor the most, were her beautiful blue eyes, which sparkled when she talked, but surprisingly, when she smiled, her teeth showed neglect and decay.

"So Loretta, I'm glad that you didn't bring Mr. Jiggs…what's his name? Oh, Riggs's." Elizabeth laughed, as she took a seat next to Alice. "That Mr. Riggs's talks too much and I don't want this to get into the newspapers." She added, with a sudden serious tone, while looking over at both Loretta and Alice.

"Anyway, so a man came to my door and said he was the Fairchild's attorney and that Fairchild had gone to some spring, but I don't remember where and something about his blood turning to water. What did he say? Anemia! Yes, he has Anemia!" Elizabeth exclaimed, with a quick hand gesture. "And that he wanted to meet me at the Post office either the next day, Wednesday or Thursday at the latest."

"What did he want?" Loretta asked, trying to play along. She already knew that this story was simply another fabricated lie, in order for Mrs. Tabor's welfare aide to be added to her bank account. The entire town tried their hardest to allow Elizabeth to keep her dignity, but still have money to survive the winters.

"Well Fairchild was a cattleman and he came to Mr. Tabor once and wanted to borrow $4,000. That was Mr. Tabor's way. He never refused anyone. He was the most wonderful man on God's earth." She explained, as she grabbed her crucifix and stared upwards.

"And just so you know Alice, I am very religious and I always wear my…Oh, the flame is going out." Elizabeth exclaimed, as she quickly jumped up and grabbed another twisted piece of newspaper and lit it with the fire from the wood stove. Walking over to the kerosene lamp, she gently slid it inside and smiled as the light burned bright again.

As she walked back towards her chair, Elizabeth pointed to a second stack of wood piled in the corner. "That pile of wood has been in here for years. I'm so afraid of running out of wood, that I keep it there and never touch it."

"So, to finish my story, Fairchild wants to settle his debt to my Tabor for $100 on the thousand, which would be $400. And with that I can start my mine back up!" Elizabeth announced, with a huge smile. "Oh, the flame is going out again…"

Watching Mrs. Tabor repeat her ballet of rolling up pieces of her despised Denver Post and setting them on fire, Alice discovered that she finally had a chance to glance around the little cabin.

The first thing she noticed was that the ceilings and walls were covered in a heavy, building paper that was stained with coal dust and soot, while the corners of the ceiling were decorated with large spider webs, that perhaps the tiny Mrs. Tabor was unable to reach.

Looking down at her feet, Alice noticed that the floor boards were wide and rough, with years of dirt and grime ground into their grain, which she assumed were rarely swept.

Looking back towards the interior door, which led to the lean-to addition, she noticed two built in tables. One held a water bucket and a few kitchen utensils, while the other held a basin that she assumed was for washing, as a small, square, wood framed mirror hung on the wall above it. And to complete the feeling that the basin was for washing, the narrow window beside the mirror was partially covered with newspaper, to keep out prying eyes.

Glancing over towards the little kitchen, Alice noticed ceiling to floor shelves filled with dust covered papers, books, pamphlets, boxes and assorted Knick Knacks, with pots and pans along the bottom shelves.

Across the room Alice noticed a stack of storage boxes and trash, which were covered over with rugs, clothes and rags, in what appeared to be an attempt to hide the items from view, as well as an image of the Virgin Mary hanging on the wall.

Surrounding the bas-relief image, were many freshly cut pine limbs, cedar berries, pine cones and leaves in a type of makeshift altar. But as Alice was taking in a mental picture of Mrs. Tabor's cabin, the elderly lady's sweet voice snapped her back to the conversation at hand.

"Oh, I wish you could have known my Tabor. He never spoke a cross word to me, he never looked cross, I never saw even a disagreeable look on his face and I hope no one ever see's one on mine." Elizabeth explained, as she caressed the crucifix around her neck and looked up at the ceiling. "His parents were English and Methodists, but for twenty years he favored the Catholic religion and he died with four Jesuit priests blessing him. What a wonderful way to die."

Turning back to her guests, Mrs. Tabor quickly changed the subject to something more sinister and the look on her face matched her tone.

"But my Tabor had his troubles and some of them were due to Mr. Moffat being a very bad man." Elizabeth explained in a cold tone, as she leaned forward in her chair. "Mr. Tabor made him rich, but he was a bad man. Now his wife was a very charming person…but Bonfil's and Tammen were crooks!"

Frederick Bonfils's and H.H. Tammen had purchased the Denver Post in 1895 and while looking for investors, David Moffat had asked Horace Tabor to invest with him, but he refused. This left a sore spot, which the Tabor's felt was the cause of so many negative stories written about them in the Newspaper.

"When my Tabor died, they wrote lies about him and attacked me and the children." Mrs. Tabor explained, with a mournful expression. "And just lately, Mr. Bonifils's wrote some more lies about me and I got down on my knees, before my bed and I prayed to my merciful God to help me bear it and to never allow him to write lies about me again."

"Did he?" Alice asked, desperate to know the answer.

"No." Elizabeth replied, as she looked up at her guest with a wicked smile on her face. "He died. And now he will never write about me again. He is dead! I believe in God, a just God! Everyone should!"

Frederick Bonfils's died in his home on February 2, 1933, at the age of 72, of encephalitis. The condition is described as an inflammation of the brain, which could be caused by a virus, herpes or rabies and can result in seizures, hallucinations, trouble speaking and death.

But it wasn't just the Tabor's who disliked the Denver Post's style of "Sensationalistic journalism."

In December 1899 both Mr. Tammen and Mr Bonfils were shot in their office by W.W. Anderson, an Attorney who represented Alfred Packer, the notorious "Man eater." The Denver Post story accused the Attorney of taking Packers life savings, as a retainer.

During the argument, Attorney Anderson had shot Tammen three times and Bonfils's twice, but was never convicted. In a strange turn of events, both shooting victims were convicted of jury tampering in their third trial against Attorney Anderson.

Then in 1900 both Mr. Bonfils and Mr. Tammen were horse whipped and hospitalized by another Attorney who didn't much like their style of "Yellow Journalism." This term describes journalism that uses little or no legitimate news and instead uses exaggerated, eye catching headlines to increase sales.

Seems the Denver Post isn't without its enemies.

Thankfully, Elizabeth Tabor could avenge her family every time she lite her kerosene lantern, by setting a piece of the newspaper on fire and watching it burn.

"Oh, I almost forgot to tell you ladies, I sprained my ankle and both of my thumbs chopping wood just before Christmas", Mrs. Tabor added, as she ran a soot covered finger along her thumb, leaving a blackened trail. "And I really have no muscle, see I never had to work, because we had plenty of money and I used to ride around in my upholstered coach. We had a coachman and a footman too." She added, as she transported herself back to that time in her life, even if it was just for a brief moment.

"One Christmas we were in our coach distributing presents to the poor in Denver and this woman holds out this baby boy, plump as butter, and asks Mr. Tabor if he would adopt the baby!" Mrs. Tabor explained with a laugh. "He of course said no."

"Mrs. Tabor, how is your ankle now?" Alice asked, which quickly snapped Elizabeth back from her memories. "My ankle? Oh, well, my leg is swollen and seems to be going up my knee." She replied, while rubbing her leg. "But I bathe it in hot water every night and put kerosene on it, which I think helps."

But as she watched Mrs. Tabor stop rubbing her leg and begin to rub her right arm, up near her shoulder, Alice begin to suspect that she might have a rheumatic condition.

"Oh, the flames going out again." Elizabeth announced, as she stood up and gleefully tore a strip of news print off a copy of The Denver Post, rolled it into a small, tight wand and ignited it with the flames of her wood stove.

As Alice listened to the childlike giggle of a small, elderly woman achieving continual revenge, she was able to finish glancing around Mrs. Tabor's cabin.

This time she focused her attention on Mrs. Tabor's bed, which appeared to be a single or double sized, iron framed bed and displayed chipped, white paint, combined with numerous scrapes. A black blanket covered the mattress, which appeared to either have defective springs or hidden piles of clothing beneath the bed covering, as it appeared lumpy.

Piled against the foot of the bed was the second pile of stacked wood, which Mrs. Tabor had been using to keep the wood stove alive and in the middle of the room was a homemade wooden table, about 3 feet x 2 feet. The surface of the table was the cleanest thing in the entire cabin and was surprisingly covered with a carefully spread out copy of The Denver Post, with a pair of either gold or brass rimmed spectacles resting on top of an open pamphlet.

A friendly ticking sound drew Alice's attention over to a Big Ben clock, which faced the visitors, as they sat near the wood stove. The sound of the ticking, mixed with the sound of the crackling fire, made the dreariness of the cabin seem not so harsh.

"Your clock is a half-hour slow." Loretta pointed out, as she pointed to the clock. "Oh, it is?" Mrs. Tabor replied as she quickly got up from her seat and turned the hands to 5:30.

"Oh, did I tell you girls about the time my Tabor delivered a message for President Lincoln? His mother told me the story years ago and she even still had the hat Horace was wearing the night it happened, which shows all the bullet holes. God saved him that night! I believe in God and I think everyone should." Elizabeth Tabor explained, as she grasped her crucifix and looked up towards the heavens.

"My Tabor was just a little boy, just about so high and just in his teens." Mrs. Tabor continued, as she held her hand up to show the height of a young child. "And the armies were drawn up in a, umm… big field, you know with soldiers everywhere and the General asked who will take this message to the other General?" She announced with a deeper voice, as she reenacted the scene.

"You see, it was very dangerous and the messenger had to get on a horse and ride as hard as he could to the other side, with people shooting at him. It was very dangerous." She added, as she looked into the eyes of her captive audience.

"But no one said a word, so the General asked again, who will take this message that says the slaves are free?" Mrs. Tabor announced, as she fluttered an imaginary paper in the air for dramatic effect.

"Then someone spoke up and said we can't take this message! We will be shot down before we get started! And that's when Mr. Tabor rushed up…he was just a little fellow… and he cried I'll take it! Give me those papers!" And he seized them, sprang upon his horse and away he went with the soldiers firing at him." Elizabeth demonstrated with a deep, stern voice and a wave of her arms.

"And you know, this was the moment the miracle arrived, because his black hat was full of holes!" Elizabeth announced, while holding her beloved crucifix tightly in her dainty hands. "I've seen the hat, Tabor's mother had it, but God saved him. I believe in God and I think everyone should."

But despite Mrs. Tabor sharing the dramatic story of her husband, as though it was fact, history has proved that the story was unfortunately false.

Historical records show that Horace Tabor was a 31 year old married man, who was running a General Store in Buckskin Joe at the time President Lincoln issued his preliminary Emancipation Proclamation, on September 22, 1862.

"Oh, and I'm going to have the history of the Tabor's all written some day! Loretta is going to help me." Elizabeth Tabor explained with a smile, as she swept her hands over towards the collection of boxes across the room. "I have it all in there, the dates and everything. And that book Silver Dollar is nothing but lies! I'm going to write the truth!"

"We will do it next summer, Mrs. Tabor." Loretta announce cheerfully, as she stood up to put on her coat.

Seeing that her guests were ready to leave, Elizabeth got up and put on her heavy coat, before entering her lean-to and unlocking the outside door. As the three women walked through the lean-to, Alice took a closer look around and noticed that numerous boxes were stacked up, all the way to the peak of the little room's roof, while the walls were lined with stacks of split firewood. The area was so cluttered, that the three women had to walk out, into the frosty winter air, single file.

After experiencing the sudden sting of winter on her face, Alice felt a tiny hand grab her arm and turned to see Mrs. Tabor and noticed a sadness in her eyes. Bending down, Alice hugged the elderly woman, as she tried not to cry.

"I see your tracks in the snow, you girls would do better to wrap your feet in gunny sacks then to trust those rubbers to keep your feet dry." Elizabeth Tabor called out, as she watched the two woman slowly wade through the deep snow, towards their car.

Loretta had parked her vehicle at the bottom of the Matchless mines driveway, as she was afraid the snow was too deep for her car to make the climb and as she slowly lifted her foot out of the snow pack and watched it sink deep with her next step, she was glad she did.

But Loretta's visits to Mrs. Tabor would come to a sudden and bitter end a few months later, after a Leadville resident let it slip out that the food boxes came from the community food bank and were in fact charity.

Loretta had discovered a box full of food sitting outside Elizabeth's Tabor's door, when she arrived to bring her another the following month and despite a desperate attempt to fix her deception, Mrs. Tabor never again would open the door for her former friend.

A SHOTGUN NAMED TRUSTY AND THE CLOAKED VISITOR

"Mrs. Tabor? Excuse me…Mrs. Tabor, are you home?" Roy Thatcher inquired, as he again knocked on the front door of Elizabeth Tabor's cabin. "Mrs. Tabor, we are here to talk to you about re-opening the mine."

Peeking out the window, Elizabeth saw two overly dressed men kicking snow away from her front door, to avoid standing in the drifts that had blown up against her cabin. The spring blizzards of 1934 had been just as nasty as always, but luckily the warmth of summer was starting to melt away all the left over patches, that lay hidden in the shadows.

Opening the window, Elizabeth peeked out and told the men she would be right out. At 79 years old, Elizabeth didn't move as fast as she used to, but she always made sure she was dressed for the weather.

And that her gun was loaded.

With a slow creak, the men finally heard the door of the Lean-to open and the tiny Mrs. Tabor appear, with her shot gun at the ready. Giving the men the once over, Elizabeth decided not to invite them into her cabin and instead silently motioned, with the barrel of her gun, for the men to have a seat outside on a nearby bench.

With their hands slightly raised, the men quickly walked over to Mrs. Tabor's selected spot, brushed off the snow and had a seat on the cold, wet wood. Keeping her eye on the men and never lowering her weapon, Elizabeth sat across from them, on a bench of her own.

"Mrs. Tabor, my name is Roy Thatcher and I'm a consulting engineer and this here is Archie Leviton, from Wyoming." The man explained, with a slight nervous tone. "Mam' could you please lower your gun? We are not here to hurt you, we just want to re-open the Matchless."

Elizabeth gave the two nervous men one more glance, before slowly lowering her gun and laying it across her lap, but she never took her eyes off the uninvited visitors.

"Mrs. Tabor, we have been granted a lease of your property by the

Elizabeth Tabor walking out of her cabin- The Denver Public Library, Western History Collection-Z-14609

heirs of the late John Mullen." Mr. Leviton began, as he held up a copy of the agreement and tried hard to rid himself of the nervous squeak his voice had suddenly developed. "We have named our new mining company the Matchless Silver Dollar Mine Inc. and with your permission would like to start bringing in new machinery."

"Can I still live in my cabin?" Elizabeth questioned, with an untrusting tone. "I have a contract inside, that both Mr. Mullen and myself signed, that says I can live here, until I die."

"Yes Mam', we will be honoring that promise Mr. Mullen made to you." Mr. Thatcher added, as he tried hard to return his voice to a more natural sounding tone.

"When did he die?" Elizabeth asked, loosening her grip on the gun.

"A few years ago Mam', he died of pneumonia back in the fall of 1929." Mr. Thatcher answered, with a quizzical look. "I think he was…82?"

Just then the creak of a car door began to fill the air and looking over towards the sound, Mrs. Tabor saw a familiar face appear from out of the back seat of the men's vehicle, which caused her to quickly jump up and draw her gun.

"Whoa, whoa, put the gun down!" Both Mr. Thatcher and Mr. Leviton pleaded, as the man from the car continued his stubborn stroll in Mrs. Tabor's direction. Pumping the shotgun and hearing the shell slide into its chamber, Elizabeth held her aim. "Get off my property, you son of a bitch!"

"Nice to see you again too, Mrs. Tabor Mam'." The man casually replied, as he stopped walking and slowly raised his hands up in a show of sarcastic surrender.

"If you have hired this man to assist you in reopening my mine, then there is no deal!" Elizabeth explained in a harsh tone, as she backed up enough to keep all three men in her sight. Confused, Archie Leviton looked over at Roy Thatcher and asked "Wait, I thought you hired him because he was familiar with the Matchless?"

"I am." The old miner replied, with a cocky tone to his voice. "I worked for old H.A.W Tabor back when this mine was pumping out millions in Silver, I just didn't get along with the Miss's very well, that's all."

"You are no longer welcome and you all need to leave my property!" Elizabeth Tabor insisted, as she motioned the men to move, once again using the barrel of her gun to point the direction. Defeated, both Mr. Thatcher and Mr. Leviton quickly began walking back to their car, while the old miner continued to stand and smile. Then, with a tip of his hat and the blowing of an arrogant kiss in her direction, he bid her good day.

Watching the car drive back to the main road, Elizabeth walked down to the end of the driveway to make sure they were gone, before she propped her shotgun upon her shoulder and headed back to her cabin.

She knew they would be back.

As the months passed, gossip began to spread through town of the possibility of the Matchless reopening, so she knew those business men had been putting the bug in peoples ears. And when a new group of men from The Shorego Mining Company came knocking on her cabin door, she was ready for them.

With a sign.

On the front door of her cabin, Elizabeth wrote in bold letters "Gone to Denver", locked the doors and windows up tight and sat quiet as a mouse.

"Mrs. Tabor, My name is J. Warsaw and I'm the President of The Matchless Silver Dollar Mines Inc. My associate Roy Thatcher came to speak to you a few months back." The man explained in a loud voice, as he assumed the elderly woman was simply hiding inside the cabin. "We understand that Mr. John Mullen promised that you could live in this cabin for as long as you wished, but we would like to offer you the chance to live like a queen, like you did when your husband was alive."

"Mrs. Tabor, we hate to see you suffer through these long winters and we would like to offer you a comfortable Hotel room in either Denver or New York City, with a modest income, which would of course come from your share of the mines profits." Mr. Warsaw added, as continued to knock on the front door of her cabin. "Mrs. Tabor, did you hear my offer? Mrs. Tabor?"

Waving him aside, a mining representative out of Denver took his turn at the door. "Mrs. Tabor, My name is Harry Schechtel and I just want to assure you that the Shorego Mining Company has only your best interests in mind Mam'." He began, as he leaned his face closer to the door, in an attempt to make himself heard more clearly. "Mrs. Tabor, your husband did so much for this community and his widow shouldn't have to live in an old, tumble down shack."

Hearing a car pull up to the cabin, the two business men turned their heads and watched a group of young tourists pounce out of their car and happily skip over to the front door of the cabin, squeeze past the men and knock on the door. "Mrs. Tabor, we loved your movie! Can we please meet you?" the group inquired with an excited shriek, as a few of the sight seer's began peeking in the windows. "Mrs. Tabor! Mrs. Tabor! We love you!"

Walking away from the circus, the two men sat down on a nearby bench, lit a cigarette and glanced around the run down property. A treasure trove of Silver lay under their feet, but it would remain untouched if one, lonely old widow doesnt agree to let them retrieve it.

But as the men watched yet another group of tourists pull up to Mrs. Tabor's cabin and begin to take pictures, they shook their heads in defeat and headed back to their car.

Luckily, as the beautiful Leadville summer turned into fall and the chipmunks finished gathering the last of their nuts for the long winter, Elizabeth Tabor was finally beginning to relax. She hadn't seen the men from the Shorego Mining Company for a few months now and she was hoping the upcoming winter blizzards would keep them at bay.

Pouring herself a hot cup of tea, Elizabeth walked over to her soot covered wall calendar and crossed off September 25th, which marked her 80th birthday. Glancing out the window, she smiled at the sight of tiny snowflakes dancing around outside her cabin, which she hoped marked the end of her visits with the Shorego mining company and their hired goons.

And as the year came to its blustery end, Elizabeth Tabor spent New Year's Eve going over her supplies and gaging how long it would be before she would have to make the track back into town, but she wasn't expecting to wake up to the sound of melting snow dripping off her roof, on January 26, 1935.

Being hit by a unexpected heat wave, Leadville experienced a high temperature of 52° degrees, when just 5 days before, the winter temperatures had dropped down to a numbing -22°. And it turned out that 1935 was hitting records, not only in Leadville, but all over the state of Colorado, as the warmest January in 48 years.

As Elizabeth's supplies continued to dwindle, she finally saw a beautiful, peacock blue sky greet her on the morning of February 20th and after wrapping herself up tight and adjusting her scarf, she headed out of the cabin and towards 7th street, the main road into town.

But she had to get out of her driveway first.

Covered in a deep snow pack, mixed with sections of melting ice and frigid puddles, Elizabeth Tabor tried her hardest to keep her balance, but failed. Picking herself up numerous times, she finally arrived at 7th street saturated with snow and cold, heavy mud, which made her burlapped covered boots difficult to manage during her mile long walk into town.

"Mrs. Tabor, my dear, are you alright?" John McMahon asked, as Elizabeth slowly walked into the Post Office and headed towards the counter. Resembling a pig that had been rolling around in a mud hole, Elizabeth Tabor appeared more bedraggled than usual and when Mr. McMahon inquired about what had happened, she simply tried to laugh it off.

"Oh, I just slipped and fell a few times coming from my cabin to the main road, that's all." She replied, as the Post Master questioned her condition.

Not much for causing a scene, Elizabeth quickly collected her mail, sent off her letters and headed over to Frank Zaitz's Mercantile to stock up on supplies. The heavy mud that covered her clothes and boots was beginning to dry and despite all her attempts to shake it loose, the weight remained and was beginning to drag down her tiny frame.

"Will this be all today Mrs. Tabor?" Elmer Kutzieb asked, as he finished placing all of Elizabeth's things into a box. With no witty response, her silence caught his attention. "Mrs. Tabor? Are you feeling ok?"

"I'm just feeling rather tired today, that's all." She replied with a forced smile. "Just tired."

Helping Mrs. Tabor into the passenger side of his delivery truck, Elmer noticed that the entire drive back up to his customer's cabin held an eerie silence, as Elizabeth chose to simply look out the trucks window instead of engaging in her usual, casual chit chat.

Pulling up to the driveway of the mine, Mr. Kuzieb found himself over 100 yards from the cabin, when his truck became stuck in the mud and snow. Asking Mrs. Tabor to remain in the truck, Elmer grabbed her box of groceries from the bed and began his careful walk to the cabin. He didn't want to risk walking his tiny, mud covered customer towards her home, until he could gage the extent of difficulty she would face, as he had no desire to have her fall again.

Upon returning to his truck, Elmer felt confident in his chosen path and held onto Mrs. Tabor as they slowly walked up to her cabin. Helping her inside, he showed her where her new box of supplies was and asked her again if she was feeling alright.

"I'm just tired, that's all…I'm just tired."

"When would you like me to return with your next order Mam'?"

Elmer Kutzieb asked, as Elizabeth began adding more wood to her stove. "Why don't you come back on April 10th, I should have enough supplies until then." She added with a smile, as she slowly stood back up and gave him a gentle pat on his arm. "April 10th should be just fine."

With a wave and a thank you, Elizabeth watched the delivery man head back to his truck, before locking her cabin door up tight and hanging up her mud encrusted coat.

So tired…

Sitting down next to her wood stove, she felt the warmth fill her body as she slowly began to untie the twine that held the muddy layers of gunny sacks over her boots.

Just so tired…

Undressing down to her chemise, Elizabeth shuffled over to her bed and crawled under the piles of soiled covers and soot stained blankets, desperate for rest.

I just need to sleep…

Please God just let me sleep…

But her pleading soon fell on deaf ears, as a black cloaked entity suddenly materialized outside the Matchless, floated towards Elizabeth Tabor's cabin and pressed the tip of his scythe against her front door.

Easily gaining entry, the Angel of Death silently glided over to Elizabeth Tabor's weary body, seized her heart and compressed it.

Bolting upright and grabbing her chest, she gasped as the sharp pain shot through her, before death teasingly loosened his grip, only to squeeze once again. To add to her torment, he then enveloped her body within his black mist and begin stealing her breath, gently returning it with a struggle, before violently ripping it away from her once again.

Desperate to breathe, Elizabeth managed to push her covers aside and escape her bed, but as Death continued his torment…the pain in her chest suddenly stopped.

Pulling his skeletal hand away from Elizabeth's heart, the Reaper turned towards the sound of a nearby soul begging for release. Glancing down at the frail body of Mrs. Tabor, he reached deep within his spectral robe and removed a gothic hour glass, which he set on the nearby table. Tapping it with the tip of his scythe, the sands that gaged Elizabeth's time left on earth began to fall, as Death vanished from her cabin.

And with the wind continuing to blow snow against the mines head frame and assist the blizzard in its arrival, the only sound that emitted from inside the cabin was the delightful crackle of the wood stove and the constant ticking of a clock, which reveled in being 30 minutes slow.

Tick, tick, tick…

But with the hands of the clock unable to add fuel to the fire, the heat from the woodstove eventually began to diminish, as the last specks of wood burned out. And with the snow continuing to dump its feathery brilliance onto the cabin, it soon created a cocoon around its silent occupant, as the thermometer begins it's decent, until it hit a frigid -8°.

Tick, tick, tick…

"Mrs. Tabor? Mrs. Tabor? Are you home?" Tom French asked, as he knocked on the front door of the cabin. "Mrs. Tabor?"

"Boost me up and I'll peak in the window." Sue Bonney asked, as Mr. French leaned his ear against the door.

Wading through the waist deep snow that surrounded the cabin, Tom lifted up his lady friend and held her still, while she looked inside the windows for any sign of Mrs. Tabor. The couple hadn't seen her in town for a while and when they walked past her cabin, Tom had noticed that there was no smoke coming out of her stove pipe.

"She's laying on the floor! Oh my God! She's on the floor!" Sue screamed, as she struggled to get down from the window. "She's on the floor Tom! Hurry, open the door!"

Lowering Sue from the almost 4 foot high snow drift, Tom trudged back over to the cabin's front door, tried to open it, but found it locked.

Taking a few steps back, he got a good start and slammed his shoulder against the door, which gave a slight groan. Rubbing his upper arm, he shook the door handle and could feel the looseness of the inside lock. With a confident expression, Tom slammed his shoulder once more into the door and almost fell into the cabins lean-too, as the lock gave way.

With a slight fear of Mrs. Tabor's shotgun, the pair of trespassers stood silent for a second and listened for any sound that might come from inside the cabin. Hearing nothing, both Tom and Sue slowly walked over to the interior door, which separated the lean-to from the main cabin and again Tom knocked and called out to Mrs. Tabor, but received no answer.

Turning the handle and listening to the latch click, the pair cautiously entering the cabin and immediately noticed the icy temperature and the stillness of the room. Seeing the lifeless body of Elizabeth Tabor on the floor, Tom ran over to it. "Mrs. Tabor? Mrs. Tabor?" he inquired in a soothing tone, as knelt down and gently placed his hand on her shoulder. "Mrs. Tabor?"

"Sue, she's dead…Oh, damn, Sue…She's frozen. Completely frozen solid", he added with a whisper, as he ran his hand down Elizabeth's bare arm and attempted to give it a squeeze. Standing back up, he removed his hat and lowered his head in an honest show of remorse.

After a moment of respectful silence, Tom placed his hat back on his head. "Sue, stay here with Mrs. Tabor and I'll walk into town and get the coroner." He said in a shushed tone, as he hadn't yet processed the frozen body that lay at his feet. "Stay with her."

As Tom buttoned his coat up tight and left the cabin, Sue wasn't sure what she was supposto do while he was gone. The tiny, partially clothed body of Mrs. Tabor was lying face down on the floor with her arms spread out, but bent in at the elbows and her fingers were clasped, as though she had suffered some type of a convulsion or had died attempting to keep warm.

Nervously looking around the room, Sue noticed that the covers on Mrs. Tabor's bed had been pulled back and rumpled, which made it appear that she had just gotten out of bed before she died, which would explain the tattered chemise she was wearing.

Leaning in the corner of the room was the rifle that Mrs. Tabor had called "My Trusty" and hanging next to it was the old bonnet Sue was so used to seeing her wear around town. The style of the bonnet was popular in the early 1900's, when people went motoring in twin-cylinder cars and chugged around town and next to it , hung Mrs. Tabor's winter jacket.

Once an expensive, tailor made coat, whose price would have kept the 1935 Mrs. Tabor in groceries for a year, now hung thread bare and worn on it's simple, wooden peg. Against the wall, Sue also saw some boxes filled with old newspapers and notes written on scraps of paper carefully stacked on a long wooden shelf.

And then she spotted the wood stove.

With a high outside of only around 22°, the inside of the cabin was frigid, but Sue knew she couldn't risk Mrs. Tabor thawing out, just to warm herself up. Taunted by the stove and its lure of a crackling fire, she simply buttoned her coat up a bit tighter and waited.

After what seemed like hours, Sue finally heard the sounds of heavy footsteps crunching in the deep snow and distant voices of numerous men approaching the cabin. Jumping up, she quickly left the frozen mausoleum that held Mrs. Tabor's body and welcomed the chance to join the living once again.

"Afternoon Mrs. Bonney, sorry we all have to meet like this." Coroner James Corbett announced, as he turned to introduce the young man he had brought up with him. "And this here is Andy Cassidy, he has been learning the trade."

"Nice to meet you Mam', sorry about Mrs. Tabor", he added, as he shook Sue's hand.

"Well, let's all go inside and see what happened", the Coroner announced with a mournful tone, as he started to walk towards the open door of the cabin's lean-too.

Heading into the cabin first, Sue quickly led Mr. Corbett over to the still body of Mrs. Tabor, which lay near the cold wood stove. Leaning down to check for a pulse, he noticed the bluish tone of her skin, which Mr. French had previously informed him about. Removing his gloves, he slid his bare hand underneath Mrs. Tabor's thin garment, which covered her back and gently laid his palm between her shoulder blades.

"Damn, your right Tom, she's frozen solid!" Mr. Corbett announced with a start, as he glanced back over at Mr. French, "Poor old girl."

Standing back up, he began looking around the room for clues to her cause of death and possibly how long she had been laying on the floor. Spotting a wall calendar, he walked over to it and noticed that Mrs. Tabor had written that she had gone into town on February 20th to visit a Mr. Zitz, which could quite possibly be a misspelling of Mr. Zaitz, who ran the local Mercantile down on Harrison Ave., as she also had listed that a boy drove her home that same day.

Across the top of the calendar it read "21 Spirits Spirits", but in looking at the rest of the calendar and Mrs. Tabor's style of note taking, it appeared to be in reference to Feburary 21 and not twenty one spirits.

She also had a note written underneath Feburary 22nd that read "MND and lady will come I got at", which hinted at a possible visit from expected company, but if her company had come, it's unlikely they caused her death, as her body showed no signs of trauma.

Glancing over to Mrs. Tabor's kitchen area, Mr. Corbett found 5 cans of soup and tomatoes, along with a 24 pound sack of flour, which would discount the possibility of her starving to death, as well as an old pocketbook that held two $1 dollar bills and a few odd coins.

Returning to inspect the position of Mrs. Tabor's body, Mr. Corbett felt that perhaps she had gotten up out of bed and sat in her rocking chair by the wood stove, only to fall onto the floor while attempting to add wood to the fire, as a few pieces of wood were within arm's reach.

"Well, her body doesn't show any signs of violence", Mr. Corbett announced, with a slight shrug. "And if she had frozen to death, I think her body would be curled up in more of a ball, instead of simply face down, with her hands curled. So, I'm just going to list her death as heart disease."

"So, what would the official description be?" Andy Cassidy asked, as he continued to write down everything the Coroner was saying in his notebook, "Oh, yeah, sorry", Mr. Corbett chuckled, as he watched his young assistant hold his pencil at the ready. "Acute Myocarditis, which is an Inflammation of the heart muscle, brought on by a viral infection."

"And why do you think she had a viral infection?" Andy asked, as he continued to write.

"Well, over on that table I found an almost empty medicine bottle, so I'm guessing Mrs. Tabor was possibly doctoring herself for a cold." Mr. Corbett replied with a shrug of uncertainty, as he walked towards the front door of the cabin.

"And time of death?" Andy inquired, as he continued to write.

"Oh, there is no way to know that Andy." The Coroner laughed, as he turned around to face his assistant. "But we will list her death as February 20th."

"But, Sir, Mrs. Tabor's last entry on her calendar was February 22st." the young man reminded him, as he pointed back over at the calendar.

"Well, she also wrote about spirits on the boarder of the calendar too, so there is no real way to prove she wrote these notes on the actual day of February 21st or 22nd." The Coroner explained, as he opened up the outside door of the cabin. "And besides, the last day she crossed off on her calendar was Feburary 19th, so the 20th works for me."

"Now if you and Mr. French would help me retrieve the cot and some blankets out of the back of my truck, we can get Mrs. Tabor wrapped up and down to the morgue, so she can thaw out." He added, as he began buttoning up his coat alittle tighter.

This is defiently not the ending anyone would have wanted for the widow of Governor H.A.W Tabor.

A TOWN FULL OF SCAVENGERS AND THE JOYFUL REUNION

Nothing travels faster than bad news.

Within minutes of Tom French alerting Leadville's Coroner James Corbett, that Mrs. Tabor had been found dead, the phone lines began lighting up like a wild fire. Surprisingly, every major Newspaper recieved word that her body had been found around 1:30pm, Thursday March 7, 1935, before the Coroner had even returned to the mortuary with her frozen, blanket wrapped corpse.

Except her family.

Desperate for an interview, a reporter from The Denver Post Newspaper contacted Elizabeth Tabor's younger brother Willard McCourt for a comment, but instead became the first person to inform him that his sister had died.

After giving the reporter a quick statement that he would handle all of his sister's arrangements, 64 year old Willard boarded the Friday morning train out of Denver and wondered what type of mad house he was going to find, when he arrived in Leadville.

"Mr. McCourt! Mr. McCourt! Will your sister be buried in

Leadville or Denver?" reporters inquired as Mr. McCourt stepped out of the open door of the train car and onto the platform. "Will she be buried next to Governor Tabor?"

"Mrs. Tabor will be buried in Leadville at either Evergreen Cemetery or St. Joseph's Cemetery, possibly on Saturday." He replied, as he addressed the eager reporters. "It hasn't yet been decided, now if you will please excuse me."

Quickly entering a waiting car, Willard headed to the Moynahan-O'Malia Mortuary to view the now thawed out body of his 80 year old sister Elizabeth. Entering the building, he was greeted by Mr. Corbett and Reverend Father Edward L. Horgan, the pastor of the Church of the Annunciation, where his sister worshiped.

After accepting condolences for his loss and visiting his sister's mortal remains, the men sat down to discuss her funeral and burial arrangements. Feeling that Elizabeth would want to be buried in Leadville, the decision was made to bury her at Saint Joseph's Catholic cemetery.

Driving up to the Cemetery, Willard McCourt chose a burial plot in front of a tall, pine tree before heading back to the Mortuary, to complete his sister's funeral arrangements. But as he entered the building, he was met by a well-dressed woman and her Lawyer.

"Mr. McCourt, my name is Mrs. Ella Mullen Weckbaugh and my sister's and I would like to not only offer you our deepest condolences for the loss off your sister, but also offer to pay for Mrs. Tabor's funeral." the woman announced, as she handed a envelope to Mr. McCourt. "As I'm sure you are aware, our father J.K. Mullen purchased your sister's Matchless Mine in order to gift it back to her, until her death and we would like to propose a change of venue, in regards to your sister's burial." The woman explained, as she watched Mr. McCourt open up the envelope and review the papers inside.

"You want to bury her down in Denver with Horace?" Mr. McCourt asked with a quizzical expression, as he continued to read the

A TOWN FULL OF SCAVENGERS AND THE JOYFUL REUNION 361

document. "Mam', I don't know if you are aware of this, but the State of Colorado lost the location of Mr. Tabor's grave years ago. Nobody even knows where his grave is."

"Yes, we are aware of this slight inconvenience, but we have put the word out in an attempt to find him." Mrs. Weckbaugh announced, with a hopeful smile. "Denver's Calvary Cemetery has been left to the weeds and there is also the rumor that Mr. Tabor's small grave marker may also have been stolen by souvenir hunters decades ago."

"Mrs. Weckbaugh, I think your intentions regarding my sister are wonderful, but we do need to get her buried." Mr. McCourt announced, with a smile. "Now I have already chosen a burial plot here in Leadville, but I would be willing to hold off on her funeral until Monday March 11th, to give you some time to locate Mr. Tabor."

But then a thought raced through his mind.

"Mrs. Weckbaugh, I would like to ask a favor, if I could?" He asked, with a hopeful expression. "My older brother Stephen McCourt is also buried in the Calvary Cemetery, after he died in 1909. If you are able to locate Horace, could you possibly also have my brothers body exhumed as well and buried next to our sister?"

"Of course, I will have my men begin looking right away." She replied, with an understanding tone to her voice.

With a smile and a handshake, Mrs. Weckbaugh headed over to a nearby phone, to contact her people in Denver, as Mr. Willard McCourt explained the new agreement with the funeral director.

After a quick explanation in regards to the proposed burial request, Mr. McCourt chose to still have the grave dug for his sister, up at Leadville's Saint Joseph's Catholic Cemetery, just in case Mr. Tabor's body couldn't be located and for Elizabeth's mass to still be held the next morning, Saturday March 9th.

Discovering they still had the go ahead to prepare Mrs. Tabor's final resting place, the grave diggers went to work.

But they had a problem.

A big problem.

The ground was frozen.

Not new to this type of inconvenience, the men began clearing the deep snow from the chosen grave site, covered the frozen earth with straw and set it on fire. Adding small logs and brush, the men encouraged the fire to burn for hours, as the top few feet of the ground slowly began to thaw. Using a long, metal drill bit, they periodically attempted to drill into the frozen ground, until they finally hit their desired depth of six feet.

Allowing the fire to die down to a smolder, a total of eight holes were drilled, each with a diameter of 1 ½ inches. Two holes were drilled at the top of the future grave, one in each corner, two at the bottom, also with one in each corner, two holes along the length of the grave, with one on each side, about half way down and two in the center.

Satisfied with the holes, two 8" long sticks of dynamite, at 50% strength, were then lowered into each hole, one stick above the other, with each hole then carefully packed with sand to prevent the dynamite from shooting straight up out of the holes like rockets, when they were detonated.

"Fire in the Hole!"

The sudden blast sent shockwaves through a town already in the throes of morning, as people held their heads down in silence, with a combined understanding that this was Mrs. Elizabeth Tabor's grave being prepared.

But while some people chose to honor the dead woman, others decided to pounce upon her now unguarded cabin and strip it bare.

News Paper reporters, photographers and souvenir hunters alike, tore into the tiny cabin looking for anything they thought might be valuable or news worthy, turning the once tidy, little home into a war zone. Elizabeth's carefully organized boxes of newspaper clippings and letters were dumped out onto the floor and riffled through, in a desperate quest to locate hidden jewelry or silver, while the numerous unopened gifts she had received, from the fans of the movie she detested, were carted off by the armload.

Like locusts, Elizabeth Tabor's trunks were torn apart, her wood stove rifled through and even the brown paper peeled off her walls, yet her supply of canned food, which could have filled a starving person's stomach, sat ignored and untouched.

But as the morning of Saturday March 9th greeted the citizens of Leadville, it reminded them that this was the last day they would ever have to look upon the dainty face of Mrs. H.A.W. Tabor. With images filling people's heads of a frozen, elderly woman lying on the floor of her tiny cabin, the viewing of her body finally gave the people of Colorado the chance to see the real Mrs. Tabor.

The Silver Queen.

Dressed in a brown crepe dress her brother Willard had purchased for her and with her feet covered in brand new black slippers, he had found tucked away inside her cabin, she painted quite a different image than the one the people of Colorado were used to seeing.

No longer was her girlish figure enveloped in layers, upon layers of soiled clothing or her beautiful strawberry blond hair tucked away underneath an ancient cap. Laid out like a queen, on the satin lining of her coffin, Elizabeth Tabor shone with the elegance of her once blessed life style.

And as Mr. McCourt stood by and watched the curious of Colorado approach his older sister's casket and listened to the many kind comments regarding her beautiful appearance, he was approached by a well-dressed man, who tapped him on the shoulder, before casually whispering in his ear.

"They found him."

Excusing himself, Willard McCourt quickly followed the man over to the funeral director and arrangements were put in place to have his sister's coffin loaded onto the next Denver bound train, as soon as Mass was complete.

Surprisingly, Mr. Tabor's lost gravesite was discovered by a 17 year old, red haired, freckled faced senior at Denver's St. Francis De Sales High school…who was also Elizabeth Tabor's pen pal.

Orville Porouix had sent a letter to Mrs. Tabor, a few years earlier, after discovering that Mr. H.A.W Tabor had done a big favor for an old relative of his and wanted to thank her. But as he learned more about the lonely widow, he asked her if they could be pen pals, which she gratefully accepted.

But Orville didn't just accidentally stumble upon Mr. Tabor's grave, he had actually been looking for it off and on for over a year, as Mrs. Tabor had asked him to find it for her and say a prayer on her behalf. And on Saturday March 9th, his search had paid off, when he finally

Elizabeth Tabor's Funeral- The Denver Public Library, Western History Collection-X-22026

found a small granite stone that read "Tabor", leaning against a rusty iron cross, surrounded by an over growth of weeds and bushes.

But Horace Tabor would still have to wait a few weeks to join his beloved Elizabeth, as someone still had to locate his brother –in- law, Stephen McCourt.

The new cemetery chosen to hold the mortal remains of the once fabulous Mr. and Mrs. Tabor, was Mount Olivet Cemetery, which had held Denver's Catholic community since 1892. Currently, Horace Tabor and his brother-in-law Stephen McCourt, laid buried in the Roman Catholic section of The Prospect Hill Cemetery, which opened in 1858.

Unfortunately, Prospect Hill's fell into great disrepair by the 1880's and the families had been ordered to have the graves moved, but with the large number of graves in the Roman Catholic section, the city of Denver sold the 40 acre plot to the Diocese, who re-named it the Mount Calvary Cemetery.

But now it simply sat weed filled and forgotten.

That is until Mrs. Elizabeth Tabor's death brought its disgraceful state back onto the front pages of the local Newspapers.

But as the dirt was being dug out Saturday afternoon, for Mrs. Tabor's newly chosen Mount Olivet grave site, her body was still laying inside the chapel of Leadville's Church of Annunciation, receiving the blessings of the Priest and bathed in the light that shone though the churches beautiful stain glass windows.

After a service filled with prayer and tradition, the church began filling with heavenly music as the congregation stood up to silently witness the removal of Elizabeth Tabor's coffin and make notice of her chosen Pallbearer's.

Taking hold of the front two handles, were Post Master John W. McMahon and Doctor Franklin J. McDonald, while the middle set of handles were held by Assistant Post Master Joseph R. Dewar and Mine Manager John Harvey. Holding the final two handles, located at the back of the coffin were Lawyer Robert McLeod and Marshall Dennis J. O'Neill.

Filing out behind the casket, the curious and the loving began heading to their vehicles, so they could follow the hearse to the cemetery, but were suddenly caught off guard as the funeral director asked for the attention of all the mourners.

"Ladies and Gentlemen, could I please have your attention? Ladies and Gentlemen? Thank you." The Director began, as Mrs. Tabor's casket was slid into the back of the waiting hearse. "I wish to inform you all, that just a few hours ago, we learned that Mrs. Horace Tabor will no longer be buried here in Leadville, but will instead be buried next to Governor Tabor, in Denver. Thank you."

As the mourners began to discuss what they just heard, Willard McCourt entered his car and followed the hearse to the Leadville train depot. With a sprinkling of mourners in attendance, Willard watched as his sister's coffin was loaded, before he accepted final condolences and found his seat on the train headed back to Denver.

Arriving that evening and with no fanfare, Elizabeth Tabor's casket was loaded into a waiting hearse at Denver's Union Station and taken between the silent gates of The Mount Olivet Cemetery, where her brother and a few on lookers braved Denver's chilly spring weather.

With the newly dug grave blessed by a nameless Catholic Priest, the observer's lower their heads, as the final prayer was given.

"O God, by whose mercy the faithful departed rest, send your holy angel to watch over this grave, through Christ our Lord."

Amen.

On April 4th, almost a month after Elizabeth was laid to rest, both Horace Tabor and Stephen McCourt's graves were exhumed, for reburial in Mount Olivet Cemetery. The only relative that stood by to witness the former Governor of Colorado's casket see the light of day once again, was Frank C. Tabor, a great-Nephew who Horace had never met.

As four grave diggers hoisted Tabor's wooden tomb out of its original grave, the well-constructed casket held strong, with only a layer of mold to indicate it had been underground for 36 years.

And the next day, with no ceremony or fanfare, both Horace Tabor and Stephen McCourt were laid to rest.

Again.

But where Horace Tabor's original grave site had held a small, $12 head stone that read "Tabor", his new grave site, which he now shared

Elizabeth Tabor's coffin being carried from the church-- (#1-Willard McCourt, #2-R.D. McLeod, #3 John Harvey, #4 Dr. Franklin J. McDonald, #5 Dennis O'Neill, #6 Joseph Dewar and #7 John W. McMahon) The Denver Public Library, Western History Collection-X-21987

Horace Tabor's coffin-86.296.338 History Colorado

with his wife Elizabeth, remained bare and unmarked.

It appeared that the people of Colorado were eager to move on from the funerals of the Tabor's and onto the chance to purchase some of the memento's that Elizabeth Tabor had tried so lovingly to preserve.

Souvenir hunters, some who had never heard of Tabor's until the movie Silver Dollar was released, developed the desire to own more artifacts, after ransacking Elizabeth Tabor's cabin up at the Matchless Mine, quickly following her death.

Mrs. Tabor's brother Willard McCourt had visited his sisters cabin

Inside Elizabeth Tabor's cabin- The Denver Public Library, Western History Collection-X-61265

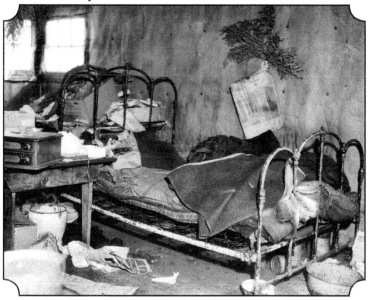

Inside Elizabeth Tabor's cabin- The Denver Public Library, Western History Collection-X-61260

the day he came up to Leadville to make her funeral arrangements, but found nothing inside that he deemed important or valuable, except the black slippers he chose to place on his sisters tiny feet.

The cabin had been locked up tight by the Sherriff numerous times, to keep out vandals and the curious, but they still managed to break in. Mr. Corbett had searched the ransacked cabin after Elizabeth Tabor's funeral and found items that could have been useful to someone, so he collected them and took them over to Sue Bonny.

Five cans of soup and tomatoes, a 24 pound sack of flour and a couple of old blankets were taken over for Sue, but as he looked around the cabin he saw a few pieces of furniture that could possibly be sold as antiques, if Ms. Bonney didn't want them.

An old coal stove, a kitchen table, four mismatched chairs, an iron bed with a mattress and a now empty trunk, thanks to the numerous thieves who continued to ransack the cabin. Even the wood stove had been knocked over, so the pipe itself could be searched for valuables.

And now the people of Colorado waited on baited breathe, as news of the Tabor mementos were being discovered, as not being inside her cabin after all, but safely in storage.

The first collection of artifacts was located in the basement of Leadville's Saint Vincent's Hospital, which revealed two boxes and 6 burlap sacks, full of things a souvenir hunter might not want, but might be important in regards to history.

Box #1- contained 3 burlap sacks.

Sack #1- One fur cape, believed to be seal (Very badly worn), one paper sack of rock specimens and one paper sack full of newspaper articles about Horace Tabor.

Sack #2- One sack of letters, one sack of legal papers, one sack of stock certificates and a collection of ore samples

Sack #3- One sack of letters, one sack of legal papers, one sack of stock certificates, a collection of ore samples and a few photo plates.

Box #2-Cooking utensils, old shoes, numerous newspapers and clippings, one album titled "Mines and Mining men of Colorado", one frame, a set of portieres (curtains made to hang from a doorway), ore specimens, writing paper and envelopes, old notes, a few towels and articles of clothing.

Large burlap sack #1-

Rolls of newspaper, a collection of empty coffee cans, a coffee can full of ground ore samples and papers dated from the World War, marked "Clean table papers".

Large burlap sack #2-

Small paper package containing a sack of private letters.

Large burlap sack #3-

Newspaper clippings about Mrs. Tabor, ore specimens and personal letters marked "Dreams and visons".

Large burlap sack #4-

Two canvas bags full of private letters

Large burlap sack #5-

Bundles of private letters and a package of letters labeled "Dreams and visons".

Large burlap sack #6-

Groceries, kitchen toaster and a few newspaper articles.

Also located in the basement of the Saint Vincent hospital were 16 trunks, which after they were sorted by the auction house, were listed by market value, instead of for their historical significance.

(This list is only for the items discovered in trunks 15 and 16.)

A Golden watch fob-weighing 5 oz. - valued at $100, for melting purposes only

A ladies gold ring containing eight small diamonds and seven sapphires- valued at below $100

A gold specimen with a plush case, weighing around ½ oz. - valued at $17.50

A filigree butterfly broach and cross- valued at below $20

Box of pens- valued below $1.50

Four unmounted cameo's, three of which are damaged- valued below $2.50

The silver Assayer's sprout- valued at $3.50

Seed pearl necklace, which is broken and many of the pearls are loose- valued below $10

Three gold pieces-valued at $23

A silver piece from "Colorado Poultry Association"- valued at $0.25

A gold breast pin- valued at $2

More trunks were also discovered at Bekins moving and Storage Company, in Denver, Colorado, which were also assessed by the auction house, by market value, instead of for their historical significance.

815 Newspapers- no market value

2,149 letters, telegrams and post cards-no market value

755 miscellaneous books, periodicals and magazines- no market value

105 copies of a book titled "Star of blood" by Silver Dollar Tabor- valued at $30

802 copies of sheet music titled "Roosevelts hunt" by Silver Dollar Tabor-valued at $30

One bundle of miscellaneous sheet music-no market value

245 items of clothing-which includes:

Mrs. Tabor's wedding dress, 35 badly damaged hats, Baby Tabor lace dress with velvet coat and hat, Mr. Tabor's dress suit and National Guard uniform with accouterments, as well as 96 articles of Mrs. Tabor's personal clothing, 46 articles of Mr. Tabor's personal clothing and 57 articles of children's personal clothing- no market value

17 items such as embroidered pillows, panels, lace etc. - no market value.

Luckily for Elizabeth Tabor, her attempt to preserve her families' possessions for history appeared to have a Silver lining after all, in the form of a newly founded group called "The Tabor Association." Their only reason for existing, was solely to preserve and purchase as many of the Tabor's relics as possible, but unfortunately, they would have to bid on them just like everyone else.

When the auctions were over and all the precious memories that Elizabeth Tabor struggled so hard to preserve were sold off to the highest bidder, even down to the little velvet bags that held her daughters baby teeth, the victorious winners displayed their new treasures and life went on.

And the memory of the Tabor's faded into history.

Five years later a man named C.E. Liesveld, who owned G &L Granite in Denver, was taking his usual stroll through the Mount Olivet Cemetery to gaze upon the tomb stones and check for possible cracks or chips.

His company made granite monuments and head stones for the graves around the state and when business was slow, he would check to see which monuments could use some work or even be upgraded.

And that's when he saw it.

Rechecking his map of the occupied graves, he discovered a double burial plot from 1935, which had never acquired a head stone.

Horace and Elizabeth Tabor.

Without a clue who the couple was and only seeing dollar signs for a potential sale, he marked it off on his sheet and headed back to the office.

But when he began looking through the cemetery records, for any possible family, he quickly realized that this grave was alittle differnt than some of the others. And after contacting the Museum, he was able to put the word out that the couple needed a grave marker.

Surprisingly, the call wasn't answered by a library or even a Historical Society, but by Denver's Mile High Optimist club.

Founded in 1916, the club focused on filling the needs of its community and to work towards bettering the World around them.

And to purchase a grave marker.

With G&L Granite donating the granite slab, the club was only responsible for the cost of the engraving and installation. C.E Liesveld offered to help them with the design and write the inscription, but it was soon evident that he wasn't really a fan of Horace Tabor.

"I never knew Senator Tabor or any members of his family, but I am a student of history", he explained during his interview for the Steamboat Pilot newspaper. "I don't believe that Tabor was a great man, but he certainly was important in the development of the state. It is just an affront to history, that his grave was not marked."

The final design for the oversized slab of granite showed a boarder that depicts a rocky ledge on the left side, that symbolizes the discovery of the mine that made him rich, the top of the stone showed a engraving of the State Capital building, to highlight his term as Governor, while the right side of the stone had a engraving of a setting sun, which represented his death.

The center of the stone read:

"Unknown to fame until approaching the age of 50, chance suddenly brought him considerable wealth and reputation. A few years later another throw of the dice as quickly returned him to his former obscurity but left in the wake a colorful character in the annals of Colorado History."

Along the bottom of the stone, the engraver added Horace A.W. 1830-1899 to the left side, above the spot where his casket now lay, where on the right side the engraver added Elizabeth Baby Doe 1854-1935 above where her casket lay. And in the center of both names, was an engraved likeness of H.A.W Tabor, facing the name of his beloved Elizabeth.

But burying a body doesn't mean the soul of the deceased has left this earthly domain for a new life amongst the angels and the Lords pearly gates.

Mr. J.K. Mullen had promised Elizabeth Tabor, back in 1928, that she could remain at the Matchless mine for as long as she wished and people were soon about to discover that the cabin up at the mine wasn't entirely vacant.

A STACK OF CHAIRS AND THE TWISTED FLASHLIGHT

"**Mrs. Tabor?**" **Greg** Turner inquired, as he began knocking on the front door of Elizabeth Tabor's cabin. "Good morning Mam', my name is Greg and I was here yesterday giving tours of your cabin. I hope it's ok if I come inside to set up."

Putting his ear to the door, he listened for any sounds that might indicate that Mrs. Tabor was not going to tolerate his desire to conduct a tour of her cabin today. Not hearing anything, he reached for his keys and that's when he noticed it.

The rope, that he had left tied to the inside wall of the lean-to, was missing.

Again.

Having grown tired of sweeping out the cabin every morning before he started his summer tours, Greg had devised a creative way to block dirt from blowing underneath the cabin's door, which involved both a piece of rope and a quilt.

Greg would take the old quilt off the bed and after rolling it up like a snake, he would fold it in half and wrap it up with a thin rope, but leave a long, excess piece sticking out in the middle. He would then carry the quilt over to the door, lay it on the floor and push the long tail of excess rope outside from underneath the door. This allowed him to then leave the cabin, close the door behind him, grab the rope, pull it until the quilt was tight against the inside of the door and then tie the rope to a nail inside the lean-to.

No longer would dirt, bugs or mice be able to slide underneath Mrs. Tabor's cabin door and wreak havoc, causing him to clean up a mess every morning.

His invention was genius.

But Greg soon learned that Mrs. Tabor enjoyed untying his rope and moving the quilt, in a sort of phantasmal game.

Curious to see what Mrs. Tabor had done inside the cabin this time, Greg Turner unlocked the door and slowly began pushing it open. "Mrs. Tabor, I know I said goodnight to you last night." He teased the deceased woman, as he heard the now familiar sound of a wooden chair scraping across the cabin's floor.

Every night, before he locked up the cabin, Greg always made sure to straighten up the pictures on the walls, fluff the pillows on the small, cast iron bed and set up all the chairs against the walls, for the visitors who would be coming the following day.

And tell Mrs. Tabor goodnight.

But when he entered the cabin that morning, he could see that its ghostly inhabitant had, once again, stacked most of the chairs up in the center of the room, minus the one she always put behind the front door. Reaching around the door, Greg managed to slide the chair out of the way, before he entered the dimly lit cabin.

Needing more light, he reached over to pull the string that hung from the ceiling, but noticed that the room remained dark.

But he wasn't surprised.

In 1917 Elizabeth Tabor's lessees had installed electric up at the mine, in order to run their newly installed machinery, but Elizabeth didn't want the electric turned on in her cabin, as she said it was simply an extra expense she couldn't afford. So she wasn't very happy when the electric was turned on after she died.

Current photo of the cabin- Photo by author

"Mrs. Tabor, like I have told you before, the Leadville Mining Museum is paying all the bills for the electric." Greg explained to the dead woman he couldn't see, as he reached over to the light bulb and found it, once again, loose in its socket. "Young lady, do you understand that if this bulb ever falls onto the floor, you're going to have glass everywhere?"

Carefully tightening the loose bulb, the room quickly illuminated and Greg soon located the quilt that was supposto of been blocking dirt from blowing into her cabin. Laying across the bed, with the rope carefully rolled up beside it, the cabin's ghostly occupant had laid the quilt down where she felt is should be.

And with an understanding smile and the shake of his head, Greg grabbed the broom and started sweeping out the cabin, before setting the chairs back against the walls.

Ever since Elizabeth Tabor's grizzly death was plastered all over the headlines, back in 1935, people had been breaking into her cabin, to either steal things or just to feel what it must have been like to live there.

So, if people really wanted to see it, Leadville decided in 1950 that it was time to fix the place up and show it to them.

Unfortunately, all of Elizabeth Tabor's belonging had already been either stolen, sold or thrown in the trash, so all that remained was the hollow shell of the cabin, that now needed restored and refurnished. After a restoration of Mrs. Tabor's former home, a group called The Leadville Assembly Inc. began offering tours on July 16, 1953, at 15 cents a person.

Matchless mine dedication ceremony-(Front row-left to right-Lee Robbins, Fred Mazzulla, Eleanor Wechbaugh, Neale Easton, Caroline Bancroft, Anna Smith, Ron Barker and Jack Thomas) The Denver Public Library, Western History Collection-X-61236

In 1988 the Shorego mining company, owned by the heirs of J.K. Mullen, had transferred the Matchless Mine claim over to the Leadville Assembly, who in turn transferred it to Leadville's National Mining Hall of Fame and Museum in 2006.

And, as an added pat on the back for a job well done, the Matchless was also listed on the National register of historic places in 2011.

But despite all the years of dedicated preservation work and Leadville's eternal quest to educate all the future generations of Coloradoan's about the Tabor's , Elizabeth still didn't want people inside her cabin.

But ghostly shotguns just don't seem to chase people off, no matter how hard she tried.

And the tourists just kept coming.

As Greg placed the final chair back on the floor, after Mrs. Tabor's stacking shenanigans from the night before, he began seeing cars pull up to the cabin, for the first tour of the day. With an ornery smile, Greg glanced in the direction he felt Mrs. Tabor might be and announced "Oh Mam, just so you know, tonight a Paranormal team called Haunted Dimensions, will be doing an investigation inside your cabin. These are people who talk to the dead, sort of like the Spiritualists you used to hear about. So, with any luck, I'll be talking with you tonight."

As the day continued, Greg gave his tour of the Matchless to school busses full of children, tourists from all across the country and even a few locals who just wanted to bring their families from out of town. But after the sun set and a full moon lite up the night, Greg welcomed another set of tourists, this time of the investigating variety.

Armed with cases full of instruments, cameras, flashlights and the newest in technology, the paranormal team exchanged their introductions with both Greg Turner and the museum's curator Kat Neilson, before setting up for a night of spiritual conversation.

One of their most useful tools the team brought into play, to communicate with the dead, was a simple flashlight, with an added twist.

Literally.

They simply took a standard flashlight, turned it on, then twisted the case just enough so that the light went off. Next, they gently shook it, to see if the light flickered on and off and if it did, it was laid on a flat surface so any ghostly visitor could turn it on when asked a question.

Next, the team handed out a collection of EMF meters, which is a hand held device that houses five different colored lights on the top, which range from yellow to red and is believed to detect spikes in electromagnetic energy.

As the team began to scan the room, a collection of digital recorders were also set up, in an attempt to catch any disembodied voices during the question and answer segment of the investigation. One of the investigators would also be holding a digital recorder, as well as wearing a set of headphones, so he could hear any ghostly response to a question and immediately re-play it back for the team.

Finally, while one team member turned on an infrared video camera, another clicked on an amazing paranormal wonder, called an Ovilus. This amazing digital device contains a dictionary of up to 3,000 pre-programed words and it is believed that spirits can answer a question by choosing a word in the machines data base, which will then appear on the screen.

"Ok everyone, let's go dark"

"Hello Mrs. Tabor, we understand that we were supposto make an appointment, but we didn't know who to call." Head investigator Tammila Wright explained, with a tension relieving laugh. "We are here in full respect and we just wish to talk to you."

"Mrs. Tabor, if it is you who is with us tonight, can you turn the EMF detector to red please?"

Nothing.

"Is there a different person here tonight?"

Nothing.

"Is Augusta Tabor here tonight?"

A loud thump noise, similar to a boot stomping on the floor, was heard echoing through the cabin, as the digital recorder picked up the first disembodied voice of the night. "That's not me"

"Mrs. Tabor? Is that you?"

In response, the flashlight quickly turned on, followed by relieved cheers and laughter from the entire paranormal team, as well as the members of the Mining Museums' staff, who were brave enough to attend.

"Can you please turn it off?"

The flashlight quickly goes dark.

"Thank you."

Just then then the Ovilus begins typing out a word on the screen, as Mrs. Tabor quickly figured out how to manipulate every electrical gadget placed in front of her.

Unhappy

"Mrs. Tabor, are you unhappy because we are in your cabin?"

The flashlight turns on.

"Mrs. Tabor, we mean no disrespect. Are you aware that you have passed?"

Just then the Ovilus displays a picture of a heart.

Leaning over to tap the lead investigator on the arm, Greg Turner whispered, "It is believed that Mrs. Tabor died of a heart attack."

"Mrs. Tabor, did you die from a problem with your heart?"

A loud stomp is heard.

"Mrs. Tabor, do you want to talk to us tonight?"

Silence.

"Mrs. Tabor, do you want us to leave?"

The flash light quickly turns back on, but is now shining brighter than before and then quickly turns back off.

"Mrs. Tabor, can you tell us why you want us to leave?"

Suddenly, another loud thump is heard, followed by an uncomfortable tension in the room. "I feel that Mrs. Tabor is yelling at us." Erick Wright, one of the paranormal investigators announced to the group, which was quickly answered by the flashlight coming back on again.

"Mrs. Tabor, we just feel bad for you, there is just so much more to life than this cabin…"

Suddenly, Erick held up the digital recorder and announced "She just said, don't come back."

As a shiver ran through the cabins visitors, a single word appeared on the Ovilus.

Greg

"Mrs. Tabor, who is Greg?"

With a smile, Erick said "She just replied that he works here. Oh wait…now she says she appreciates him."

Feeling a beam of pride, Greg Turner couldn't help but smile.

Desperate to continue the heated conversation, the investigator asked "Are you here with any other spirits?"

The flash light clicks on.

"I just picked up the sounds of a woman humming and the creak of a rocking chair," the investigator holding the digital recorder announced, with a smile. "Wait, wait…she just said that's my chair."

"Mrs. Tabor, can you tell us who else is here with you?"

Just then the man holding the digital recorder held up his hand, to request silence and replayed the name he had just heard, before he looked over at both Greg Turner and the Museum's curator Kat Neilson and asked a question that solidified the entire investigation.

"Who is Jacob?"

Just then, loud boot steps were heard walking across the cabin's wooden floor and when they stopped, the flashlight turned on.

Then turned back off.

"She's with Jacob?" Greg whispered to Kat, as they both try to keep their voices down. "I thought she would be with Horace."

"Mrs. Tabor, are you the one who moves the furniture at night when the tour guides don't say goodnight to you." Investigator Tammila asked, unaware of the private conversation going on between the museums staff members.

Again the recorder catches a reply.

"She just said that's Jacob."

Suddenly the digital recorder is filled with a loud, angry male voice, which is trying to communicate in a foreign language. Despite repeatedly playing back the recording for the group, nobody can determine what the voice is saying.

"I'm guessing that would be Jacob Sands." Greg Turner explained, as he turned around and pointed to a framed picture on the wall behind them. "He was Elizabeth Tabor's lover, when she was married to her first husband Harvey Doe. His full name was Jacob Sandelowsky, but he shortened it to Sands, after he emigrated here from Poland. So that language you caught is probably Polish."

"Can I ask Mrs. Tabor a question?" Greg asked the paranormal team, who instantly approved his request.

"Mrs. Tabor, this is Greg. Was it you that smashed my hand, when I was trying to lock down the outside window shutters on your cabin?"

The flashlight quickly turns on, then off again.

"She just said I can't see." The investigator holding the digital recorder announced, with a huge smile. "She can't see!"

Holding his hand out for the group, Greg presented his scabbed knuckles as proof of Mrs. Tabor's admitted guilt. "I just never realize that closing the shutters would keep the dead from seeing out the windows."

As the night continued, the questions started to become repetitive and Mrs. Tabor become bored of her uninvited guests. The digital recorder began picking up the sounds of water sloshing in a tub and footsteps, both heavy and light. "I think she has moved on to doing her house hold chores", the investigator informed the team, as he played back the recording.

"Maybe it's time to move onto the black smith's shop, next to the cabin."

As part of the team walked out of the cabin and over to their new location, Greg pulled out a couple of pictures he had taken in the building months earlier, which showed a ghostly fog swirling around. The fourth picture he showed them was of a face, looking at him through the cabin's window. "This is the window right next to the door. I took this when I arrived for work awhile back."

With the equipment ready, the lights were turned out and the questions began. But, to keep the investigation interesting, a few team members remained behind in the cabin and kept track of the time when questions were answered or noises were heard.

And they got the response they were expecting.

Elizabeth Tabor was traveling between the two buildings.

Back in the cabin, the investigators were asking Mrs. Tabor where she had met her husband Horace, which she finally acknowledged that she had met in Nevadaville, with a click of the flashlight and then stopped talking. Seconds later, the team in the shop began talking to the ghost of a young boy who had died after working in the mine.

"Do you know Greg? The Tour guide?"

Thump

Then instantly, the Ovilus spits out a word.

Problem

"Is there more than one of you guys here tonight?"

Thump

"Did you do a lot of different jobs here?"

Thump

"You said you had a problem, were you injured?"

The Ovilus quickly produces a word

Slightly

"Were you injured in the mine?"

Eleven

Community
Pale
Finger

"Wait, wait, I think I know what he is saying." Greg announced with a proud tone to his voice, as he began to question the ghost further. "Back in the old days, young boys ranging from nine to thirteen year's old worked in the mines packing dynamite and he just said Pale. Pale was also a word used to describe gangrene."

Thump

"Did you live in the community?"

Thump

"Did you die from an injured finger, which turned into gangrene?"

Thump

With a smile, Greg held his shoulders back just alittle bit straighter, happy that his extensive history of the area had finally came in handy.

But as the night continued and the spirits appeared to of become bored with the constant questioning, the team finished up their paranormal investigation and began packing up their gear. As they did, the paranormal team asked Greg Turner why he thought Elizabeth Tabor was spending eternity with Jacob Sands and not her husband Horace.

Suddenly remembering a piece of history, Greg went over to a cabinet and after rifling through a stack of papers , pulled out a copy of an old letter, which Jacob had sent to Elizabeth Tabor.

"My darling love, I remain yours and ever."

Jake

If you would like to visit the Matchless mine and maybe try to contact Mrs. Elizabeth Tabor or Jacob Sands yourself, the mine is open for tours from Memorial Day through Labor Day. Versions of the Ovilus are also available free, as an App for your cell phone or you can purchase one from any Ghost hunting supply store.

All three paranormal investigations, discussed in this chapter, as well as the ghostly photographs, can be viewed on YouTube, under "Walking History of the Matchless Mine. Mov."

Good luck and happy hunting!

If you wish to visit the Matchless Mine, please contact:
The National Mining Hall of Fame and Museum
120 west 9th street
Leadville, Colorado 80461
1-719-486-1229

If you wish to visit more locations owned or favored by the Tabor's, Leadville is home to many buildings, which are open to the public.

The Vendome Hotel/ Tabor Grand Hotel
701 Harrison Ave.
Leadville, Colorado

The Tabor Opera House
308 Harrison Ave.
Leadville, Colorado

The Church of the Annunciation
609 Poplar Street
Leadville, Colorado

Horace and Augusta Tabor's former home
116 East 5th Street
Leadville, Colorado

If you wish to view the Silent movies that Silver Dollar Tabor starred in, while she lived in Colorado Springs, they can be viewed,

by appointment, at The Colorado College.
The Colorado College
Charles L. Tutt Library
14 East Cache la Poudre Street
Colorado Springs, Colorado
1-719-389-6000
http://www.coloradocollege.edu/library

Elizabeth Tabor's personal recipes and home remedies

While researching the life of Mrs. Elizabeth Tabor, I discovered many recipes and home remedies that were written in her own handwriting. The only item she mentions that she would buy at the grocery store instead of make herself, was an item called "Orange sugar", but I included it because I loved her description of it.

Orange Sugar

The clipping reads, "This sugar is prepared from selected fruit and is guaranteed pure and can be used in any quantity with safety. To make a delicious drink, use from one teaspoon to three teaspoons of this sugar to an ordinary glass of water."

"This is like the nectar of the God's, described by Homer." - Elizabeth Tabor

Cream Hash

To make good, please have the meat chopped rather fine and put into a saucepan with sufficient stock to cover.

Cover the saucepan, allow the hash to come slowly to steaming point and keep it there for about 5 minutes. Then add to each pint of meat, a tablespoon of salt, a quarter of a teaspoon of pepper and a teaspoon of grated onion. Serve on toast.

Rocks

1 cup drippings
½ cup white sugar
½ cup brown sugar
Two eggs
Level teaspoon soda in cup

Bring the water to a boil, then add one Tablespoon ground cinnamon, one cup chopped nuts, one cup chopped raisins and 3 cups of flour. Drop from a teaspoon, into a buttered pan and bake in a moderate oven. You can add a Tablespoon vanilla or other flavoring.

Potatoes on Half Shell

Bake any large potatoes, cut in halves and scrape out insides and mash. Season well with cream or milk, butter, salt, pepper. Make fairly thin. Beat well until very light. Then add the stiffly beaten whites of three eggs, well folded and put back into potato shells. Grate cheese over them and brown this. Is for 8.

Large potatoes can be made and browned later in the day.

Tomato Soup

1/2 pint tomatoes boil on simmer until water is gone. Add small ½ handful of soda. Now add one quart milk, butter the size of a walnut, salt, pepper.

Later, as it comes to a boil, cook on double broiler after milk is added.

Beer

12 lbs. of Barley
Handful of loose hop beans
One shunk of beef

In order to better understand this odd recipe, I contacted the Florence, Colorado Microbrewery for answers. Their Brew master explained that in order to make a beer out of this, it would require yeast and water, which this recipe does not mention.

In regards to the added shunk of beef, he feels that it may have simply been added for flavor, as he has heard of oysters being added to the brewing process. He went on to explain that the beef would not cause the Barley and hops to ferment and if the recipe was made as listed, it would be more of a soup base than a beer.

Homemade Corned Beef

Soak either ham or salt pork overnight. Put fresh beef in hot water with salt meat and let boil till done. Add any vegetables you wish.

Corn Griddle Cakes

Scald two cups of corn meal with 1 -3/4 cups boiling water. Let stand, without stirring, until cool.

One levelspoon sugar
One levelspoon salt
One full levelspoon butter
Two eggs
Two levelspoon's baking powder

Cream butter and sugar when meal is cool. Add one cup flour, stir, then add eggs, well beaten and enough milk to make thin batter. Last, add baking powder.

Peanut Candy

Two cups granulated sugar
Two bags of chopped peanuts

Melt sugar, stirring continuously. Add peanuts and pour on melted butter. Use 4x sugar is best.

Sponge Cake

One cup sugar in pan first
Seven separated, yolks only
Beat milk and sugar hard and long
One cup flour-mix

Beat awhile. Stiff

Add One tablespoon butter and one teaspoon Flanassiz. Bake from 35-45 minutes. Moderate oven.

Bread

One sifler of Rye flour
One cup or alittle more molasses's
Canary seeds
Annes seeds

While flour make stiff, stir in milk and palalu water and one cake yeast. Set overnight.

In the morning pull all in. Let rise again, then make loaves and raise long time and bake.

Carimal Jewny (Caramels)

Two cups sugar
¾ cups milk
Butter the size of an egg
Flavor vanilla

Boil until it hairs, beat until cold.

Suet Budding

One cup molasses
Two cups sweet milk
Two cups Suet milk
Two eggs
One teaspoon soda in molasses
Two teaspoons cream of Tartar in flour
One quart flour, in one teaspoon dose
Two teaspoons cinnamon

Two cups stored raisins, floured

Steam for two hour's

Chocolate fudge

2 ¼ cups granulated sugar
One small square chocolate
One cup cream
¼ cup butter

Mix. Cook 10-15 minutes

Lemon sauce

One large cup sugar
½ cup butter
One egg
One lemon. All the juice and half the grated peel
One teaspoon Nutmeg
Three kitchen spoonful's of boiling water

Cream butter and sugar together. Peal in eggs, whipped light with lemon and nutmeg and beat hard 10 minutes. Add spoonful at a time in the boiling water. Put in bowl set in of Leadville? Keep hot, stir constantly. Not boil.

Ice cream cake

Make a sponge cake, baked ½ inch thick and let get 2 cold.
One pint thick sweet cream
Flavor vanilla

Blanch and chop one lb. of almonds. Add to cream and vanilla. Put on very thick between each layer.

Dinner white cake

1 ½ cups granulated sugar- measure after sifting
One cups of white eggs
One cup of water
½ cup butter- even and exact
Three cups flour- after sifting 4 times
Two teaspoons baking powder

Cream butter light then add water, flour and one cup of sugar, alittle at a time. Beating hard all the time. Beat whites very light and add the ½ cup of sugar. Put these last with pinch of salt and ½ teaspoon vanilla. Put baking powder in milk and flour. Bake.

Maple Fudge

Two cups Maple sugar- not syrup
One cup cream

Boil and add butter. Boil for 10-15 minutes, beat well and place in buttered pan. Cut into quarters.

Home remedies

For a cough or a cold

Raw linseed oil
Honey and paregoric- equal parts

Mix and put 2-3 drops on the roof of the tongue often.

"Mrs. Morse said it's wonderful."-Elizabeth Tabor

TO PROTECT FROM BAD AIR

Buy Oxide of sodium. Put in ¼ oz. in a little cotton bag and sew it on a miners cap. He can work down in any mine, where the air is bad and foul. It will last one day.

TO THICKEN THE BLOOD

Take Eupatorium and Iron.

FOR RHEUMATISM

Wine of Colchicum seed put into cherry wine. Add 20 drops in cold water every four hours.

(Written on the back of a an Spillane Undertakers card)

CORN CURE

Acid- Salicylic or Lalicylic acid. Mix with cold water or lard of Vaseline.

TO TAKE THE BAD EFFECTS OF COCAINE GIVEN FOR FIXING TEETH OR ANY OTHER REASON

Grind black mustard seeds. Add one big Tablespoon full of black mustard seeds to cup of cold water and drink it, after using cocaine or other opioids.

Soft Bones

Flax seed, milk, lemon juice, lump of sugar or the best honey. Drink all the time as your only food. Morning and night.

For Rheumatism

Use Venus Turpentine on chamois skin and place a piece on each wrist over pulse and on each foot. With Turpentine on soles, change each piece, every day until well.

Endnotes

A Painted Sky and the Blind Folded Mystic

1. Colorado Magazine- The opening of the Tabor Grand Opera house- 1881
2. Booklet- The Saga of H.A.W Tabor -by Rene L. Coquoz 1973
3. Horace Tabor love letter to Elizabeth Tabor- 2/18/1883 Tabor Collection, Denver History Museum
4. Telluride Journal 10/21/1899 "Dr. McIvor-Tyndall"
5. Salida Mail Volume XXVIII # 92 – 4/21/1908 "Whispers from the shadowland."
6. Ouray Herald 10/12/1899
7. Book- "Augusta Tabor- a pioneering Woman." By Betty Moyniban- Cordillera Press 1988
8. San Miguel Examiner Volume XIV #15 -10/21/1899 "World's greatest Palmist is here."

The Vial of Ink and a Broken Promise

9. Sacred Heart Catholic Church pamphlet
10. Salida mail Volume XXVIII #92 4/21/1908
11. Telluride Journal 10/21/1899
12. San Miguel Examiner Volume XIV # 15 10/21/1899
13. Herald Democrat 7/27/1899
14. Silverite Plain Dealer 10/6/1899
15. Book-"The complete guide to Palmistry."-by Robin Gile and

Lisa Lenard -Alpha books 1999
16. Ancestory.com- Peter McCourt 1818-1883
17. Ancestory.com- Elizabeth Anderson Nellis 1826-1910
18. Book- "The legend of Baby Doe."-by John Burke-G.P. Putnam's and Sons. 1974
19. Book- "The two lives of Baby Doe."-by Gorgon Langley Hall- Macrae Smith Company. 1962
20. http://www.Victorian –era.org
21. Letter from Harvey Doe to his parents-3/29/1880- Stephen Hart Library,Tabor Collection
22. http://www.austin diocese.org
23. http://www.Catholic company.com

Buckets of Soapy Water and the Dead Politician

24. Central City Newspaper "Town Talk" 10/1877
25. Divorce papers- William H. Doe Jr against Elizabeth B. Doe- Stephen Hart Library Tabor Collection
26. Leadville Daily Herald –"Death of Lieutenant Governor Elect Robinson "- 11/30/1880
27. Book- "Horace Tabor."- by Duane A. Smith- Colorado Associated University Press- 1973
28. Book- "Colorado- A history of the Centennial State"-by Carl Abbott, J. Leonard and Thomas J. Noel-University Press-2013
29. Book- "The Legend of Baby Doe-the life and times of the Silver Queen of the West." By John Burke- G.P Putman Son's- 1974
30. http://www.history colorado.org
31. Photo- Augusta Tabor's home. Denver Library x-22040
32. http://www.w lcollege.ilm.edu

HIDDEN BOXES OF DIAMONDS AND A SHOT TO THE HEART

33. Book-"Augusta Tabor: Pioneering Woman." By Betty Moynihan- Cordillera Press- 1988
34. Book- "The saga of H.A.W Tabor." By Rene. L. Coquoz- Johnson Publishing-1973
35. Silver cliff weekly Herald 4/27/1882
36. http://www.senate.gov
37. http://www.colorado.gov
38. http://www.history colo.
39. The Flume- Fairplay, Colorado "Review of events 1879-1880"-11/26/1885
40. Ancestory.com-The McCourt family tree
41. http://www.slfp.com/old courthouse.html
42. http://www.nps.gov
43. Rocky Mountain Sun 12/23/1882
44. Leadville Daily Herald 1/4/1883
45. Dolores News "Tabor's disgrace."-3/10/1883

MASSIVE MARBLE FIRE PLACES AND SPARKLING CHANDELIERS

46. Book- "Augusta Tabor: A Pioneering Woman."-by Betty Moynihan-Cordillera Press- 1988
47. Book-"The saga of H.A.W Tabor." –by Rene L. Coquoz-Johnson Publishing-1973
48. Leadville Daily Herald 1/4/1883
49. Photo of Augusta Tabor's Broadway home-Denver Library Archives-X-22040
50. http://www. colorado.gov
51. http://www.coloradoencyclopedia.org
52. http://www.mayo clinic.org
53. http://www.senate.gov

54. http://www.cbsnews.com
55. Sierra Joural (Rosita) 2/1/1883
56. Montezuma Millrun 3/3/1883
57. http://www.biography.com/people/james-garfield
58. Monezuma Millrun 2/10/1883
59. Book- "A little book of tribute verses." Page 240- Field

Canvas backed duck and a child bride

60. http://www.beginning catholic.com
61. Leadville Daily Herald 3/6/1883
62. Ancestory.com –McCourt family tree
63. http://www.biography.com
64. Henry Teller letter-3/8/1883- Teller Collection- State Historical Society
65. Journal of the Executive proceedings of the Senate of the United States of America-D. Green-1901
66. Book-"The two lives of Baby Doe."-by Gordon Langley Hall- Macrae Smith Company- 1962
67. http://www.catholic divorce.com
68. http://www.st.matthcw cathedral.org
69. http://www.washington.intercontinental.com
70. http://www.catholic.org
71. http://www.cuf.org
72. Book-"The Holy Bible."
73. http://www.econdolence.com
74. Fort Collins Courier 3/8/1883
75. Montezuma Millrun 3/3/1883
76. Book-"The Saga of H.A.W Tabor." By Rene L. Coquoz- Johnson Publishing- 1973

A Murdered Priest and a Handful of Gold Coins

77. Book-"The two lives of Baby Doe."-by Gordon Langley Hall- Macrae Smith Company- 1962
78. Leadville Daily Herald 5/25/1884
79. http://www.menominee-nsn.gov
80. Book-" Lizzie McCourt: Baby Does legend begins."-by James L. Metz-Polemics Press-2013
81. Castle Rock Journal 2/6/1884
82. Book- "History of Colorado Volume 1."- by Wilbur Fiske Stone- S.J.Clarke-2013
83. http://www.econdolence.org
84. Book-" Horace Tabor." –by Duane Smith-Colorado Associated University Press-1973
85. http://www.catholic news agency.com
86. http://www.find a grave.com
87. http://www.mayo clinic.org

Peacock Feathers and the Two Dead Brothers

88. http://www.a catholic infant baptism service-saint aloysius church.org
89. http://www.sacraments of inition.baptismfor the dying.awaken to prayer.org
90. Book-"Silver Dollar Tabor."-by Evelyn E. Livingston Furman
91. Book- "The two lives of Baby Doe."-by Gordon Langley Hall
92. Central City Newspaper- The Mining reporter- "Town Talk."
93. http://www.Blessings of parents after miscarriage.globalcatholic network.org
94. Handwritten note describing her first born son-Stephen Hart Library-Tabor collection
95. Book-"The unexpected President: The life and times of Chester

A. Arthur."-by Scott s. Greenerger
96. http://www.guinness world records.com
97. East London Advertiser 3/31/1888
98. The Star- "A white chapel horror." 8/7/1888
99. Book-"Silver Dollar Tabor."-by Evelyn E. Livingston Furman
100. http://www.Catholic prayer-restore my child to health catholic.org

WHEN THE BOUGH BREAKS, SILVER WILL FALL

101. Book-"Catholic Funeral ediquette."-by Marian T. Horvalt PHD
102. http://www. Caholic.org
103. http://www.Our Catholic prayers.org
104. Book-" The two lives of Baby Doe." –by Gordon Langley Hall
105. Book- "Chronicles of the builders of the common wealth- a historical study."-by Hubert Howe Bancroft
106. Book-" History of the life of Horace Austin Warner Tabor."- by Hubert Howe Bancroft
107. Book- "America in the gilded age."-by Sean Dennis Cashman
108. Fort Collins Courier 1/29/1891 –" A forgotten Senator."
109. Book- "Democracy in desperation: The depression of 1893."- by Douglas Steeples and David O' Whiten.
110. Book-"Augusta Tabor: A pioneer woman." –by Betty Moynihan
111. Aspen weekly times 5/12/1894 –"Still holds on."
112. Book-"Florence and Cripple Creek railroad: Forty miles to fortune." –by Russ Collman and Dell A.McCoy.
113. Book-" Cripple Creek: a quick history of the worlds greatest gold camp." –by Leland Feitz
114. Aspen weekly times 5/19/1894 –"Tabor settled."
115. Ancestory.com Horace Tabor family tree
116. Boulder daily Camera 2/2/1895
117. Aspen weekly times 11/9/1895-"Senator Tabor gets time."

118. Book-"Cosmic conscience or the Man-God whom we wait."- by Alexandar J. McIvor-Tyndall
119. Aspen Tribune 5/20/1896-"Order made for witness."
120. Aspen Tribune 5/22/1896- "Tabor is in Arizona."
121. Boulder Daily Camera 6/8/1896-"A defeat for Tabor."
122. Aspen Weekly Times 6/13/1896- "The Tabor estate."
123. Leadville daily/evening chronicle 6/11/1896-"Fight for the Matchless."

STACKS OF FIREWOOD AND A SHOVEL FULL OF GOLD

124. http://www.haunted Colorado.com
125. http://www.hotel Jerome.aubergeresorts.com
126. Aspen Daily Times 6/12/1896
127. Aspen Weekly Times 6/13/1896 "The Tabor mines."
128. Aspen Tribune 6/14/1896 "Tabor loses suit."
129. Aspen Tribune 6/16/1896 "Ten days extention."
130. Boulder Daily Camera 6/23/1896 "Tabor sold out."
131. Boulder Daily Camera 9/11/1896 "Tabor loses all."
132. Aspen weekly Times 9/5/1896 "The Tabor estate passes."
133. http://www.weather.gov
134. Book- "Silver Dollar Tabor"-by Evelyn E. Livingston Furman
135. Daily Journal (Telluride) 3/24/1897 "The Tabor property."
136. Colorado Transcript 2/23/1898 "Tabor star rising."
137. Book- "The king of Cripple Creek."- by Marshall Spague
138. Colorado Transcript 10/20/1897
139. Book- "Guide to Colorado Ghost towns and mining camps"-by Perry Eberhart-Sage Books-1959
140. Book- "Thirty years of American Diplomacy." –by Allan Nevins-Harper brothers-1930
141. Daily Sentinel 1/14/1898 "Tabor nominated to be Post Master."
142. Daily Sentinel Volume 5 #47- 1/20/1898 "Tabor takes charge."

143. Daily Sentinel Volume #42- 1/24/1898 "Denver's Post Master."
144. Booklet- "Chronic Catarrah-Its symptoms, causes and effects." –by Doctor Lighthill
145. Booklet- "Face pain: The challenge of facial pain"-by Doctor Wesley E. Shankland- Omega publishing-2001

Cups of Leeches and the Ring of Flowers

146. Aspen Tribune 4/11/1899 "Death of Senator Tabor."
147. Aspen weekly Times 4/15/1899 "Death of HAW Tabor."
148. Booklet- History of appendicitis vermiformis: Its diseases and treatment."- by Arthur C. McCarty MD.- University of Louisville-1927
149. Herald Democrat 4/10/1899 "Tabor is dying."
150. Basalt Journal 4/15/1899 "Ex-Senator Tabor dies of appendicitis."
151. Daily Journal (Telluride) 4/10/1899
152. Herald Democrat 4/10/1899 "Tabor is dying."
153. Daily Journal (Telluride) 4/10/1899 "Former Senator Tabor dead."
154. Herald Democrat 4/11/1899 "Early bonanza king gone to his last home."
155. Aspen Tribune 4/11/1899 "Tabor death."
156. Rifle Reveille 4/14/1899 "Ex-Senator Tabor dies of appendicitis."
157. Aspen weekly times 4/15/1899 "Tabor funeral."
158. Aspen weekly Times 4/15/1899 "View Tabor's remains."
159. The Daily news 4/11/1899 "Death of postmaster HAW Tabor."
160. Durango Democrat 4/18/1899
161. Ouray Herald 4/13/1899 "HAW Tabor dead ."
162. Herald Democrat 4/14/1899 "Tabor funeral."
163. Aspen Tribune 4/15/1899 "Tabor funeral a large one."
164. Herald Democrat 4/15/1899 "A state tribute to dead Tabor."
165. The Daily News 4/15/1899 "Tabor was buried with high honors."

166. http://Baptism for the dying catholic family faith .org
167. Book- "The Victorian book of the dead."- by Chris Woodyard
168. http://www.prayers for the dead.catholic-saints.net
169. Book- "Catholic Social teachings"-by Charles E. Curran- George Towns Press-2002
170. Booklet- "Catholic Funeral guidelines." –by Diocese of Wilmington Reverend W. Francis Malooly-Catholic book publishing-1989
171. Booklet- "Preparing the body for a home funeral" -by Crossings: caring for your own

TINS OF CHEWING TOBACCO AND A DIAMOND FIT FOR A QUEEN

172. Herald Democrat 4/18/1899
173. Herald Democrat 4/12/1899 "Body of Tabor to lie in state."
174. Aspen weekly times 4/15/1899 "Funeral of Senator Tabor."
175. Herald Democrat 5/10/1899 "Tabors diamonds."
176. Aspen Tribune 5/24/1899 "Mrs. Tabor is not post master."
177. Colorado Transcript 5/10/1899 "Gossip from Denver and State Capital."
178. Craig Courier Volume 4 #48 5/28/1899 "Editorial and otherwise."
179. Julesburg Grit 6/22/1899 "The Hand of retribution."
180. Park County Bulletin 6/23/1899 "Tabor block sold."
181. Herald Democrat 7/9/1899 "Senator Tabors will."
182. Herald Democrat 12/24/1899 "Personals."
183. Herald Democrat 9/26/1899 "Mines at our door."
184. Personal letter-Tabor collection-Denver Historical society
185. Yuma Pioneer 2/16/1900
186. New Castle Nonpareil 2/15/1900
187. Herald Democrat 6/8/1900 "In the district court."
188. Glenwood post 11/17/1900 "On the verge of poverty."

189. Colorado Transcripts 4/10/1901 "Tabors creditors take matchless mine."
190. Herald Democrat 6/8/1901 "To work matchless."
191. Colorado Transcript 6/12/1901 "Matchless mine saved to Mrs. Tabor by a kind friend."
192. Book- "The king of Cripple creek." –by Marshall Sprague- Magazine Associates-1994
193. Colorado Transcripts 6/12/1901 "W.S. Stratton saves the matchless mine."
194. Weekly courier 6/13/1901 "Winfield Scott Stratton."
195. Eagle County Blade 6/13/1901 "W.S. Stratton saves the matchless mine."
196. Daily Journal (Telluride) 6/26/1901
197. Salida Mail Volume XXII #7 6/28/1901
198. Aspen Daily Times 6/29/1901 "Mrs. Tabor Troubles."
199. Herald Democrat 7/3/1901 "After he sulphide."
200. Aspen Daily times 7/9/1901 "Mrs. Tabors luck."
201. Aspen Daily times 7/11/1901

Stolen mining stocks and a dead millionaire

202. Herald Democrat 7/9/1901 "Mrs. Tabor told that she has a bonanza at Leadville and lessees stealing ore."
203. Yuma Pioneer 8/2/1901 "Mrs. Tabor loses Matchless."
204. Carbonate Chronicle 8/5/1901 "The weekly story of happenings in our great industry."
205. Herald Democrat 4/3/1901 "Widow met it and money raised in Leadville not needed."
206. Colorado Transcript 2/6/1901 "Summery of the work of the Colorado Legislature."
207. Aspen Daily times 2/6/1901
208. Aspen Democrat 2/9/1901 "The state will pay."

209. Herald Democrat 1/31/1901 "Tabor funeral bill state of Colorado called upon to meet account."
210. Herald Democrat 2/1/1901
211. Herald Democrat 12/14/1901 "Briefs from the wires."
212. Weekly courier 12/19/1901 "Western news notes."
213. Herald Democrat 1/30/1901 "Downtown shaft will soon be started."
214. Herald Democrat 6/13/1902 "Fryer hill a hive."
215. Herald Democrat 4/10/1902 "Mrs. Tabor heavy suits."
216. Encyclopedia Britannica "Maid of Erin silver mine co."
217. Herald Democrat 5/30/1902 "Trimble and Mrs. Tabor."
218. Herald Democrat 5/25/1902 "Widows quest."
219. Silverton Standard 6/28/1902 "Personal."
220. Silverton Standard 7/12/1902 "Mines and mining in San Juan."
221. Herald Democrat 7/18/1902 "Contracts for theater."
222. Herald Democrat 1/23/2013 "Silver cord mine manager had idea for Yak tunnel."
223. Herald Democrat 8/15/1902 "Mines and mining."
224. Summit county Journal 8/23/1902 "Personal."
225. Breckenridge Bulletin 9/13/1902 "Deeds. Patents and mining locations."
226. Book- "The King of Cripple creek."-by Marshall Sprague- Magazine Associates- 1994

The Man Who Owned the Earth

227. Herald Democrat 11/8/1902 "Mrs. Tabor settles suit."
228. Herald Democrat 1/18/1903
229. Herald Democrat 1/29/1903 "Mrs. Tabor's suit against D.H. Moffat."
230. Rifle Reveille 2/6/1903 "Mrs. Tabor sues for millions."
231. Herald Democrat 2/14/1903 "Wants Millions."

232. Herald Democrat 2/6/1903 "The Tabor suit for millions."
233. Herald Democrat 3/8/1903 "Angry widow and lawyer."
234. Weekly Courier 6/10/1903 "Mrs. Tabor suit."
235. Herald Democrat 6/9/1903 "Mrs. Tabor loses."
236. Aspen Democrat 4/21/1903 "Moffat owns the Earth."
237. 2Herald Democrat 6/12/1903
238. Aspen Democrat 6/12/1903 "Still owns matchless."
239. Durango Wage Earner 6/11/1903
240. Herald Democrat 6/24/1903
241. Ouray Herald 6/19/1903 "Red Rogers group."
242. Herald Democrat 8/30/1903 "Personal mention."
243. Herald Democrat 11/26/1903 "Turns down Tabor claim."
244. Book- "Silver Dollar Tabor."-by Evclyn E. Livingston-The National writers press- 1982
245. htttp://www. History.com/1893 Chicago World's fair

A DEADLY SNOWBALL FIGHT AND THE LOVING HAND OF GOD

246. Herald Democrat 3/6/1904 "Matchless Mine more lawsuits."
247. Herald Democrat 11/29/1903 "Italian sues Mrs. Tabor."
248. Herald Democrat 5/5/1904 "Matchless Mine Mrs. Tabor suit."
249. Herald Democrat 12/10/1904 "Fire at the Matchless."
250. Herald Democrat 12/13/1904 "Personal mention."
251. Herald Democrat 12/10/1904 "Boys throw snowballs old man falls dead."
252. Daily Journal (Telluride) 1/25/1905
253. Telluride Journal 1/26/1905
254. Aspen Daily Times 2/4/1905 "In memory of Governor Tabor."
255. Elbert County Banner 2/17/1905 "House Bills."
256. Herald Democrat 5/10/1905 "A rich strike in Silver Cord."
257. Herald Democrat 7/16/1905 "Personal mention."
258. Herald Democrat 9/29/1905

259. Summit County Journal 10/7/1905
260. Herald Democrat 10/11/1905 "Finds rich ore in old property."
261. Herald Democrat 11/17/1905 "Schedules increased."
262. Herald Democrat 10/27/1905 "Some producers of Fryer Hill."
263. Aspen Daily Times 3/16/1906
264. Aspen Daily Times 3/16/1906 "Regains fortune."
265. Silverton Standard 4/28/1906 "Reported to have sold Red Rogers for $1,000,000 but story not substantiated at Denver or here.
266. Silver Standard 4/28/1906 "Mrs. Tabor in luck."
267. Herald Democrat 10/22/1906 "List of delinquent taxes 1905."
268. Eagle County Blade 5/2/1907 "Keeps old scrapbook."
269. Castle Rock Journal 5/3/ 1907
270. Telluride Journal 5/2/1907
271. Herald Democrat 5/26/1907 "It is best in Colorado."
272. Telluride Journal 5/30/1907
273. Herald democrat 6/5/1907 "Tonnage for past months."
274. Herald Democrat 6/23/1907 "Will work successful."
275. Herald Democrat 6/23/1907 "Around the city."
276. Herald Democrat 7/26/1907 "Big drill hole north of city."
277. Herald Democrat 12/17/1907 "Sells jewels at auction."
278. Summit County Journal 12/21/1907 "Jewels bought by John T. Mason 1572 Race street for $8,750."

President Roosevelt's Hunt and the Scientific Method

279. Herald Democrat 5/6/1908 "Personal mention."
280. Herald Democrat 6/9/1908 "Starr strikes valuable ore."
281. Herald Democrat 8/7/1908 "Filed for record."
282. Herald Democrat 8/13/1908 "Leadville girl writes new song."
283. Herald Democrat 11/28/1908 "Matchless mine again in court."
284. Aspen Daily Times 12/10/1908 "Matchless lessess in possession."
285. Herald Democrat 11/29/1908 "Work to start after court decides

on injunction case-accident ties up big 6
286. Durango Democrat 12/12/1908 "Matchless mine in hands of lessees."
287. Herald Democrat 12/13/1908 "Gold is found in alps group."
288. Herald Democrat 6/13/1909 "Narrow escape for the Tabor's."
289. Herald Democrat 12/9/1909 "Around the city."
290. Herald Democrat 1/8/1910 "Found mysterious bomb."
291. Herald Democrat 2/17/1910 "Monument to Tabor."
292. Herald Democrat 2/22/1910 "That Tabor memorial."
293. Salida Record Volume XXVII #46 -3/18/1910
294. Herald Democrat 12/9/1910 "Tabor luck my yet hold good."
295. Letter from Silver Dollar to her sister Lily 12/29/1906 –Denver Historical society-Tabor collection
296. http://www.webmd.com
297. http://www.belmarra health.com

STOLEN VIRTUE AND THE TAXIDERMIED LION

298. Telluride Journal 3/23/1911 "David Moffat is dead."
299. Eagle Valley Enterprise 3/24/1911 "David Moffat dies in the east."
300. Telluride Journal 3/30/1911
301. Telluride Journal 3/23/1911 "In the death of Moffat."
302. Kiowa County Press 9/10/1911 "Windy city appalled her."
303. Herald Democrat 8/3/1913 "Personal mention."
304. Herald Democrat 1/1/1914 "Here's to you by Silver Dollar Tabor."
305. Herald Democrat 2/15/1914 "Society."
306. Silver Dollar's letter to Priscilla Ranch Colorado historical society Tabor Collection
307. Book- "Silver Dollar Tabor."-by Evelyn E. Livington Furman- The national writers press-1982

308. Book-"An illustrated history of hairstyles 1830-1930.by Marian L. Doyle-Schiffer-Pub LTD.-2003
309. http://www.cathoic.org
310. The Evening Chronicle 6/9/1880 "Turn-Hale."
311. Encyclopedia Britannica-"Turnvereins."
312. Salida Mail Volume XXXIV #77-2/27/1914 "Popular wedding occurs in Denver."
313. Herald Democrat 3/24/1914 "Around the city."
314. Herald Democrat 3/27/1914
315. Wray Rattler 4/30/1914 "Mrs. Tabor sues Moffat estate."
316. Carbonate Chronicle 5/18/1914 "Had hard fall from horse."
317. Herald Democrat 6/1/1914
318. Herald Democrat 7/5/1914
319. Two letters from Silver Dollar Tabor to her mother-4/20/1914-Colorado historical society Tabor collection
320. Herald Democrat 8/31/1911"Harrison Dewar personal mention."
321. Herald Democrat 11/19/1905 "Newsboys beat Light foots."
322. Herald Democrat 12/17/1905
323. Herald Democrat 9/20/1909 "Run at driving club yesterday afternoon."

A RIVER FULL OF QUICKSAND AND THE LOST RING

324. Herald Democrat 9/13/1914 "Personal mention."
325. Carbonate Chronicle 9/6/1915
326. Canon City Daily Record 6/3/2015 "Film industry once thrived in Fremont County."
327. http://www.Indb.com
328. http://www.all movie.com
329. Silver Dollar's letter to her mother from Chicago 9/27/1915
330. Letter to Elizabeth Tabor from Ollie Underwood 8/27/1915

331. Letter to Elizabeth Tabor from Ollie Underwood 9/2/1915
332. Book- "Denver's lakeside Amusement park."-by David Forsyth- University Press of Colorado-2016
333. Letter from Silver Dollar to her mother 9/27/1915
334. Herald Democrat 9/4/1915 "Silver Dollar Tabor 24 Denver is nursing a deeply discolored eye."
335. Herald Democrat 10/11/1915 "Matchless plant destroyed by fire."
336. Letter from Silver Dollar Tabor to her mother 11/8/1914
337. Book-"Silver Dollar Tabor."-by Evelyn E. Livingston Furman- National writers press-1982

Frozen Boa Constrictors and Another Bought of Appendicitis

338. Inventory list #8186-Elizabeth Tabor's personal property –The State historical society of Colorado
339. http://www.guinness world records.com/greatest tempature range in a day
340. Daily Journal (Telluride) 4/25/1916 "Taking children to home."
341. Daily Journal (Telluride) 5/3/1916
342. Ancestory.com-Cornelius Dunham Tabor Family tree
343. Ancestory.com-Vernia Tabor 1920 Census records
344. Ancestory.com- Milton B. Tabor Death certificate
345. Ancestory.com Zelmar. Vernia and Noah Tabor Orphange census 1910
346. Historic post card of Boa Constictor with story
347. Montrose Daily press Volume VII #133 12/8/1914
348. Colorado Transcript 10/12/1916 "Mountain view."
349. Colorado Transcript 11/23/1916 "Mountain view."
350. Ancestory.com Madge Tabor family tree
351. Ancestory.com Charles M. Tabor family tree
352. The Matchless Mine, Leadville. Colorado stabilization and

improvement project "Baby Doe cabin." Floor plan and sections- National Mining museum, Leadville, Colorado.
353. Carbonate Chronicle 12/4/1916 "Around the city."
354. Booklet- "Leadville's tales from the old timers."-by Mrs. Helen Skala and Dora Krocesky
355. Ancestory.com James Ryan family tree
356. Letter from Silver Dollar Tabor to her mother 2/14/1916-Colorado historical society Tabor collection.
357. Letter from Silver Dollar Tabor to her mother 5/12/1916- Colorado historical society Tabor collection.
358. Book-"Feathered Omens: Messenger birds from the spirit world."-by Ted Andrews- Hawk Publishing- 2009

An angry circus midget and the dead German fighter pilot

359. Lettter from Silver Dollar Tabor to her mother 7/14/1917-Colorado historical society Tabor collection
360. U.S. Department of State Archives "Pancho Villa Expedition- Mexican Expedition or punative expedition." U.S. Army
361. Ancestory.com Eva W. James
362. Ancestory.com Numa James
363. Ancestory.com Evan Shade James family tree
364. Book "The Denver posse of Westerners 1969 year book- Volume #25." -Johnson publishing (A visit from Baby Doe- Originally titled "Baby Doe slept in my bed"-by Numa L. James)
365. Colorado transcript 8/16/1917 "State news in brief."
366. Carbonate Chronicle 8/20/1917 "Around the city."
367. Herald Democrat 8/13/1917 "Around the city."
368. Herald Democrat 8/13/1917 "Circus midget whips Wildman and giant."
369. Oak creek times 9/20/1918
370. Eagle Valley Enterprise 9/13/1918 "Western mining and oil news."

371. Wet Mountain Tribune 9/13/1918 "Western mining and oil news."
372. San Juan Prospector 9/21/1917 "Colorado State news."
373. Herald Democrat 9/17/1917 "Around the city."
374. Carbonate Chronicle 12/31/1917 "The Matchless."
375. http://www.webmd.com/lung/tb/tuberculosis-symptoms
376. John Francis Campion papers-University of Colorado, Boulder archives
377. Booklet-"Mines and mining." By John G. Canfield 1967
378. Book-"Richthofen: A true story of the red Baron."-by William E. Burrows. Rupert Hart-Davis publishing-1970
379. San Juan Prospector 8/9/1918
380. Book-"The family Romanov: Murder, rebellious and the fall of Imperial Russia." –by Condace Fleming- Schwartz and Wade publishing-2014

Freshly baked pie and the diamond necklace

381. Book-"The history of Narrative film."-by David Cook-W.W. Norton Publishing-2004
382. Book-"Dark tide: The great Boston Molasses flood of 1919."- by Stephen Puleo- Beacon Press-2004
383. Letter from Silver Dollar to her mother 2/28/1919-Colorado History museum Tabor Collection
384. Book-"A shattered peace: Versailles and the price we pay today."- by David A. Andelman- Wiley Publishing-2014
385. Book-"The Tabor Opera house- A captivating history." –by Evelyn E. Livingston Furman- National writers press-1984
386. Interview with Mrs. Rose O'Connel(Mahoney) by Mr. Victor Wisemen April 4, 2011
387. Ancestory.com- Rose O'Connel (Mahoney)-1920 census records
388. Ancestory.com- John F. Mahoney- 1920 census records

389. Oak Creek times 2/21/1920 "Tabor diamond is stolen."
390. Book-"Woodrow Wilson: A medical and psychological biography."-by Edwin A. Weinstein-Princeton University Press-1981
391. Book-"Silver Dollar Tabor."-by Evelyn E. Livingston-Furman-The National Writers Press-1982
392. Letter from Silver Dollar Tabor to her mother 9/16/1920-Colorado historical museum Tabor Collection

A BOX FULL OF POMEGRANATES AND THE BROKEN STEAMER TRUNK

393. Book-"Fortune telling with tea leaves: a beginner's guide."-by Sophia Buckland-Create space publishing-2016
394. http://www.cemetary of choice.com/Maude Tabor Virgo
395. Booklet-"Centers for disease control and prevention Syphilis fact sheet."
396. http://www.catholic.org/Saint Anthony
397. Silver Dollar Tabor letter's to her mother 11/20/1920, 1/15/1921, 11/5/1921, 2/18,1922 and 4/22/1922- Colorado Historical Archives Tabor collection
398. 398. Ancestory.com – Matilda McCourt Family tree
399. Carbonate Chronicle 3/27/1922 "Old lady's fortune swept away by trial."
400. Great Falls daily Tribune 12/20/1919" Mother buried daughter under shingles."
401. Ancestory.com -Sarah Tabor 1910 Census
402. Ancestory.com -Joseph C. Virgo 1910 Census
403. Ancestory.com -Luther Tabor family tree
404. Ancestory.com-Cornelius Dunham Tabor family tree
405. Eagle Valley Enterprise 2/11/1921 "General."
406.

MESH CAGES FULL OF TEA AND A PRESCRIPTION FOR WHISKEY

407. Book-"Tabor Opera house."-by Evelyn E. Livingston-Furman- National writers press-1972
408. Oral history-Lake County, Colorado Public Library collection- Interview with Charles H. Schlaepfer
409. Ancestory.com- Charlie H. Koch family tree
410. Ancestory.com-Fred G. Pfannschmid family tree
411. Herald Democrat Grocery ad for Koch and Pfannenschmid Grocery 11/11/1912
412. Ancestory.com business directory – Fred G. Pfannenschmid
413. Book-"A history of Leadville Theater."-by Gretchen Scanlon- History Press-2012
414. Book-"Fortune telling with tea leaves-a beginner's guide."-by Sophia Buckland-Create space publishing-2016
415. Book." The last call-the rise and fall of prohibition."-by Daniel O'Krent- Scribner Publishing-2011
416. Silver Dollar Tabor's letter's to her mother- 10/19/1922, 11/9/1922, 12/1922, 4/1923, 5/15/1923, 10/11/1923, 12/1923,1/18/1925,4/18/1925 and 8/4/1925- Colorado History society Tabor collection
417. http://www.Catholic.org

THE STENCH OF EMBALMING FLUID AND THE HEART WRENCHING LIE

418. Interview with Mrs. Rose O'Connel (Mahoney) by Mr. Victor Wisemen April 4, 2011
419. Chicago daily Tribune 9/21/1925
420. Chicago Tribune 9/25/1925 "Strange death of Ruth Tabor laid to mishap."
421. Aspen Daily Times 9/21/1925 "Death of Silver Dollar Tabor due to shock."

422. Milwaukee Times 9/22/1925
423. Aspen times 9/22/1925 "Daughter of Colorado mining camps escapes a pauper's grave."
424. Routt County Sentinel 10/9/1925
425. Routt County Sentinel 10/2/1925
426. Denver Times (Longmont) Volume XXXI #236- 9/21/1925" Murder theory is given up in Tabor death."
427. Fairplay Flume 10/2/1925
428. Booklet –"History of the Sacred Heart church."-obtained by author at front desk of The Sacred Heart Catholic Church, Denver, Colorado
429. http://www.catholic.org
430. http://www.our catholic prayers.com
431. Book-"Praying with the saints for the holy souls in purgatory."- by Susan Tassone- Our Sunday visitor publishing-2009
432. Author interview with William James, son of Numa James and Grandson of Eva James.
433. The Scroll Annual 1927 (Yearbook) Washington High School, Milwaukee, Wisconsin. Caroline Last-pages 157,158 and 160.
434. Map of Route of Denver, Colorado Tramway Corp., Including schedule-Denver Public Library archives
435. The Scroll Annual 1928 (Yearbook) Washington High School, Milwaukee, Wisconsin. John Last-pages 68,136,140 and 203
436. Colorado business hall of fame-J.K. Mullen-National Mining Hall of Fame and Museum-Historical Archives, Leadville, Colorado
437. Book-"Silver Dollar Tabor."-by Evelyn E. Livingston Furman- National writers press- 1982

A TUB OF LARD AND THE DANCING SQUIRREL'S

438. Aspen daily Times 8/10/1928 "Colorado News of interest"

439. Eagle Valley Enterprise 1/4/1929
440. Oak Creek Times 7/19/1928 "News of interest."
441. Author interview with William James, son of Numa James, Grandson of Eva James
442. Holy Cross Trail Volume 17 #14- 4/2/1927
443. J.K. Mullen Colorado Business Hall of fame- Leadville national mining hall of fame and Museum, archive's, Leadville, Colorado
444. Book-"What did they mean by that? A Dictionary of historical and genealogical terms."-by Paul Drake-Heritage books-2004
445. Ancestory.com-Peter McCourt family tree
446. Book-"Denver posse of the Westener's annual 1969 Volume 25."-Johnson Publishing-Story written by Numa James-"A visit from Baby Doe."(originally titled Baby Doe slept in my bed.")
447. Steamboat Pilot 4/4/1930 "Watcher at Tabor Mine found dead."
448. Interview conducted by Mr. Victor Wisemen with Mrs. Rose O'Connel (Mahoney) 2011
449. Article written by Helen Hunt Jackson for The Atlantic Monthly "To Leadville."-May 1879.
450. Book-"Augusta Tabor:A Pioneering woman."-by Betty Moynihan-Cordillera Press-1988
451. Booklet-"Tales from the old times."-by Mrs. Helen Skala and Mrs. Dora Krocesky-1972
452. Interview with John Martain by Dave Kanzeg-May 1994
453. http://www.find a grave/Peter McCourt
454. Ancestory.com Emma F. Fellows McCourt family tree
455. The Daily Western (Oshkosh) 4/8/1929
456. Steam Boat pilot 4/26/1929
457. Ancestory.com Bertha Roberts 1920 and 1930 census
458. Ancestory.com Elmer E. Kutzleb 1930 census
459. Interview with Bertha Roberts for Leadville Colorado Historical Oral history collection-1982

The Deadly Brain Tumor Heard Around the World

460. Steamboat pilot 3/11/1932 "New book deals with Silver and Tabors."
461. The Denver Post Archives 11/2/2012 "Colorado women win the right to vote in November 7,1893 election."
462. Book-"Molly Brown-unraveling the myth."-by Kristen Iversen-Johnson books-1999
463. Booklet-"Leadvilles Tales from the old timers."-by Mrs. Helen Skala and Mrs. Dora Krocesky-1972-Interview with Bridgie Ryan by authors
464. Steamboat Pilot 12/9/1932 "Leadville relics taken to Denver for Silver Dollar."
465. Book-"Silver Dollar."-by David Karsner-Crown Publishers-1932
466. The Republican 3/1/1883
467. http://www.catalog.AFI.com/silverdollar1932
468. Book-"Little Caesar:A biography of Edward G. Robinson."-by Allen L. Garsberg-Scarecrow press-2004
469. Book-"Bebe Daniels:Hollwoods good little bad girl."-by Charles L. Epting-McFarland press-2016
470. Steamboat pilot 1/6/1933"Girl tries to visit Mrs. Tabor."
471. The Denver Post 3/8/1935 "Girl is first to see Mrs. Tabor in death."
472. Interview with Mrs. Rose O'Connel (Mahoney) by Mr.Victor Wisemen-2011
473. Interview with Wallace and James Murcray for Leadville, Colorado's oral history collection

Laughing while the Denver Post burns

474. Steamboat Pilot 1/13/1933 "Wants famous Matchless ore."
475. Steamboat Pilot 2/24/1933

476. Steamboat Pilot 3/10/1933 "At the Chief."
477. Steamboat Pilot 3/17/1933 "Silver Dollar had large crowds at Chief Theater."
478. Steamboat Pilot 8/18/1933 "Mrs. Tabor will not see visitors."
479. Steamboat Pilot 8/11/1933 "Local news."
480. Steamboat Pilot 10/27/1933 "Mrs. Tabor will not take gift."
481. http://www.catholic.org/saints
482. http://www.ColoradoVirtualLibrary.Org/Helen Bonfils:Denver Post Co. Owner and Philanthrapist.
483. Book-"The emancipation proclamation."-by Abraham Lincoln-reprinted by Applewood books-1998
484. Interview with Alice Mae Thomas for Leadville Colorado oral history collection pages 42-51

A SHOTGUN NAMED TRUSTY AND THE CLOAKED VISITOR

485. Denver Post 3/13/1934 "Baby Doe drives men from mine."
486. Steamboat Pilot 1/19/1934 "Mrs. Tabor and the Matchless mine."
487. Steamboat Pilot 5/11/1934 "Mrs. Tabor will not leave the Matchless."
488. Steamboat Pilot 3/23/1934 "Mrs. Tabor uses gun to protect Matchless Mine."
489. Steamboat Pilot 6/15/1934 "Mrs. Tabor offered luxury but has not accepted yet."
490. Eagle Valley Enterprise 6/22/1934 "News of Silver State."
491. http://www.Colorado business Hall of fame-J.K. Mullen.org
492. Denver Post 3/8/1935 "Mrs.Tabor always a devout Catholic."
493. Denver Post 3/8/1935 "Mrs.Tabor silent in her later years."
494. Denver Post 3/8/1935 "Girl is first to see Mrs. Tabor in death."
495. Herald Democrat 2/26/1935 "Around the city-Cold wave moderates."

496. Steamboat Pilot 3/15/1935 "Mrs. Tabor dies in cabin at mine."
497. Denver Post 3/8/1935 "Queen of Colorado's silver boom perishes after 36 year vigil."
498. Interview with John Martain by D. Kanzeg –May 1994 (in regards to Coroner Jim Corbert and Andy Cassidy)
499. Denver Post 3/8/1935 "Had left note Feburary 20th saying went to town."
500. Elizabeth Tabor Death certificate-Leadville, Colorado public library
501. Letter written to Mr. Ernest Morris 3/27/1935 regarding Shorego Mining Company
502. http://www.heart.org
503. http://www.urban dictionary.com/Grim Reaper
504. Herald Democrat 2/22/1935 "January was warmest in 48 years in state."
505. Herald Democrat 11/9/1921 "Frank Zaitz Mercantile Co."

THE BROWN CREPED DRESS AND A BRAND NEW PAIR OF BLACK SLIPPERS

506. Author interview with Mr. Kent at Colorado Quarries, Canon City, Colorado (In regards to the use of dynamite to excavate a frozen burial plot)
507. Canon City Daily Record 3/9/1935 "Grave for Baby Doe is blasted from hillside in Leadville cemetery."
508. Interview with Alice Mae Thomas for Leadville, Colorado oral history collection
509. Denver Post 3/9/1935 "Plans laid to exhume Silver Kings body for burial side by side."
510. Denver Post 3/8/1935 "Friends of Baby Doe are eager for her to have a fitting burial."
511. Denver Post 3/9/1935 "Youth finds marker from Tabors grave."

512. http://www.internment.net/mount calvary cemetary Denver, Colorado
513. Photo of Elizabeth Tabor's Catholic mass, preceeding her burial-Denver Library phot collection
514. Ancestory.com Stephen Henry McCourt family tree
515. Ancestory.com John Harvey family tree
516. Ancestory.com John W. McMahon family tree
517. Ancestory.com Robert McLeod family tree
518. Ancestory.com Dennis J.O'Neill family tree
519. Salt Lake Tribune 4/5/1935 "Tabor body removed from grave for burial beside that of "Baby Doe."
520. Steamboat Pilot 3/21/1940 "Monument erected for the Tabor's"
521. Letter to Mr. Ernest Morris in regards to the vandilizm of the Matchless mine-3/27/1935 Leadville, Colorado public library collection
522. Letter to the Honorable Thos. Evans , Judge of Leadville's County Court ,in regards to the contents of Mrs. Elizabeth Tabor's trunks, bags and boxes-Leadville, Colorado library collection
523. Steamboat Pilot 9/20/1935 "Sell Tabor Relics at public auction."
524. http://www.Catholic.org
525. http://Mile hi optimus Denver.org

A STACK OF CHAIRS AND THE TWISTED FLASHLIGHT

526. Walking tour of the Matchless Mine. Mov-Walking history series-Youtube.com Video down loaded 8/31/2013
527. http://www.mining hall of fame.org
528. http://www.ghosts101.com/ghosts-flashlights-on-off
529. http://www.ghost stop.com/k2-deluxe-emf-meter
530. http://www.ghost shop.com/product/ovilus
531. Herald Democrat 7/18/2012 "Story of Baby Doe to be revealed."
532. Personal interview with former Matchless Mine Tour guide Greg

Turner by author

ELIZABETH TABOR'S PERSONAL RECIPIES AND HOME REMEDIES

533. Shopping lists and recipies Box MSS 614. Horace Tabor Collection, FF 1068 # 1-14, box 34. Denver History Museum archives
534. Prescriptions and cures etc. MSS 614 Horace Tabor collection. FF1069 # 1-16 and FF 1071 # 1-9

CPSIA information can be obtained
at www.ICGtesting.com
Printed in the USA
LVHW051551290920
667417LV00011B/850